A SHIP'S LOG BOOK

by

Captain Frank F. Farrar

Edited by Dorothy B. Maxwell

Tales of the sea by an irreverent, conniving, dedicated Merchant Marine
captain who shipped out at sixteen for a chance to wrestle rusty tubs
through wild waves from the fierce Pentland Firth
to steamy South American jungles by way of World War II.

―――――――――――――――――――――

Laced with photographs from Captain Farrar's mischievous and
exciting days at sea, spiced with vintage photos
from the National Archives/U.S. Naval Historical Center.

Published by
Great Outdoors Publishing Co.
4747 - 28th Street North
Saint Petersburg, Florida 33714

Great Outdoors Publishing Company
4747 - 28th Street North
Saint Petersburg, Florida 33714

©1988 by Frank F. Farrar

Library of Congress Catalog Card Number 88-081968

ISBN: 0-8200-1036-7 (paperback)
ISBN: 0-8200-1037-5 (hardcover)

Photo credits:
Pages 85, 89, 93, 111, 120, 136, 173, 187, 238: Official U.S. Navy photographs;
Pages 41 & 269, *A Careless Word – A Needless Sinking*, Capt. Arthur R. Moore;
Pages 177 & 178, Sperry Marine, Inc.; Page 198, Wide World Photos;
Page 220, *Chapman Piloting*, 57th edition;
Pages 250 & 251, U.S. Defense Mapping Agency (*Sailing Directions [Enroute] for the East Coast of South America*, 3rd edition);
Page 262, Defense Mapping Agency Hydrographic/Topographic Center
(*American Practical Navigator*, originally by Nathaniel Bowditch;
Page 263, Walter Stoy.

DEDICATION

For some time I've pondered who to dedicate these stories to. There is no one I can thank, because I wrote them all alone.

Then it came to me. I'll dedicate them to the men and ships that they came from.

So, these stories are in memory of my many shipmates and the ships we sailed together.

CONTENTS

ILLUSTRATIONS

FOREWORD

The largest gap which we have in our knowledge of America's merchant marine is for the period which encompasses the early years of steam-driven cargo ships; that is, the years from 1860 up to and including World War II. Records of the trade routings of the earlier days, the ships, and of the men who sailed them are disappointingly lacking. The later World War II is no exception to this sparsity.

Custom House statistics disclose that at the outbreak of the Civil War, 66.5% of our foreign commerce was carried in American bottoms. Then followed the so-called "flight from the flag," a result of high insurance rates brought about by the threat of Confederate raiders. By 1870, American bottoms carried only 33% of our foreign trade, a complete reversal of the proud position our merchant fleet had held before the war. By 1890, American shipping accounted for less than 13% of exports and imports.

When we mobilized for the war with Spain in 1898, we suffered the humiliation of having to send a large part of our troops to Cuba and Puerto Rico on ships purchased from British companies. We learned then that a nation surrounded by the sea was ill-fitted to wage war upon foreign shores without a merchant fleet suited for troop lift and resupply. With peace, the lesson was soon neglected, and we allowed our merchant marine to again degenerate into a coastal transport system.

By 1915, U.S. shipping company participation in our carriage of foreign trade was back to the dismal point where it had been in 1890. In an attempt to alleviate that disparity and to prepare us for war should we become directly involved, Congress passed The Shipping Act of 1916. Its preamble read:

"To establish a United States Shipping Board for the purpose of encouraging, developing, and creating a naval auxiliary and naval reserve and a merchant marine to meet the requirements of the commerce of the United States within its territories and possessions and with foreign countries ... "

This time, better prepared than in 1898, we entered the World War in 1917. By the time the conflict ended, we had a merchant fleet which rivaled that of the major maritime powers. But our shipping position, at 43% in foreign trade by 1920, still did not meet the parity it should have had. By 1928, the volume of our trade carried in our own ships had dropped to 34%. Congress hoped that the Jones-White Act would provide a cure by funneling federal subsidies (in the form of mail contracts) to those ship owners engaged in the Atlantic Trade. But before the effect of that assistance could be realized, along came the world depression and most of the hopes evaporated.

In 1931, over 4,500,000 Americans were out of work. No solution was in sight to alleviate the unemployment. Shipping, as is usually the case in such a time, was one of the first industries to feel the pinch. During that same year, Japan chose to march into Manchuria, a direct violation of the Kellogg-Briand Pact which had as its purpose the outlawing of war. Japan, a signatory to the Pact, had – by its invasion of another – stepped across that threshhold which would lead the world again to war.

It was also during that year (1931) that Frank Farrar entered the maritime industry when, as a 16-year-old, he walked up the gangway of his first ship. His subsequent career from deck boy to master would include the Great Depression, World War II, and the immediate years that followed. He was destined to witness during that time an ascendency of America's shipping industry to the point in 1945 when, as a nation, we boasted the largest tonnage of any merchant fleet in history. He was sad witness to that fleet's postwar decline, back to the level of a third rate maritime power.

Farrar's experiences, told here in essay form, speak not only of the years of peace and war, but they also relate the change in one man's attitudes as he progresses from fo'c'sle to master's cabin. In a low key style that reflects the writer's professionalism as a mariner, he episodically describes the experiences he best remembers.

Captain Farrar goes a long way in filling a void in the literature of the seaman's occupation. His work is invaluable in aiding us to understand the human element of that era which has regrettably been so neglected by technical historians.

Charles Dana Gibson
May 1988

PREFACE

The writer begs the forgiveness of the reader for any inaccuracies of dates, places, and the characters, all of whom were real.

One's memory can play tricks, and some of the events took place upwards of fifty years ago.

It has been most difficult to stick to the truth. It is tempting to exaggerate, but to my recollection all the happenings took place as I have described them.

Captain Frank F. Farrar
Melbourne Beach
Florida, 1988

ACKNOWLEDGMENTS

First and foremost, my three staunch and faithful friends. Without their unflagging support and encouragement, this book would never have come into being. They are my publisher, Charles Allyn, my editor, Dorothy Maxwell, and my friend, author and maritime historian Captain Charles Dana Gibson.

Two more who kept me going: Mrs. Gloria McCallum and my wife. They did all the tedious typing, proofreading, and correction of my atrocious spelling. They also flattered me outrageously, which always helps.

I am very grateful to you all.

F.F.F.

For fools rush in
where angels fear to tread.

Alexander Pope

—1—

EASTBOUND TO THE BALTIC
(STUCK IN THE ICE)

The log book of a deepwater vessel is like a skeleton. Dry bones —
a framework of terse phrases. The body, the flesh and blood, are hidden
between the lines, concealed by stilted, abbreviated notations.

To the initiated, though, there are stories of high adventure to be
found in those tattered, salt-stained chronicles. One accustomed to
reading between the lines may come on deeds of heroism, of danger,
suffering, and misery. Death, too, is often present, peering over the
shoulder of some tired, forgotten deck officer as he makes his brief entries
by the fitful light of a swaying lamp.

I am a shipmaster who has "swallowed the anchor," a term used
by seafarers for one who has left the sea and come ashore. Tonight, as I
sit before the fireplace, safe and warm on dry land, the urge to reminisce
about such things is strong.

In the bookcase beside me are several old log books from my voyages. Taking one at random, I idly turn the pages. As my eyes skim over
the entries made so long ago, I am no longer aware of the fire and the
warmth. I am again a young captain, worried, tired, and more than just
a little apprehensive. My gaze centers on an entry made one cold, wintry
day.

"SS *Theodore Parker* – Feb. 5th – Noon position, Lat. 58-
41 North, Long. 9-23 West – Sea slight – Course 089° – Speed
10.3 knots – Approaching Pentland Firth – 4:00 p.m., on
soundings, 150 fathoms – sighted the Flannen Light bearing 173° – Radio Direction Finder bearing of the Butt of
Lewis, 100°– Soundings, 75 fathoms – Vessel two miles
inside course – Changed course to 087°."

In my mind's eye I am once more on the bridge of that rusty tramp,
loaded to her marks with coal, bound from Norfolk to Copenhagen.

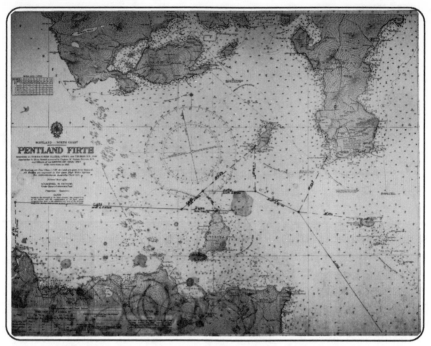

A bad place for an old, slow ship. Coffee mug stains bear mute evidence.

At the outset of the voyage I had made my decision to proceed by way of Pentland Firth, a narrow, desolate strip of water separating the northern tip of Scotland from the Orkney Islands, rather than go by way of the south of England and the English Channel.

Pentland Firth is one of the world's worst places to navigate, but my destination was a day's run shorter by this route ... and I was young, ambitious, and anxious to show my owners that they had chosen wisely when they placed me in command.

Yet, suddenly I was not so sure.

The *Sailing Directions*, which I had been studying all the way up the Great Circle route, had nothing encouraging to say. The Firth was not to be taken lightly. Heavy fog prevailed most of the time. The passage was very narrow and obstructed by two rocky islands. No anchorages were available in the locality. But these were minor when compared to the fearful tides for which the Firth is noted.

Twice in every 24 hours the tidal flow from the North Sea rushes through this bottleneck on its way to and from the Atlantic Ocean, amassing, in the Firth, the incredible rate of ten knots! The *Sailing Directions* explain very clearly that when this tremendous flow of water passing over a shallow bottom meets with winds in the opposite direction, even slight winds, a sea sweeps up which has swamped and capsized many a vessel. Throughout, caution and prudence are emphasized.

But – for this trip, the die had been cast. Already, the Flannens, a group of islands lying off the Northwest coast of Scotland, were in sight, and the Firth itself was only 12 hours over the horizon.

Night was coming on: February, a winter's night. The sea churned treacherously, but all was snug below decks and all was secured topside.

The day watch would be coming off to a brightly lighted mess room and a hot supper. As I stood, keeping my own watch there on that black, windswept bridge, I had no regrets about what I was doing. No thoughts of lights and warmth and home crept into my mind.

On his way off deck, the first mate stopped at my elbow. "I'll be glad to stand while you slip below for a bite, sir," he offered.

I shook my head. "Thanks, no." A feeling of elation, born partly of fear, buoyed me and made me disdain his suggestion. He slipped below and I was alone with my thoughts again.

These feelings that I had could be compared to those of a craftsman's fierce pride in his creation, of a job well done. Was it work for work's sake that I was doing? Maybe, but I was experiencing pride and satisfaction a bit prematurely; the job was yet to be done. And was it such a feat? Ships traversed this passage daily. Why should I, standing there, feel that this was such a challenge? Probably, it would be fair to say, it was because it was my first time.

I only know that I felt good. I was about to do something that was quite commonplace, that was expected of me, that I was paid to do. Yet at the same time, it *was* momentous. This first voyage of so many to Scandinavia was what I had wished and hoped for all my life – the chance to be master of my own ship. Now here it was. What wonderful, terrible, unknowable events would come next?

The mate had thoughtfully taken the chair from his stateroom, lengthened the legs, and had it installed on the bridge for my comfort. (Oddly enough, I had done the same thing for my Old Man when I was mate.) Settled comfortably in the chair, I took stock. The night was dark but clear. The sea was slight with a moderate ground swell. *Plans must be made,* I reminded myself. It was just an anxious thought: they had already all been made.

Daily during the voyage, I had charted the courses through the Firth and committed them to memory because once a vessel starts through, there is no time to go into the chart room and mess around with parallel rulers and dividers. Sharp turns abound and there would be no time for reflection and indecision. But now, the whole night was still before me and inaction made me restless.

Go over everything again. Make sure.

Lying across my knees was a small chart of the area. All the courses, bearings, and distances had been carefully inked in. Tide tables were at hand. Another peek at them, with the mate holding the flashlight, verified what I had known for a week. A fair tide, just commencing and therefore weak, would occur at 6 the next morning. An ideal time to transit the Firth. Just con her through like an automobile on a curving stretch of road. *Nothing to it,* I reassured myself. All this occupied only ten minutes. The long night still stretched ahead.

I summoned the chief engineer for a discussion on speed, propeller revolutions per minute, and the stupidity of engineers as compared to the super-intelligence of all deck officers. He tramped off the bridge afterward, muttering something like what would "they" do without engines.

Feeling better, but still restless, I sent for the chief steward and complained bitterly about the way eggs were bring fried on this ship. "Not fit for a dog, Steward."

Quietness settled in. The best part of an hour had passed. Somewhat mollified by my unnecessary display of authority, I decided a sandwich or two would be in order. The steward will never believe that it wasn't spite, because unthinkingly, I ordered a couple of fried egg sandwiches.

"9:20 p.m., sighted Cape Wrath – Cross bearings of the Cape and the Butt of Lewis indicates vessel one mile outside of course - Speed 11 knots."

Cape Wrath is one of the bleakest spots to be found on this earth. Here against its headlands beats the whole Western Ocean. Gales originating in Labrador and Newfoundland sweep eastward, skirting the southern tip of Greenland, gaining force and piling huge seas before them. Nothing obstructs them until they reach Cape Wrath. It is written that the seas pounding on the northwest coast of Scotland have sent spray a hundred feet into the air with the spume carried over a mile inland. No wonder wool sheared from sheep raised on the Outer Hebrides Islands is considered the world's finest.

Tonight, the Cape in the moonlight looked as if it had been subjected to such treatment for thousands of years, as indeed it had. Black and foreboding, it reached westward, daring the sea to destroy it.

"3:30 a.m., sighted Dunnet Head Light, the western entrance to Pentland Firth – Speed reduced to reach the Head at approximately 6:15 a.m. the beginning of the tide."

Slowly, the night was passing. Four o'clock was approaching, time for the chief mate to return for his morning watch. He would be most welcome because he would bring his own coffee percolator on the bridge with him. As it had always been my habit at sea to take early morning star sights, I had become quite accustomed on this trip to the chief's strong, black 4:30 a.m. brew.

At the appointed hour, the mate heaved himself up the ladder, grunting at the chill and darkness. He and the second mate hurriedly went through the time-honored business of changing the watch. The course was so-and-so. Such had been sighted or was in sight. Nodding in my direction, "The Old Man has the bridge," the second mumbled goodnight and went below to write up his log.

The chief mate checked the compasses and running lights, and saw to it that the lookout was properly posted. Then he set his pot to boil and soon the fragrance of brewing coffee made me stretch up out of my chair and stomp around the bridge in anticipation.

"Mister," I said as we leaned against the wind dodger soon afterward, warming our hands on steaming mugs, "not that I anticipate any untoward incidents this morning, but it wouldn't do any harm if you broke out the ship's carpenter and had the anchors cleared away. Then, on the off chance that we got into difficulty, those insurance people couldn't say that every precaution hadn't been taken."

Responding to orders, Chips, the carpenter, shortly reported to the bridge. He and the mate went forward to the fo'c'sle head where they removed the devil's claws and hawse pipe stoppers. (Strange words here tonight.)

Left alone on the bridge except for the helmsman, I paced back and forth, mentally anticipating the next couple of hours. As I completed a turn of the bridge, my foot stumbled against the engine room telegraph. Guiltily, I brought up short. It was perfectly normal to stumble in such pitch darkness, but I remembered other ships where I had been the helmsman. The most minute move of the Old Man was always observed. "Is the ship O.K.? Does he know what he's doing? Is he worried?" With deadly accuracy the Old Man's thoughts, attitude, and capability were deduced by the man at the wheel, and like wildfire were transmitted below decks: no cause for nervousness; everything anticipated, planned for. Just another voyage.

I resumed my pacing, but with slow, deliberate steps. I observed to the helmsman, oh so very carefully, that by the feel of the morning the day should break clear and fine. His answering grunt was noncommittal and therefore reassuring. His apparent lack of interest was sure proof that he, and hence the entire ship's company, felt that things were as they should be.

"5:40 a.m., Resumed full speed – 5:50 a.m., Tor Ness bearing 066°– Dunnet Head bearing 119°– Vessel is 3/4 mile outside course and 5-1/2 miles west of Dunnet Head, the entrance to the Firth – 6:20 a.m., Dunnet Head abeam - Entered Pentland Firth with Stroma and the Skerries on range bearing 093°."

Strange Scottish names: Stroma, Tor Ness, Swilkie Point, Tarf's Tail. But now there was no time to think about that – no time except for doing.

We entered the Firth at 6:20 a.m. on course 093°. At 6:45 a.m., with Swona bearing 065 degrees, course was changed to 065°. Nine minutes later, with Stroma abeam, course was changed to 090°. At 7:02 a.m Tarf's Tail was abeam and the course was changed to 125°. At 7:10 a.m. Swilkie Point bore 226°. Course changed to 146°. At 7:45 a.m. Duncansby Head bore 302°. Course again changed to 099°, and we were clear of Pentland Firth, all squared away nine degrees south of East for our next landfall, the Norwegian coast.

"6:20 a.m., entered the Firth; 7:45 a.m., all clear." One hour and twenty-five minutes! There had been anxious moments during that almost hour-and-a-half. A deeply laden tramp with old engines doesn't respond to the helm as you would wish.

The logbook states: "Vessel entered Firth Stroma and the Skerries on range bearing 093°." Stroma is a rocky, uninhabited island smack in the middle of Pentland Firth. Some miles beyond it there is a lighthouse on another rocky, wave-swept reef, the Skerries. The idea is to line them up on a bearing of 093° and then steer that course; in other words, to head directly for the island of Stroma. This course must be held until another island, Swona, just to the left of Stroma, bears 065°. Then hard aport on course 065° and head straight for it.

All this is done in very close quarters. The vessel is held on course until the last minute, heading right for an unfriendly shore where any ship would surely be lost. Then, quick, up with the helm and hope she answers in time. In the early morning light the land seems far too close, especially after two weeks of open sea.

After a surreptitious glance at the helmsman to see if he was listening, I very casually shouted to the mate on the bow to secure the anchors. When he returned to the bridge I managed to appear slightly bored (an air all skippers are expected to assume).

"Well, Mister, she's all yours. I believe I'll slip below for a bit of breakfast."

Once I reached the comparative privacy of the chart room I gave myself over to a brief session of self-satisfaction. I had done it! And without a hitch, nor with the slightest sign of nerves or muddle. Little did I know, as I swung down the companionway to the saloon and breakfast, that within two days we would be confronted with something all seafarers dread – ICE!

For now, in our oblivion of what was to come, we wallowed along in the peculiar North Sea swell all day and night. The next morning the southwestern coast of Norway reared up over the horizon. The log book merely states, "10:50 a.m., Sighted land three points on the Port bow – Soundings, 81 fathoms."

Simple words. Yet the great painters of history would have sought in vain among the tubes on their palettes trying to duplicate the color and grandeur there. Authors famed for their descriptive passages would lack the words to describe the mountains as they looked from seaward on a clear wintry day.

When we first saw it, we were at least 40 miles away. Despite the distance, we could plainly see the snowcaps in sharp contrast to the deep purple of the rock. As the ship drew nearer, the purple color, an illusion caused by great distances, gradually changed. The sun reflected from the snow on the ridges, making the ravines, or fjords, assume all the colors of the spectrum. It was a breathtaking sight.

As a rule, most seamen are a phlegmatic, unappreciative lot. The wonder and beauty of the seven seas almost invariably elicit at the most a bored shrug or a cursory glance, but usually nothing. On this particular cold morning, though, something about this spectacle, now broad on the port bow, seemed to affect the entire crew. Looking aft from the flying bridge, I was amazed to see sailors, firemen, even those whose watch it was below, all absorbed in this wondrous sight. Even the cook was at the rail, his thin cotton singlet showing white against his blue skin, his apron flapping wildly in the winter wind. The cold and the wind told their common sense that this was crazy.

"Go below where it's warm."
"But wait, look there!"
"Never saw anything like it."
"Aw, it's only a bunch of mountains."

Yet they all continued to watch the ever-changing colors, as fascinated as I was.

Through my many years as a sailor, I knew of the pride a seaman takes in never exhibiting any surprise, fear, or any other emotion. I don't know why, nor do I especially condone it. Nevertheless, it's very real.

Why, there on the bridge, I was doing the same thing. Deliberate steps – 12 paces to port, sniff the wind, look briefly at the coastline – 12 paces to starboard. To any bystander, I might have been waiting for a streetcar. Yet this never-to-be-forgotten scene was being so vividly imprinted on my mind I would never forget it.

I wondered if the Vikings, those stalwart Norsemen returning home from their voyages, saw what I saw. Did their imaginations run wild, and did they exaggerate because it was home? They had ventured halfway around the world in their frail cockleshells. After months and months of terrible hardship and privation this same scene confronted them on their return. What were their feelings way back then? Could theirs have been the same as ours?

All that afternoon we steamed along the southern coast of Norway, maintaining a distance off of about seven miles. Then: "4:20 p.m., Radio report indicates ice in Kattegat serious."

After several years at sea, I was finally to meet that arch enemy of shipping. Tall tales are told in fo'c'sles about vessels being caught by ice. Some were caught fast for days and weeks. Some were lost.

Sparks, the radio man, tuned in on the local Norwegian and Danish frequencies. The air was full of reports verifying my fears. The floe ice was solid all the way from Skaw south to beyond Copenhagen. Sparks handed me a report fresh in from a Danish ice-breaker.

"Low-powered steamers may expect difficulty navigating in ice. No immediate possibility of ice-breaker assistance due to commitments in lower Kattegat and in Copenhagen harbor. Recommend taking pilot at the Skaw."

I visualized the locality. Directly south of Norway, separated by an eastern arm of the North Sea, is the coast of Jutland, a part of Denmark. This body of water is called the Skagerrak. The northeastern tip of Jutland, the Skaw, is the entrance proper to the north-south body of water called the Kattegat. It is bordered on the east by Sweden, and on the west by Denmark.

Just before reaching Copenhagen, the Kattegat narrows to a ten-mile wide stretch of water known as the Oresund near where Shakespeare's "Hamlet" is set. Kronborg Castle, where Hamlet gave his famous soliloquy, is still there. Had we passed close enough we could readily have recognized it. From here, we had only to pass Hven Island before making our approach to Copenhagen. Yet I had little time for such calm thoughts. The ice and the worry lay heavy on me.

Sparks handed me another radiogram, this time from the Danish pilot vessel which normally was stationed off Skagen Light. She had been driven westward by the ice. If I desired a pilot, she would meet us at a little fishing village in Jutland, Hirtshals.

Hurriedly consulting the chart, I told Sparks to arrange the rendezvous. A new course was laid out from the ship's dead reckoning position to Hirtshalls. As soon as we had hauled 'round on the new course, I took stock of the situation.

Unfortunately, we didn't have a large-scale chart of Hirtshals' harbor, such as it was. We had only a coast chart which, except for sunken wrecks, omitted most of the detail and information necessary to make a landfall. The Sailing Directions were equally vague, Hirtshals being only a fishing hamlet. Because our approach would be made in darkness, any such landmarks would be useless, but it would have been nice to have them anyway, to know what was there.

What looked to be a comparatively safe anchorage was pricked on the chart, and bearings laid off to the light on the harbor mole and to the one lighthouse in the vicinity. All this had just been completed when the second mate stuck his head in the chart room.

"'Hirtshal's Light ahead, sir."

I nodded acknowledgment. Ascending to the bridge, I was gratified to see that the night, although bitterly cold, was clear and fine. On a Slow Ahead bell, cross bearings indicated we were in position. The chief mate finally bellowed that "she had fetched up," meaning that the ship had settled to her moorings and was safely at anchor.

Not knowing just when the pilot vessel would arrive, we relaxed for a while. The anchor watch was set. There was no wind and consequently no swell – a blessing when lying at anchor on an unprotected shore. Had there been a typical North Sea winter blizzard, things would have been quite different. Thankful for this brief respite, the mate and I draped ourselves comfortably over the chart room table. His never-failing coffee percolator bubbled softly as we talked the night into dawn.

Typically, it had been a night with no sleep. To people on shore, accustomed to regular hours of work and sleep, it is unbelievable that seamen can so abuse themselves. Actually, it's surprising how little sleep the body requires. We slept, whenever possible, like hunting hounds: short naps, a few winks, most of the time in our clothes. Sounds uncivilized to say that we thrived on such fare, but we did. Seamen regularly do such things, as they must in such adverse conditions as high seas, constant gales, and badly-loaded ships.

It was early afternoon before the second mate sighted what looked to be a pilot vessel heading in. From the bridge, a quick look through the glasses was enough to identify a typical North Sea pilot boat – sort of a European schooner rig: black, rakish, but oh so seaworthy. The chief mate was already up on the fo'c'sle head with Chips, ready to heave in the anchor.

The small vessel came up on our lee quarter. There was a brief flapping of sails, the growl of her powerful diesels, and in a moment she was fast alongside. Smart work. Those Danes are fine sailormen. The pilot clambered up the ladder and his vessel cast off, her sails filling rapidly.

The pilot was a fairly young Dane, blonde, ruddy-complexioned, and with an air about him of knowing his business. I asked him about the ice. He said it was bad enough, but that if the wind remained light we had a good chance of getting through.

It was now up to me to decide. Should I radio my owners? Under the terms of my Charter Party the ship was not required to navigate in ice. The master could, at his discretion, nominate the nearest port free of ice as the port of discharge. On the other hand, this would put the charterer to great expense.

What should I do? No good seaman knowingly takes his vessel into danger. I weighed everything as carefully as I could and finally resolved to proceed to my original destination, ice or no ice.

The anchor was hove up and the engines put on Full Ahead as we squared away for the Skaw, the Kattegat, and the ice. It was a brilliant, sunny afternoon. We steamed eastward with the late afternoon sun astern of us. Shortly before 5 o'clock I thought I saw a bright streak on the horizon dead ahead. Picking up the glasses, I looked again.

I felt that old, familiar feeling in the pit of my stomach like the one you get in an elevator when it drops quickly. As far as the eye could see there stretched an unbroken sea of ice! I jumped for the engine room telegraph and rang up Slow Ahead.

"No!" the pilot countered. "You mustn't slow down. You'll need every bit of speed and power you have to maintain headway through the ice."

"But we can't just go bashing full speed into that solid mass."

He smiled slightly. "This is your first encounter with ice?" It certainly wasn't this. Many times before we made port I was to be thankful for his judgment and advice.

With many misgivings, I ordered the engines put back on Full Ahead. The chief engineer was instructed that from now on, everything was to be cracked on and no monkey business about holding reserve power up his sleeve.

We were approaching the ice rapidly, and the nearer we got, the more concerned I became. It seemed as though we were streaming full speed for a solid wall. I paced back and forth, forgetting this time to be deliberate. I was worried and didn't care if the helmsman did know it. My hand itched to ring the engines down again. We had over 9,000 tons of coal in our holds. The ship herself weighed another 3,000 tons. And here we were, all 12,000 tons, helling along at 11 knots!

In a matter of minutes, we were up to the ice. The bows crunched through the first of it. The ship shuddered, slowed. Then the powerful propeller took up its beat again. The noise of five-inch-thick ice grinding along our sides was deafening. We had to shout to make ourselves heard. We were making knots, though, for by 10 o'clock that night we had raised the Swedish coastline. Vinga Light was abeam and we were proceeding. Slowly, to be sure, and with enough noise to awaken all good sailors who had been sleeping in Davy Jones's locker since the beginning of time, but we were definitely making headway.

Then came the moment I'd feared.

"7:44 a.m., Fast in heavy ice." A brief statement: stuck in the ice. An ignominious situation to say the least, with no mention of the dire straits in which we now found ourselves.

On our port, not too far away, lay the rocky coast of Sweden. There was a slight breeze blowing on shore. The pilot didn't make me feel a bit better when he told story after story of ships being lost when the wind blew hard enough to move the ice shoreward, carrying ships with it until their bottoms were ripped out on the rocks. Sometimes, after a vessel had impaled herself on the reefs the ice literally buried her, the wind forcing the ice against her sides and up and over her decks until she disappeared.

The chief engineer was summoned to the bridge again. This time the conference held no sarcasm. First, it was apparent that no immediate assistance could be expected from an ice-breaker. Second, we were in no danger as long as the wind remained light. The question to be answered was, "How do we get out of this mess?" The ice was too thick for our engines to cope with. The chief said that was reason enough to "break the seals."

All ships' boilers are inspected periodically by government inspectors who decide what the maximum boiler pressure shall be. The safety relief valves are set to that pressure, then they're sealed with official seals. The engineer who breaks them, or the captain who orders them broken, is subject to investigation and possible loss of license should he not be able to show the grave necessity for such a step.

Not wanting to involve the chief and myself in lengthy investigations and hearings when we returned to the States, I resolved that we would first have one more try at breaking free without breaking the seals.

Full Astern! As the engines revved up, heaving against the seemingly immovable force of the ice, everything on the ship started flapping and vibrating from the powerful thrust. The funnel just behind me seemed to be trying to shake itself down. The shrouds on the mast quivered like giant fiddle strings. Water boiled under the stern and poured up over the ice. We didn't budge.

"Full Ahead, and give it to her, Chief!"

Still no movement, nothing discernable at all.

Leaving the engines on Full, I picked out an ice hummock alongside and fastened my eye on it.

There ... *it moved* ... didn't it?

But it was only my imagination, stimulated by hope.

I'll count to 20, I said to myself, *and then call it quits. After that, we'll just have to pray that an ice-breaker can reach us before the weather worsens.*

Slowly, I counted. When I reached 20, I sneaked another peek at the ice hummock. No change. *Oh, well, I meant that I'd count to 20 by fives. One, two, three, four, five – one; one, two, three, four, five – two ...* (it had worked when I was a kid). As I counted, I leaned over the bridge rail with what I hoped was a proper skipper's look: unconcerned, a bit bored, with confidence oozing out all over. Actually, cold sweat was oozing and I was scared.

The bridge telephone jangled, interrupting my counting. It was the sailor on the bow, shouting so loudly that we could hear him without picking up the receiver. *"We're moving!"* To say that I was relieved would be a masterpiece of understatement. Slowly but surely, we had started crunching our way through.

Still, the ordeal was nowhere near being over. The business of getting underway, getting stuck again, backing and filling to free ourselves, went on for over a week. A typical entry was discouraging: "Proceeding in heavy ice. Backing and filling with engines to break vessel free. Distance made good this day, one mile." One mile after 24 hours of struggling!

Finally there came a time when we would have been grateful for that single mile – because at last we could move no more. An urgent radio message was dispatched, requesting the assistance of an ice-breaker.

About midnight, the mate on watch reported a ship approaching at high speed. I growled, "Nonsense. Can't you recognize a low-flying plane when you see one, stupid? What vessel is proceeding through this ice at all, let alone at high speed?"

Just as I spoke, the running lights of a ship flashed by the chart room porthole. Astounded, I bounded out onto the bridge. There was a Danish ice-breaker rounding our stern. He proceeded completely around us, breaking the ice loose. As he swung alongside, our crew dropped a rope ladder on his deck. Her skipper mounted the ladder and stepped aboard, a veritable giant of a man, dressed in a great fur coat, fur hat, and skin boots.

"Hello, Captain," he boomed. "Having trouble?"

We repaired to my quarters for coffee spiked with aquavit, a fiery Danish drink which he had thoughtfully brought with him, while we discussed what would happen next. What he proposed was fantastic. He was going to take us in tow - all 12,000-odd tons of us – and we were not to use our engines at all.

"Leave everything to me," he said with a bold grin.

Surely, the man was mad. Yet he was such a commanding figure and so full of confidence that I was partially convinced. After all, what could we lose? Certain signals between the ships were agreed on; he returned to his vessel.

The mate broke out all hands, and went forward to take the ice-breaker's towing cable aboard. It was made fast and the Dane went slowly ahead. Just as the cable came taut, her skipper roared back at us, "Captain, I'll tow you at five knots. A pound of tobacco on it!"

Safe in Copenhagen at last, with only light ice at the dock.

And he did exactly that. He towed us all the way to Copenhagen, into the harbor, alongside the dock, averaging five knots! I would never have believed it possible. The ice was four to five feet thick in places, yet we never used our engines once. He did it with his ship and his skill, and that of his crew, alone.

Once we were safely tied up to the dock, the big Dane came aboard again. He held an empty pipe in his enormous hand.

"My tobacco!" he demanded with hearty good nature.

"Welcome aboard!" I told him gladly. This was a debt I was more than happy to pay. Good pipe tobacco was scarce in Denmark. We had a couple of quick snorts of his aquavit, then I loaded him down with two cases of good American pipe tobacco.

What a man he was! And such a superb seaman. What he did for us was commonplace to him, an everyday occurrence during the ice season. To him our rescue had been no trouble, just the completion of another vessel's eastbound passage of the Eastern Ocean. He was a rare figure by today's standards. Nothing was impossible to him.

My mind shifts back to the present as a log falls through the andirons. Red sparks shoot up the chimney. The house is very still. I realize with a start that I can no longer see to read. The firelight is nothing but a red glow. I feel loathe to return to the present, yet except for that magnificent Dane, the predicament of being caught in the ice is not one that I remember with any great joy.

Seagoing habits, acquired from years at sea, are part of me, just as the memories are. Going to the door, I sniff the weather: clear and dry with an earthy smell of spring in the air. The next day will break clear and fine, but why should I care? Safe on land, let it blow and howl. I return to my chair and my thoughts are caught in that smell of earth just coming to life.

That flicker of spring in the air smells just like a river I once sailed up in British Guiana. The rich scent untangles a new bit of memory from among all those dancing through my mind – monkeys chattering and green birds screeching in trees that formed a solid canopy over the ship as we glided through the dark, still water.

That voyage, too, almost ended in disaster.

But that's another story.

"Drive her, Johnny, drive her."
Old Sea Chanty

—2—

A COUPLE OF CLOSE CALLS

On that voyage we were bound from Savannah, Georgia, down to Port McKenzie, in British Guiana, there to load a full cargo of aluminum ore consigned to Port Alfred, Canada.

The chief engineer and I were standing on deck, idly plying tooth-picks in an endeavor to dislodge pieces of overcooked breakfast bacon, when the agent's runner came up the gangway. I was to come to the office as soon as convenient; the vessel's next assignment had been received from our Boston owners. This was welcome news. We had been lying at dock for several days enduring Georgia heat. Inactivity had begun to pall.

It was therefore with alacrity that, after a quick shower and a change into shore clothes, I emerged from the semi-darkness of the dock shed onto a waterfront street. The soaring temperature influenced me to indulge in the luxury of a taxi. My owners, being Bostonian, were nat-urally conservative. Consequently, they looked with high favor at voyage expense accounts which itemized "trolly carfare" and "bus ticket" instead of "taxi."

During the short ride to the office, I made a mental wager that this assignment would take us southward. It seemed always to be my mis-fortune to be in northern waters during the winter months, half-frozen and miserable. When the fine weather arrived, away we'd go, bound for the Equator where the bugs and prickly heat rash lay in wait.

Sure enough, it was to be a hot-weather trip. I glanced through our sailing orders from the marine superintendent, set aside the Traffic Department's instructions in connection with the Charter Party, and bade the agent good morning. Our business concluded, on the way back to the ship I bemoaned the fact that at this time of year the North Atlantic trade routes were enjoying fine, settled weather, and the skippers up there were sleeping in their bunks all night instead of battling hurricanes down in the Caribbean where we were bound.

Back on board, I held a conference with the chief engineer, the mate, and the steward. We were instructed to proceed forthwith when "in all respects ready for sea." From our owners, this meant *tout de suite.*

We were bound from Savannah to Port McKenzie to load aluminum ore.

The chief reported his engines ready to go, no stores needed. The steward began his stores list, and the mate reported a full crew with everything ship-shape and Bristol fashion. Only one matter remained to be settled: bunkers.

In order to ascertain fuel oil requirements, the distance between ports must be known. The chief followed me into the chartroom for what turned out to be a search in vain. Although we were fully equipped with charts, we couldn't find Port McKenzie on any of them. Puzzled, I sent the second mate ashore to phone the agent. Maybe a mistake had been made in copying our owner's teletyped orders. The mate returned; Port McKenzie it was. The chief drummed his fingers on the table and sucked his teeth. Obviously, he had a nincompoop skipper who, if he couldn't even locate the port on the chart, was assuredly incapable of sailing a ship there. He had that typical engineer's look spread all over his silly face.

Finally, I located McKenzie in an atlas. It was so far up the Demerara River in British Guiana that the chartmakers had omitted it! Turning to the chief, I gave him the distances involved and requested that he check his tanks and report his requirements. "That is," I observed off-handedly, "if you can read." Oh, me! When Kipling said, "East is East and West is West and never the twain shall meet," he must have been thinking of engineers and deck officers in the Merchant Service.

The chief went off to sound his tanks while I sat down in my day room to write a last letter to my son. He was in school in New Hampshire, and it was now a year and a half since I had seen him. Such are the vagaries of a tramp steamer.

At lunch, the chief and I compared notes and agreed that sufficient bunkers were on board to take us from Savannah to McKenzie, and from there 'round to Trinidad, where we were to complete loading. Trinidad, being a major fuel port, was a much cheaper place than Savannah to bunker for the voyage to Canada.

Then we held an extraordinary conversation. I would like to think that I started things off, but if I stick to the truth, it was the chief. The essence of it was that ever since engines were introduced into ships, engineers and captains had been differing, bickering, arguing. There was mutual distrust, jealousy, and misunderstanding between the two departments, both of whom had the same interest: the ship. I have sailed with dozens of fine, capable engineers, *good* chiefs, firsts, and seconds who, day and night, year after year, keep our propellers churning the waters of the seven seas. This was not one of them, but I didn't know it at the time. In a burst of magnanimity, we resolved that on this vessel, the differences would cease. We would become one happy family with one purpose, one goal: the furtherance of our owner's interests.

I like to think that we were both completely sincere, but in fact what we had was a sort of armed truce. Both sides, in effect, adopted the attitude: "I'll go along with this insane alliance so long as 'he' doesn't get out of line." Our voyage might have turned out very differently had we stuck with our resolve. Later on, the ship was almost lost twice because of engineers and the lack of complete cooperation and trust between them and the deck. But we knew none of that when we made our truce.

All that afternoon, the second mate and I studied charts, laid off courses, and planned our voyage. All hands were readying the ship for sea. As we were in ballast and therefore light, everything was battened down and secured because a light ship caught in a tropical hurricane will roll and pitch badly. The work made for a busy and eventful day. The die had been cast, but our destiny as charted by the Master Navigator was not divulged to us. Knowing what I do now, that was just as well.

The only log book entry recording all this read as follows:

"SS *Augustus P. Loring* – August 5th – Received this day orders and charter party to proceed when in all respects ready for sea to Port McKenzie, British Guiana, there to load for Port Alfred, Canada. Vessel being made ready for sea."

That evening, our last in Savannah, was spent in desultory conversation while sprawled in canvas deck chairs under a bright Georgia moon. The temperature hovered around 100. The general theme of that talk was our newly-formed pact between engine room and deck and of how we would henceforth be one happy family. Afterward, turning in for the night, my misgivings on the matter were pricked by the unpleasant discovery that some stupid engineer had, as usual, turned the wrong valve in the engine room. My radiators were smoking hot and the room was like a furnace. Dragging my mattress to the wheelhouse, I prepared for an uncomfortable night. As I drowsily swatted mosquitoes, I remembered my grandfather who, after a lifetime in sail said, "Steamboats are fine, but look what they spawned," meaning engineers.

The next morning I went ashore to clear the ship at the Customs House and pay a last visit to our agent. The United States Shipping Commissioner returned to the ship with me to sign the crew on Articles. By noon, all was accomplished and it was time to go. Leaving the saloon after a quick lunch, I could hear the mate's familiar order: "Fore and aft, Bosun, all hands."

The sailing of a cargo ship is a run-of-the-mill affair, nothing like the glamorous passenger ships with their parties, streamers, and bunting, with crowds of friends waving from the pier. For us the lines were simply cast off, a tow boat swung us down river, and we were away. As we passed the center of the city and drew abreast of our agent's office building, I gave three mournful blasts of farewell on the ship's whistle. The agent had been kind and helpful during our stay in Savannah, and the Lord only knew when we might return.

The pilot got off at the river's mouth, and we took our official departure from the Savannah Light vessel. At sea again: a comfortable, old-shoe feeling in spite of the midsummer sun making a griddle out of our steel decks.

The days passed pleasantly. We were making our southing and easting, passing well to the east of Cuba and the Bahamas, through the Mona Passage into the Caribbean. Puerto Rico lay just over the horizon on our port. Although still out of sight, we used it to excellent advantage for radio bearings to verify our celestial observations. We were making a fine passage right on course. The weather remained perfect, and the sea was like blue glass.

All hands, including myself, were down to shorts. The tropical sun blazed down day after day, turning us all a dark brown. That is, everyone except the second mate. He was an old salt who had spent a lifetime at sea. His face and hands were the color of old, polished mahogany, but the rest of his body looked like the thin, blue-white skimmed milk that farmers feed to their pigs. Being second mate, he stood the noon to 4:00 p.m. watch on the bridge. He buttoned his shirt tightly at the neck and wrists and remained under cover in the wheelhouse, coming out only when necessary to take an azimuth or shoot the sun with his sextant, after which he scurried back into the shade, for all the world like an old mole. I used to spend the afternoon on the bridge taking advantage of the beautiful weather. As my hide blackened and my hair bleached, he muttered doleful predictions of sun stroke, skin cancer, and what he called "a frying of a man's brain."

In a few days we were off the mouth of the Demerara River in British Guiana. A little brown-skinned pilot boarded us and guided the ship to just inside the river. We dropped anchor off the port of Georgetown, famous for rum that's as potent as lightning, yet slips down the throat of the unwary as smoothly as Vermont maple syrup. We went through the formalities of Customs and Immigration.

Then we exchanged one pilot for two, black as ebony. It seemed that as one's latitude grew less toward the equator, the color of the inhabitants grew darker. Our new pilots padded up the bridge in their bare feet. Splayed toes, spread like fingers, did not indicate any close acquaintance with shoes. Their speech was delightful, a cultured British accent rolling out with beautiful resonance, softly slurred by Negro idioms.

When I asked why we needed two pilots for the upriver passage, their explanation was anything but reassuring: they proposed to do their own steering. I was most reluctant to agree to any such arrangement, pointing out that our quartermasters were familiar with the feel of our ship and knew just how much wheel was needed to execute a steering order. In turn, they presented logical arguments that finally persuaded me.

The river abounded in sudden turns and shoals, they said. The tide rushing up on the flood and then streaming seaward on the ebb created a hazard. They negotiated this daily on different ships, each with its own steering peculiarities. With that settled, one pilot stationed himself at the wheel while the other politely asked me to have the mate heave up the anchor, if it was convenient.

Our trip up the jungle river was memorable. The heat and oppressive humidity excepted, it was like a National Geographic account. Virgin jungle came right down to the edge of the water, so lush and impenetrable that we could see no more than a couple of feet inland. Our ears were assaulted by a cacophony of noise from teeming life engaged in an unceasing struggle for survival. The noise reached a crescendo at dusk with the buzzing and humming of myriad insects, punctuated by the hoarse coughs and grunts of alligators. The screams and snarls of unseen animals, and the screeching and crying of thousands of birds, made conversation well nigh impossible.

We reached a shallow part of the river where we had to anchor to await the arrival of flood tide. The pilot explained that even though our ship was in ballast and not drawing much water, and could therefore proceed safely at any stage of the tide, he would rather wait for more water. I heartily agreed, and dispatched the long-suffering mate forward to drop the hook.

The mate had spent the entire day in the holds with the crew, readying them to receive the cargo. On that hangs a tale which I'll come to in a moment, because something happened down in #5 lower hold which, weeks later, almost caused the ship to founder on her way up to Canada with a full load of ore.

After dinner, I rejoined the mate on the bridge where he was standing anchor watch. We discussed his progress in the cargo holds. He was a bit concerned at finding a small amount of water in the bilges of #5 lower hold. The ore we were to load had to be delivered dry, or claims would result.

Since this water was obviously only condensation that had collected on the ship's steel sides and run down into the bilges, he had sent word to the engine room to put a suction on #5. The big bilge pump labored mightily, but nothing happened. The water remained. One of the engineers went into the hold with the mate to see first-hand what the trouble was. The strainers were all free, so the engine force decided that the valve in the bilge was either out of order or plugged.

Even as we passed time on the bridge, one of the assistant engineers was down in #5 dismantling the valve. Shortly before midnight he reported that he had found the trouble, reassembled the valve, and pumped out the water. We were ready to load. Looking back, had I known what was done in that hold by that careless man, violence would have been done that night.

We were underway by dawn. Dawn in the tropics is an experience to a sailor. Out on the open sea, daybreak is a gradual thing. The blackness slowly changes to gray. Little by little the horizon becomes perceptible. To the east, a first faint glow shows itself. A deep red shades off to purple. The sky brightens. Clouds may be massed like black mountains against the western horizon. I always used to liken those clouds to the passing of the night. Night sank over the western horizon just as day broke over the eastern rim of the sea. There was plenty of time to observe the beautiful, changing details of the coming of a new day.

Here in a jungle river, it was quite different. There was no far-flung horizon toward which one could watch and wait and hope. There were only trees and creepers, vines and mosses, almost meeting overhead. One moment there was pitch blackness and the dank, rotting smell of the river. The next, it was broad daylight. So quickly did day come that I found myself squinting as you do upon stepping out of a movie house into the afternoon glare.

All day we proceeded up the river. Mile after mile of monotony, repetition. Here and there were a few clearings. Log canoes pulled up on the mud banks gave indications that people were hereabouts. How did these people live? And on what? And for what in this steaming jungle?

Yet, maybe they were happier and more content than the residents of Park Avenue with all their wealth and power.

By late afternoon we were close to our destination. The pilots explained that the ship had to be turned around before docking so that when loading was completed, it would only be necessary to cast off. Because the river was quite narrow and the current fairly strong, I asked them how they proposed to turn the ship. Just as I spoke, the ship rounded a bend and we had arrived. As I remember it, the pilots never answered my question. There was no time. First it was "Hard right!" Then, "Full astern, wheel midships!!" The vessel answered beautifully. We seemed to spin around like a big, floating top, and then it was done. Maybe they never wore shoes, but by God those pilots could handle a ship.

We tied up to a new, efficient-looking wharf that ran parallel to the river bank. All sorts of conveyors, tracks, and overhead structural steel testified to the inroads made by 20th century technology even in this remore corner of the world.

We were not going to be loading my favorite cargo here. Aluminum ore is called bauxite. It is very valuable and very necessary to the welfare of the world. To a sailor, it is also the most devilish stuff ever loaded on a ship. It can penetrate the most minute cracks and crevices. As it is also an excellent abrasive, it damages any machinery with which it comes in contact.

All night long, thousands of tons were dumped into the holds. There was no sleeping. The heat was stifling. By daylight, the choking dust covered everything. Though it looked like snow, it didn't melt. Breakfast was eggs with bauxite. Chewing them produced a gritting sensation that was nauseous. Every stateroom was powdered with the stuff, even though every door and porthole had been dogged fast.

Shortly before noon our cargo was aboard. The loading schedule at the port called for a ship to arrive and depart simultaneously with the ice going out of the St. Lawrence River in Canada and freezing up. The schedule had to be maintained day and night, seven days a week, come hell or high water. Otherwise, the big, sprawling aluminum plant in Canada might grind to a halt just when the possession of aluminum or the lack of it could mean the difference between a free world, and slavery and oppression.

Off we went down the river, then, taking the same trip in reverse. The ship was only about three-quarters loaded because a mud bank off the mouth of the river had defied dredging. Big, deep-water vessels such as ours were required to go with only a partial load 'round to Chagaramus on the island of Trinidad to load the remainder of our bauxite, brought around by small inter-island steamers and stockpiled there.

We dropped swiftly down the river, and before I knew it we were again anchored off Georgetown. Again the usual formalities were gone through: crew lists, manifests, carbon copies to everyone including the Lord Himself, it seemed.

At the last minute a large launch came alongside with 12 passengers for Port of Spain, British families bound home on leave either to Canada or to England. As we were not due to depart until the next morning, the passengers, the chief, and myself congregated in the saloon and got acquainted. Several couples had children with them who were soon tucked into their bunks. Fortunately for us our passengers were experienced travelers, and as such came plentifully supplied with Georgetown's famous rum. The steward rounded up sufficient glasses, ice cubes were pilfered from the crew's mess, and (in a manner of speaking) the ice was broken.

It's a peculiar thing about women on board a ship. Seamen are not exactly savages. Most of us are fairly normal, have an average education, know good manners, and are in general gentlemen. Yet on board a ship, being almost always exclusively a community of males, even the plainest woman looks devastating. By the same token, I think that to any woman on a cargo ship, the officers and crew take on an aura of adventure and glamour which we don't at all deserve.

These phenomena, together with the insidious effect of the rum, produced a delightful evening for all of us. All, that is, except the husbands who were thoroughly disgusted with the gay talk and dancing indulged in by their otherwise devoted and sensible spouses. We, the crew, felt that we were really the gay dogs who could have been much more charming had not these doltish husbands been present. (Wasn't it Puck who said, "What fools these mortals be!"?) Oh, well, if the truth must be told, the phonograph was silenced and all hands were properly abed before midnight.

The next morning our brown pilot replaced the local black ones and the anchor was hove up. While getting underway, the pilot explained the method of getting over the river bar. I was astounded. I was also very annoyed at the charterers for not having explained the situation to me prior to loading.

To explain briefly, the ship was drawing about four more feet of water than there was over the bar. The pilot, very nonchalantly, drawled that it was only soft mud. He said it was imperative to maintain maximum speed and under no conditions reduce that speed while dragging over the bar. Should the vessel lose her headway, it would be impossible to get her moving again and the falling tide would leave her hanging on the hump, possibly with a broken back. A fine kettle of fish!

There was no turning back now. I told the chief engineer of the situation and impressed upon him the importance of maintaining speed. He went off to instruct the engineer on watch. This particular engineer was a native of Poland. He spoke very broken English and when excited lapsed immediately into Polish, a failing that was shortly almost to prove our undoing.

We passed out of the river mouth and headed for the bar. I telephoned the engine room and instructed the Pole to "hook her up," a seagoing expression that means on a steamer what "cracking on" meant in the days of sail. In other words, "give her the works!"

In many ways, the next few minutes were the same as when we first entered the ice up in the Baltic. We hit the mud bank full speed, but in the distance of hardly a ship's length we had slowed to a crawl. Unconsciously I leaned forward, urging the ship on.

Suddenly the engines stopped. The pilot yelled and I jumped for the telegraph. It was still on Full Ahead. Savagely, I yanked the handle back and forth and slammed it back on Full. Grabbing the telephone, I spun the crank. A flood of Polish poured out, then came a click as the engineer hung up. All the while the pilot was yelling, "Please, Captain, you must get the engines going! We only have a short time before the tide leaves us!"

The phone jangled. Picking up the receiver, I snarled my opinion of all engineers. The chief's voice interrupted my cursing. It seemed that the Pole had not fully understood the chief's explanation of how we were to pass over the bar, so when we hit the mud he assumed that the ship had run aground. Without any orders from the bridge, on his own initiative he stopped the engines. To do this without an order is unthinkable, but he had done it.

Now to really foul things up, the chief told me that because we had lost headway, the main condenser intake was plugged with mud and he couldn't give us any revolutions at all at the moment. My remarks of the next couple of minutes to the engine room destroyed for all time my chances of ever passing through the Pearly Gates. Fortunately for all of us, the chief hung up on me and went to work.

I paced back and forth like a wild man, helpless to do anything. The pilot cowered in the wing of the bridge and avoided me. I had just glanced at my watch for the hundredth time when I heard the telegraph jingle. The handles swung from Full Ahead around to Full Astern and then back to Full Ahead again. Those bells were sweet music: they meant that the propeller was turning. But was it too late? Maybe the tide had fallen too much for us ever to get under way again. What an ignoble way to end my seagoing career: "Lost his ship on a mud bank within sight of shore. No, no fog or storm, just stupidity."

As the beat of the wheel increased, I anxiously watched the bearing of a landmark nearby. *Please change.* It did! By God, we were moving! Slowly the ship inched herself along. She gave a final lurch and we were in deep water. *Whew!* The past hour had taken years off my life. Such experiences become part of a man and remain woven in the fiber of him for the rest of his life. I knew the rage and the fear of those awful moments would never leave me.

When the pilot's little launch appeared ahead, we stopped to let him off. I know he was glad to go.

Our course was shaped for the island of Tobago, a beautiful spot in the eastern Caribbean. We were to make a left turn at Tobago, passing between it and Trinidad. Our course from the pilot station off the mouth of the Demerara River to Tobago exposed us to the strength of the South Equatorial Current, one of the major currents of the world. The South Equatorial corresponds in many ways to the Gulf Stream in that, although its direction and limits are fairly constant, its velocity varies considerably according to the wind.

The chief mate and I hovered long over the chartroom table, figuring the effect of the current on our speed and course. We finally set the course and estimated our time of arrival off Tobago. About supper time a haze settled down, not quite so thick as fog but still bad. Darkness closed in. The haze was confusing, for we were not sure how much visibility there was. At times we felt we could see for miles if there was anything to see; at others we felt hemmed in by thick fog. We took advantage of the one Radio Direction Finder station in the locality, but because of its direction in relation to our position it was not much help.

We were steaming along, occasionally blowing the fog whistle and peering into the murk, when the chief mate remarked, "It's clearing up, Skipper. There's a star just over the foremast."

"Fine," said I, "because we should be up to Tobago within the hour and we've got to pick up the lighthouse."

Idly, I watched the star as the foremast swung in answer to the ship's roll past it.

Then, suddenly: "What's that!" I roared. "That star is blinking! Full Astern! Stop engines!" What we had mistaken for a star was the lighthouse up on the cliffs. We were right under it! The current had fooled us.

"That was close, Mister," I muttered. "Lucky for us that the haze cleared when it did. All those little kids down below in their bunks ... Supposing we had gone bashing into those cliffs!"

I shuddered in the darkness. Another experience to file in memory, maybe to return and haunt, jeering: "Poor judgment. You shouldn't have been so lucky." Mistakes in judgment at sea are rarely allowed. The gods who rule on such matters are not lenient. They have never heard the phrase: "one more chance." I guess maybe they had recessed for a few moments – or perhaps looked the other way – just when we raised Tobago.

Without further incident, we rounded the northern coast of Trinidad and headed down to Port of Spain, the island's capital and principal port. Soon we were at anchor off the city. Once more the business of Quarantine, Customs, and Immigration, then our new friends, the passengers, left in a flurry of farewells.

We upped anchor and steamed over to the port, if it can be called such, of Chaguaramus, about ten miles from Port of Spain. It was a duplicate of Port McKenzie, another bauxite pier. Once more there was no sleep through the night.

When morning came, the ship was low in the water. She was loaded to her tropical marks, which is fully laden with only enough reserve buoyancy to keep her afloat. For the last time the lines were cast off. We swung slowly away from the pier. The ship was very sluggish and slow to answer the helm, but finally we got her headed around and clear of the harbor. We took our departure from Trinidad and laid off the course for the voyage north to Canada.

Our course took us near the beautiful Windward and Leeward Islands of Grenada, Santa Lucia, Saint Vincent, Barbados, Guadaloupe, and Antigua. As I noted them on the chart, I thought of the days of the Buccaneers, Captain Kidd, Blackbeard, Robinson Crusoe, pieces of eight, fifteen men on a deadman's chest. Those were the days! High adventure, gold, beautiful captives who whiled away the hours with the victors. Boyhood memories, long since dispelled by reality. Our current reality was a rust bucket full of ore waddling her way up the 60th meridian of west longitude toward Sable Island, the graveyard of the Atlantic.

Day after day we steamed up the 60th meridian, averaging a steady ten knots. We were enjoying beautiful weather again with a sea like blue glass. It was on one of these beautiful mornings that an incident snapped all of us out of the lethargy into which we had fallen.

We were about five or six days out of Trinidad. The third mate had the morning watch and I was on the bridge with him, enjoying the beautiful weather. Chips, the carpenter, came up to report his bilge soundings. He gave his list to the third mate. I listened idly as the mate rang up the engine room and instructed them to put a suction on #5 lower hold. It is customary to pump a bilge whenever the soundings exceed six or eight inches. So far on this voyage all the holds had remained practically dry, showing an inch or two. Evidently, condensation was increasing as we approached cooler waters.

Soon, through the engine room skylight, I heard the big, powerful bilge pump thumping away. After a bit it stopped, and the engineer phoned up to the third mate and asked if he had pumped long enough. The third blew his whistle for Chips and sent him aft to sound #5 again. Pretty soon Chips came flying back up the ladder shouting, "There's something wrong. She's showing two feet now!"

I grabbed Chip's sounding rod and line, and ran aft to sound the bilge myself. Sure enough, there were 25 inches of water down in the bauxite. Hurrying back to the bridge, I summoned the chief mate and chief engineer and told them what was happening. We decided to try sounding again.

The chief mate stationed himself aft with the sounding rod and the chief engineer went below to his pump. Again the signal to pump was given. A half-hour later the mate reported that there seemed to be no change; if anything, the water had gone down only an inch or two. We decided to leave the pump on. It was only in the light of later events that we realized the water hadn't gone down at all. It was coming in fast and permeating the bauxite.

At 4:30 that afternoon Chip made his customary rounds, sounding all the holds. Again he came flying up to the bridge where the mate and I were arguing the respective merits of reciprocating engines versus turbines. Chip shouted from the lower bridge ladder: "Five feet, Captain! Five feet in #5."

Immediately I ordered the pump stopped. Now what? A ship loaded as deeply as we were wouldn't need much water in her to sink her. Mentally I calculated the weight of five feet of water in a hold the size of #5. The result wasn't reassuring. A little more and we would slip beneath the waves like a stone.

In view of the seriousness of the situation, I ordered all the boats swung out and additional provisions stowed in them. All hands were alerted to remain dressed and ready to abandon ship. Another conference was held. Had we sprung a leak? Struck a submerged derelict?

All at once, a peculiar fact became apparent to me: the only time water came in was when the pump was operating. The chief engineer scoffed at the thought and pressed for pumping again. Something made me ignore his idea. Instead, a man was stationed at the #5 bilge sounding pipe with orders to sound the hold every fifteen minutes. We kept this up day and night until we approached Canada two weeks later. No more water came in and no further attempts were made to pump any out.

The solution to the mystery appeared after the ship was discharged. But more about that later in its proper place. In the meantime, we were fast approaching Sable Island off the coast of Cape Breton.

Sable Island: a lighthouse, shifting sands, gales, fog, and a few wild horses surviving God only knows how. Two days south of Sable we ran into the usual pea soup fog that prevails most of the time. With good reason, Sable has an excellent Radio Direction Finder station, and I took full advantage of it.

This was in the days before radar, but we had a first-class Radio Direction Finder (RDF) and a modern fathometer. We proceeded right up to the island and passed it a half-mile on our port hand. Then, with the RDF indicating we were clear, we put the helm hard left and headed northwest for Cabot Strait and the Gulf of St. Lawrence. All this while the fog was so thick the bow was invisible from the bridge. I felt that I had turned in a fair piece of seamanship. Felt it in my own mind. It was times like these that paid me my wages. I would have gone to sea for no wages, just for the chance of doing such things.

Through Cabot Straits and across the Gulf of St. Lawrence we sailed, never seeing a thing. Bird Island lay close to on the starboard hand. We knew we were on course, thanks to our fathometer. The hundred-fathom curve there is a direct-course line clear of land. We had only to stay on it and keep the fog horn going.

I was getting pretty weary. Three days and nights of cold Newfoundland fog had penetrated my bones and I felt stiff and old. According to our dead reckoning, Anticosti Island was now just off the starboard bows. It would soon be time to turn and head up the St. Lawrence River.

At last, just before dawn, the fog lifted. About time, too. Several shore lights and beacons were clearly visible and a quick check showed us on course. I took one more look around to make sure that the fog had cleared before dragging my weary bones down the ladder to my room.

Tired as I was, as I dropped my boots with a thump I couldn't help wondering, "How did that water get into #5?" It was an uneasy sleep that finally claimed me, for even now the water just might be gaining.

By the time I awoke we had passed Cape Chat and were steaming up the broad St. Lawrence, heading for Father Point, the pilot station. The fog had cleared completely and the air was so clear it seemed to sparkle. We were shortly to be treated to one of the rare sights of the sea.

A short distance ahead of us was an old British tramp steamer, also heading for Father Point. She looked to be three or four miles ahead, perhaps more, but close enough so I could note the details of her poop without my binoculars.

I had never been up here before, so I dug out the *Sailing Directions* again. I read that the Quarantine and Immigration officials would board us with the pilot while the ship remained underway on a slow bell. In other words, we would not come to anchor.

Returning to the bridge, I reasoned that the Britisher just ahead would arrive only a few minutes before us and would be occupied the best part of an hour clearing Quarantine. Meanwhile, we would be forced to maneuver about until he finished. I figured it would be much more sensible for us to slow down so as to arrive an hour or so after he did. That way, he would be finished and out of the way, leaving us plenty of room to steam about. Accordingly, I put the engines on half speed.

An hour or so later, the buildings and dock of Father Point appeared clearly on the left bank. Oddly, the Britisher hadn't pulled away from us at all. He was still just ahead. I rang the engines down to Slow Ahead. Pretty soon we saw our friend up ahead veer to the left, heading into the Point. We could see the pilot boat getting underway. The two vessels closed and we saw the Canadian officials climbing up the Jacob's ladder. Not wanting to crowd in, I put the engines on stop. After a while, we saw the Quarantine people climbing down the ladder into their boat. The Britisher pulled back out in the river and I rang up Full Ahead. Then an odd thing happened: after steaming ahead for the next 2-1/2 hours at ten knots, we still weren't up to the Point!

When at last the pilot came aboard he told us that on very rare occasions, especially after an unusually thick fog, something happens to the air on the river, something to do with refraction of light, dryness, temperature. Anway, it increases visibility to unheard-of distances. Sometimes, he said, you can clearly distinguish landmarks 40 miles away! I believed him, for that British steamer was probably between 20 and 30 miles ahead of us, yet I would have sworn she was only four miles off at most. This was one of those things like waterspouts, St. Elmo's fire, and sea serpents that you hear about in fo'c'sles but rarely encounter even in a lifetime at sea.

We were now in store for another rare treat. Port Alfred, our destination, was located way up the Saguenay River, a tributary of the St. Lawrence into which it empties a short distance above Father Point. It is a bit confusing to use the word "above" because, although the traveler is steaming up the St. Lawrence, he is heading almost due South. The Saguenay, therefore, angles off in a generally northwest direction up into the province of Quebec. The Saguenay is considered one of the most scenic trips in the world. In summer, excursion steamers leave Montreal daily for the overnight trip down the St. Lawrence and up the Saguenay to Port Alfred for an overnight stay before returning the next day.

Our pilot was a small, cheerful French Canadian who, as we steamed along, explained the highlights of this renowned river. First, it is incredibly deep: 600 feet in places. Imagine a river 100 fathoms deep! It was cut out of the mountains thousands and thousands of years before by a glacier. I like to think of that glacier as a gigantic ship with a razor-sharp keel 600 feet deep. As the glacier-ship meandered southward, it sliced this crack now known as the Saguenay. Now, so many years later, we appreciated the beautiful trip that was its legacy, winding between high cliffs, some barren and some rocky, some covered with spruce, hemlock, and pine.

Just before sunset, our pilot told us we were approaching "The Shrine." Many, many years ago, he told us, a wealthy traveler was crossing the iced-over river. At midstream the ice went out, pitching him and his horse among the grinding floes. He had only one chance in a million of surviving. Hope dies hard, though, and as he struggled for his life in the swiftly running, icy water, he vowed that if the Lord spared him he would erect a statue of the Virgin Mary on the river bank.

Miraculously, he washed ashore, alive. True to his word he had a mammoth figure built, and as we came around the bend just then we saw it. The pilot said it was the custom for all ships to pull over close to the cliffs and blow three long blasts on the whistle while the hands said a silent prayer. Most travelers also threw coins in the river for luck. A quaint custom, but it appealed to me.

I nodded to the helmsman and we swung left. When we were abreast of the statue, I leaned on the whistle cord. Three mournful blasts echoed and re-echoed between the cliffs as I dropped a few coins over the rail and into the water. Looking up at the figure, I breathed my own silent prayer, "Please, God, no fog on this river." With 600 fathoms I couldn't anchor. And with no room to maneuver I would surely slam into the cliffs and lose my ship if we did have fog.

Was it my imagination or did I detect the ghost of a smile as a bend in the river hid the statue from view as we slid by? I choose to think she smiled, for we not only arrived at Port Alfred in good weather, but came safely back down the river as well. I remember that when we again drew abeam of the statue on our way down, I circled my forefinger and thumb and waved in the manner of fellow conspirators.

Meanwhile, Port Alfred. Another bauxite pier. We had no sooner tied up when giant clam shell grabs began digging us out. Now the mystery in #5 was about to be solved.

Soon after the grabs began discharging, they struck water-soaked bauxite. What a mess! An analysis verified what we already knew: sea water had gotten in. All the wet ore had to be kept apart from the remainder of the cargo. It was later dried and used, but as several hundred tons were involved my owners eventually paid a very substantial claim.

Now, when at last the hold was emptied, the chief mate and I went down the ladders to the bottom and immediately to the bilge boxes. Everything seemed to be in order beneath the box covers. The mate straightened up, and for no particular reason swung his flashlight around. Light glinted from a small metal object resting on one of the frames just above the bilges. I think we both realized at the same instant what had happened.

Remember the night down in the jungle river? The night one of the assistant engineers repaired the bilge valve? When he reassembled the valve he forgot to replace what is known as a non-returnable blank. These blanks allow water to pass in only one direction through the valve. Without that blank, instead of water being pumped from the bilge through the bilge manifold and into the sea, the reverse had taken place. We had been pumping the Atlantic Ocean into the ship! A few more hours of pumping and Lloyds of London would have tolled the bell for us as they do for every casualty of the sea that results in a ship being lost.

—3—

ORDERS TO ASSUME COMMAND

When I received my first letter to assume command, my feelings were indescribable. Elation, pride, overwhelming joy, gratefulness ... any word I could think of was inadequate. This was the culmination of all that had gone before, all that I had dreamed of, worked for, yearned for. With that letter from Captain Litchfield, the marine superintendent, all my dreams came true. I had finally made it!

I had sailed as chief mate long enough. Maybe too long. I had stayed on one ship that slogged the North Atlantic back and forth, then did a long stint in the Mediterranean. On another long stint the ship got stuck for several months during the Normandy Invasion. There were other ships and other voyages of two or three months each. It was time I sat for my master's ticket, so I paid off and went home to study.

Study I did, day and night. My living room floor was strewn with papers, books, navigational tables. The examination for master was unlike the ones for third, second, and chief mate I'd already sat for. The list of subjects was so long I wondered how it could all be crammed in my head.

On top of this, two other obstacles faced me. First was the time limit: five days. Unfortunately, I'm a slow writer. Teachers were only partially successful in attempting to switch me from being a left-hander to a righty in my early school years. As a result, I print with my right hand, which slows me considerably.

The other obstacle was equally frustrating. Before World War II, celestial navigation was a tedious business. The task of solving a spherical triangle involved trigonometry. This meant using the logarithms table of the trigonometric functions, which were carried out to five decimal points. A poor second mate, rousted out of his bunk after only a couple of hours sleep, found himself struggling with the cosecant of this or sine of that. The whole was subtracted from the cotangent of something-or-other. It was slow work, and the margin of error was considerable.

Then, early in the war, marvelous books appeared in chart rooms all over the seas: Dreisenstock's *H.O. 208, H.O. 211*, and finally *H.O. 214*. These books of tables solved all the trigonometric functions. Also about this time the *Air Almanac* made its appearance. It was far superior to the old *Nautical Almanac*. Equipped with a set of *H.O. 214*, the *Air Almanac*, and accurate chronometer time thanks to radio ticks from NSS, navigation had become a relative cinch. Shoot the sun with your sextant, note the chronometer time, enter the tables for a couple of quick and simple calculations, and presto – there was a fine LOP (Line of Position).

The trouble was, in those days the examiners wouldn't let us use these wonderful new books. Despite the fact that we had become rusty with them, we had to use the logarithmic tables. The Coast Guard had taken over the duties of the Steamboat Inspection Service administered by the Department of Commerce. They did it by putting the civilian Steamboat Inspection men into Coast Guard uniforms. These ex-civil servants were not unlike Supreme Court judges in that change of any kind among them evolved very slowly. They were not yet ready to recognize the value of the new tables.

So it was back to the Bowditch for me. I still have the list of required subjects. It looked endless.

Latitude by Polaris
Ex-Meridian
Longitude by chronometer (Sun, Moon, Star)
Sumner Line (Fix)
Great Circle sailing
Fuel consumption
Stability and Hull construction
Ocean winds
Weather and Currents
Navigation laws
Seamanship

On and on it went. The very last on the long, long list was the most ominous: "Miscellaneous." How do you study for that one?

Day after day, night after night, I struggled and memorized until my head was about to burst. Finally, I knew I was as ready as I'd ever be.

The next morning, a Monday, I took a bus to Boston and offered myself up to the examiner promptly at 8 a.m. I was directed to a room that looked just like a schoolroom: rows of desks facing forward. The examiner motioned me forward. He looked so forbidding and grim. He nodded as I presented my discharges, then went over them carefully to make sure I had served the required time. Already, there were several other men in the room either writing furiously or gazing into space with their faces screwed up in the effort of recalling an elusive answer.

There were four index card boxes on the examiner's desk, labeled "Third Mate," "Second Mate," "Chief Mate," and "Master." He selected a card from the "Master" box and handed it to me along with two sheets of paper.

"Write your answer on one sheet. Use the other for scratch. When you finish, bring both sheets and get another card. You may work at your own pace. However, if you haven't finished by 4 p.m. Friday, you will have failed. Good luck!"

I began spilling out everything I had memorized onto those lined sheets. As soon as I had finished one card, it was silently taken from me and replaced with another. At noon I dashed downstairs to a cafeteria for a quick bowl of soup. I left two notebooks with the cashier, one containing my notes, the other blank. During the morning I could tell from the way the cards were running what subject would be next, so I'd skim over the notes. In the other notebook I scribbled all the questions I could remember. I also noted navigational problems and their answers. I had done this when I sat for my chief mate's ticket. I had an idea then in the back of my head that if shipping got tough, maybe I'd start a navigation school with this information for men seeking to upgrade their tickets.

The week dragged on. Every night I'd study until late, going over and over the subjects yet to be faced. The next day I'd write and compute. My nerves were winding tighter and tighter. Yet when Thursday rolled around I figured I would finish that afternoon. In spite of my slow handwriting, I had been sailing along at a pretty good clip. When I went up for my last card of the day I asked the examiner if I was ahead or behind schedule.

"Mmm," said he, snapping the box shut. "Same time tomorrow, 8 a.m." That's all I got out of him.

Friday. The last day. Would I make it? I was so nervous that the first two cards seemed impossible to answer. Finally I got my second wind and stepped up the pace. I could tell from the last few cards on navigational laws that I was coming down the home stretch. No going for soup today. About 2:30 p.m. I walked up to His Lordship's desk and handed in my current card and answer.

"That will be all," he said. "Please return to your seat."

My God, was I finished? "What about Miscellaneous?" I stuttered.

"Mister, I give out cards at my discretion. On any given subject I might give two, four, or any amount until your answers satisfy me that you have or have not grasped the subject. If you want more cards I'll be quite happy to oblige, up to 4 p.m."

"Oh no, sir, I ... "

"Well, just go sit down. It's been a tiring week."

Though I hadn't realized it, he had been correcting my papers as fast as I turned them in. Not ten minutes later he said, "You," pointing a bony finger toward me. I marched up to the desk, trying vainly to stop my legs from shaking. They were trembling so badly my pants were flapping as though a half gale was blowing. The examiner finished scribbling on a card.

"Take this to the next office. They'll process your new ticket."

"You mean, Sir ... you mean I've passed?"

He never looked up. "Out. First door on your left."

I walked out of that room 40 feet tall, new words echoing in my head: *Master! You will address me as Captain, damn your eyes!*

An enlisted man made out my ticket, had it signed by the commander, Officer in Charge of Marine Inspection, slipped it into a manilla envelope, and handed it to me.

"There you are, Cap."

"Captain," I shot back.

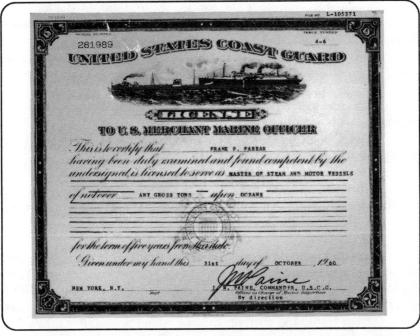

At last! The culmination of all I had worked for. (Since the current license must be relinquished with each 5-year renewal, this is my last one, not my first.)

Monday morning, right on the stroke of nine, the phone rang.

"Captain Farrar?"

Captain! How did whoever it was know? "Yes?"

"This is Captain Litchfield's secretary. The Captain would like to see you in an hour if you can make it. 'Bye."

Make it? Nobody *ever* keeps Captain Litchfield waiting. I was out the door in five minutes, plowing through the snow to the bus stop. I arrived at 40 Central Street with ten minutes to spare. In the elevator, the operator said, "Cold morning, Captain."

As I entered the outer office, the switchboard operator flung me a "Hi, Captain."

What the hell was going on? I entered Captain Litchfield's outer office, and was greeted by his kindly, gray-haired secretary. "Please be seated, Captain. The Captain will see you shortly."

The whole damned city of Boston seemed to know something I didn't. A man didn't rate being called Captain until he had a command, even if he did have the ticket.

The secretary spent a few moments in the inner office, then out she bounced. "Captain Litchfield is on long distance, but he thought you'd like to read this while you wait."

I opened the envelope she handed me and unfolded a letter addressed to "Captain Frank Farrar." Typed in capital letters on the face of it was, "ORDERS TO ASSUME COMMAND."

Usually, I'm pretty stoic. But when I read that I choked up and my eyes got all blurred. Smiling, the secretary came over with a small paper cup.

"Congratulations, Captain. You're not the first one to feel this way, you know. A few more have come before you."

"Thank you very much." I downed the contents of the cup. It was very good Scotch whiskey.

"The Captain, poor dear, has been working 12 hours a day all through the War, and sometimes at night. On his way home, he'll stop here first for a little sip," the secretary explained. "There he is buzzing for you now. Go straight in, please."

Captain Litchfield is one of the finest, most able men I have ever known. He had been one of Eastern's crack skippers on the New York-Boston overnight run, a killer if ever there was one. Sail from the North River at 5 p.m. down around the Battery, through Hell's Gate, up the East River with its traffic and currents to Long Island Sound, Buzzard's Bay, and through the Cape Cod Canal, thence to Boston. Gales, fog and more fog – nothing stopped him. Even with the responsibility for a thousand passengers weighing him down. When the war came and the company took on dozens of Libertys and Victorys, he took on the almost impossible job of crewing, sorting, repairing, and dispatching them. By God, he was equal to it.

Now, as always, he was pressed for time. But his remarks made me glow. "You've been a good chief mate. You will also be a good master. If you need me, write or call. The very best to you in your first command.

Now, be off. If you hurry, you can catch the 7 p.m. train out of South Station for Charleston." A quick handshake, a walloping thump on the back and I was out the door. What a great guy! I vowed then and there that I'd never let him down.

Back home on the bus again. It was snowing like blazes, and already we had a foot on the ground from the last storm. The bus slithered to a stop. Up the hill I trudged, kicking the snow gleefully. Walking on clouds, I was.

In no time I had my seabag and suitcase packed. My boy was at school in Waltham, Massachusetts. I got the principal to bring him to the phone. I said "So long" to him, and asked him to pick up his sled at the bottom of the hill. I flung my seabag and suitcase on the sled, buttoned my overcoat, and was off down the hill again, sextant box in one hand, the other pulling the sled.

As Litchfield knew I would, I made that 7 p.m. southbound train. I checked my seabag and suitcase through in the baggage car and fought through to a coach seat. There were no berths available.

There would be little sleep on this train tonight. Servicemen were prowling the aisles, drinking out of bottles in brown paper bags. I placed my sextant box on my lap and carefully smoothed out the precious letter. I gloated over it, drooled over it. It was real!

I was to proceed with all possible dispatch to Charleston, South Carolina, there to assume command of the SS *Augustus P. Loring*, presently loading for Brest, France. Upon arriving, I was to go to the Customs House and sign the ship's register. That little exercise would make me officially and legally her master.

The next morning I staggered off the train, stiff and sore from a sleepless night in the coach. Clutching my sextant, I went to claim my baggage. It couldn't be found, nor was it ever found until two years later. Then it turned up in Boston, moldy and worthless. Meanwhile, there I was facing a winter crossing of the North Atlantic with nothing but the old brown suit and topcoat on my back. Some of the euphoria started to leak out.

I headed first to the Customs House and signed the ship's register. Next stop was the agent's office, where I discovered to my horror that we were to sail that night as soon as loading was completed. The ship had been stored and bunkered. The previous skipper was waiting on board to turn over the inventory.

"Order me a tow boat for 11 p.m.," I told the agent. Then it was off for a quick sandwich, and back to the Customs House to clear the ship.

Once aboard, I had a quick session with the outgoing skipper and signed for his inventory. Then to the chief engineer: more than enough bunkers, he told me. Chief steward? We were stored for three months.

Finally, I met with the chief mate. I was well impressed with him: a Harvard graduate and a real proper Bostonian. In the chart room he showed me the course laid out by the previous skipper. It was an ultra-conservative course. Southeast to latitude 33 North off Bermuda, east and then northerly to the Azores, then Brest. I changed that. We would stick our snout northerly, all the way up to a point south of Newfoundland, following a Great Circle course eastward. That meant a winter crossing of the Western Ocean with all its gales and raging storms.

I impressed on the mate the necessity of battening down, especially the lifeboats. By the time we finished, supper on board was over so we went ashore for a bite.

I was worn out from lack of sleep and the tension of being a green shipmaster about to embark on his first command. We went into the first restaurant we came to, both of us in a hurry. My eggs were OK, but when I chomped down on a piece of tough, stringy bacon my bridgework broke in two pieces. This voyage was starting off just great. No clothes – now no teeth! Without the bridge I looked like a jack-o-lantern, two fangs on each side.

Back at the ship, I raided the slop chest for long underwear, oil-skins, work shoes, and a razor. I'd make do with what I found.

The ship was a beehive of activity. All hands were battening down and securing for sea. A towboat was alongside, her stack huffing quietly. I shared coffee with the pilot in the saloon. Promptly at 11 p.m. the mate came in. "The ship's ready for sea, Captain. Gangway's up, lines singled up. We're ready to go."

"Right-o, Mister. Let's go!" I hadn't gotten used to being addressed as Captain, but how sweet it was!

The pilot and I made our way up to the bridge. "Mister, ring up Stand By on the engine, please."

"Stand By. Aye."

And off we went into the winter night. We dropped off the pilot and hauled around on our northerly course up toward a point south of Newfoundland. There we would commence our Great Circle course across the North Atlantic, amid the winter gales ready to pounce out of the northwest.

Pounce they did! That entire voyage was an unending struggle with the weather. The gales never stopped. Both of our port lifeboats were stove in. The portside accommodation ladder washed away. All the wooden life rafts were smashed to bits and swept over the side.

One wild night our chief mate, the Boston Brahmin, asked me to relieve him because the stern light had burned out. I had just crawled into the wheelhouse myself after being on deck. God, that wind was fierce!

"Mister, the hell with the stern light. No ship is going to run up on us in this gale. Let it go 'til it moderates."

But he insisted, and out he went. The best part of an hour went by before he returned, soaked to the hide, a big lump on his temple. In a masterful understatement, his only comment was, "Wretched evening, Capt'n."

Wretched!

Day and night I kept to the bridge, conning the ship, easing the helm, and adjusting our engine revolutions to the weather. And still it blew, always from the port quarter. I began to think somebody had put a curse on us. Part of an old sea chanty kept running through my tired head:

"And out of the North she come.
It blew the tar right off the spars;
And the spars right off the masts.
Buckets and pails, and kegs of nails
Went by in the wintry blast."

The next day, Sparks brought me a message from our owners. "Cancel Brest. Proceed to Le Havre for discharge." OK with me. Besides, Le Havre was an easier port to get into.

Course was changed to our new destination. But that was all that changed. The weather remained foul. The wind was still Force 6 to 8, now a little more on the beam.

We entered the English Channel, hoping for a break, but it just got worse. The seas in those waters are different from the open Atlantic. Their short, vicious waves hit like solid iron. What little sleep I got was lying on my bunk with just my shoes off. Folded at the foot of my bunk was a very fancy blanket. It was royal blue, with a big, gold seal of the War Shipping Administration embossed on it. I'd pull it over me for an hour or two. When I got up, I'd fold it again. I didn't know it at the time, but the cabin steward spread the word below decks in hushed tones: "He ain't human. Hasn't been in his bunk since we left Charleston!"

Finally, one cold, wintry day we picked our way into Le Havre and dropped anchor. Sparks had radioed our E.T.A., so the agent had to know we had arrived. Yet we lay there unacknowledged for four days, licking our wounds. At last, one morning out came a towboat whose skipper acted as harbor pilot. In short order he had us alongside. The French agent put in an appearance and gave me a ride up to the port officials' building. He told me we were to discharge only enough tonnage to lighten our draft so we could proceed up the Seine River to Rouen, where we would complete discharge.

On the way up the river, the pilot told me about a phenomenon that happens every day in the lower part of the Seine. Called *Le Muscaret* ("the bore" in English), it is a cresting wave, potentially dangerous, which rushes down the river at incredible speed. This phenomenon, found in only two or three other rivers in the world, is caused by the down-flowing current meeting the rushing incoming tidal flow.

We got near Rouen about mid-afternoon. Because it is a tidal port, its locks can only be opened when the tide is right. Set into the river bottom is a series of pile clusters called "moles." A small boat tied our lines fore and aft to the moles where we waited for the locks to open. The pilot warned me to have the engine ready, men standing by the lines, ready to take action if the force of *Le Muscaret* parted our lines. Properly impressed, I made all arrangements.

We were sitting in the saloon waiting for supper when the pilot jumped up. "Here she comes – *Le Muscaret!*"

We rushed out to an awesome sight: a wall of water roaring down the river. The ship surged back on her moorings, but held fast. *Le Muscaret* disappeared down river, but not from memory.

The rest of my first command was quite ordinary. I took in the sights of Rouen. It is truly a magnificent town, fortunately spared by the Germans. After discharging, we steamed across the English Channel, up into the Bristol Channel to Newport Mons in Wales for 2000 tons of ballast. Then it was off to Cardiff to bunker for Philadelphia.

Our return home via the Southern Route was just another voyage. But though it was run-of-the mill for a tramp steamer, to me it was the greatest experience of my life.

Still is.

Tall oaks from little acorns grow.

David Everett

—4—

BACKWARD TO THE CAREFREE DAYS

My childhood was spent on the coast of New England, mostly within sight and sound of the sea. My father would point seaward and tell me that just beyond the horizon lay Spain, Portugal, Africa. I used to sit on the rocks and stare eastward, conjuring pictures of those far-off lands. Some day I would go and see them for myself. I wondered if they would be like my geography books described them.

By the time I entered high school I had become a confirmed reader of sea stories. I read everything I could lay my hands on pertaining to ships. I knew all about Donald McKay's famous clipper ships. I could quote from memory passages from their log books chronicling their record-breaking voyages around the Horn. All the tales of the whaling ships were familiar to me. When the wind howled 'round the eaves at night during a Northeaster I imagined I was a sailor making sail down in the Roaring Forties.

I was a great disappointment to my father, who planned that after high school I would enter Massachusetts Institute of Technology and become an engineer. I was stubborn and willful, as so many of us are at 16.

Without his knowledge, I canvassed all the shipping companies in Boston seeking a berth. On Saturdays I used to call at the offices of the port captains in Boston.

Finally, a month before high school graduation I was promised a berth as a deck boy on the SS *Seattle Spirit*. The ship was due to sail the day after graduation exercises. I waited until the night before to announce my plans. Oh, how that storm raged! It went on and on, but my stubbornness prevailed. Two days later, a skinny, scared kid, I stood at the head of the pier and looked up the rusty sides of my new home.

I will never forget my first meeting with Mr. Kelly, the chief mate. The product of an Irish father and a French Canadian-Indian mother, he looked like an ugly, mahogany-skinned bull. He glared at me as I stepped off the gangway onto the midships deck.

"So you're the new boy, huh? Stow your gear in the fo'c'sle and report to the bosun."

Those were the only words of welcome I received. He looked so cranky I didn't dare to ask him where the fo'c'sle was. Instead, I timidly started forward.

His roar brought me up short. "Aft, you dummy!"

I turned back and sneaked by him, half expecting a kick in the rear. Clutching my one suitcase, I made my way aft under the poop deck. Just inside a big iron door I spied the mess room. Inside was a little man noisily washing dishes. He turned out to be George, the messboy. Like most of the messboys of those times, he was Greek. (I later learned that no matter what their real names, aboard ship all Greeks are called either George or Nick.)

George showed me where the sailor's fo'c'sle was. It was a long, dimly lit room all the way aft on the starboard side. Double decker iron bunks lined one side, crude wooden lockers occupied the other. The place was deserted. I quickly changed, putting on a brand new pair of dungarees. That big chief mate had taken all the starch out of me and now I didn't dare go out again, 'though I knew everyone was on deck, working.

While I stood there getting up my courage, someone entered. I couldn't believe my eyes. Even though the doorway was of conventional size, he had to stoop to get through! I found out later that the bosun (for that's who this was) was six feet eight. He was stripped to the waist. And of all the fine figures of men I've since seen, he outstripped them all. He looked like a combination Greek god and professional weightlifter. The muscles across his shoulders rippled like brown snakes. He barked at me in a foreign tongue. When I didn't answer he spoke again, this time in a guttural, broken English.

"You are de new boy, ja? Vat's your name?"

He was a German, a native of Hamburg. I soon found out that almost the entire crew were Germans. These were days in which immigration laws were not rigidly enforced. Because this particular ship was running regularly to Hamburg and Bremen, it was natural that a good chief mate would take advantage of the fact that Germany had come upon evil times economically, and hire some of the thousands of good German seamen that were on the beach in Hamburg.

My boyhood days were over. The bosun had me out on deck in no time, and in one day I was a man, doing a man's work. That night we all sat down at the long table in the messroom for supper. As befitted a boy, I sat at the foot of the table. The bosun presided at the head. Then came the oldest able seaman and so on, down to the ship's boy. After swinging a chipping hammer all day, my appetite was as sharp as a razor.

The messboy brought in a big pan of meat and gravy. The bosun forked several pieces onto his plate and passed it on to the first A.B. When the pan finally reached me I stabbed my fork down into the thick gravy, drooling. Nothing was left, only gravy. I looked up the table. All hands were busy eating. The bosun saw me looking and growled, "Vat's de matter, boy?" I replied that there was no meat and I was hungry. Mopping up the last of his plate with a piece of bread occupied him for a minute. Then he told me that on a ship men eat before boys, and boys eat what men leave, so if I wanted to eat I'd better become a man. Brutal and direct.

All right, I said to myself. *I'll show him. I'll learn everything there is to learn and I'll work harder than anyone else. I will be a man.*

The SS Seattle Spirit was built in Seattle, Washington, in 1919. She measured 410 feet from stem to stern, had a 54' beam, and measured 28' to the water line.

The next morning at dawn we sailed for Hamburg. As ship's boy, I wasn't put on watch but was assigned to work on deck with the bosun. He was a slave master and I his slave. The work was heavy. Great hawsers and coils of tackle had to be stowed below. The cargo handling gear had to be put away. And always that gigantic bosun loomed over me. When lifting something heavy he would always have his end up first. Then would come the "Lift, boy. Vat's de matter? You tired?"

For a while I hated him. I longed to push him over the side and used to imagine how easy it would be. *Wait till he's close to the rail. A quick lunge and he'll be gone, off my back.*

Then, without my quite knowing when or why, I began to admire him, and so commenced to emulate him. I didn't talk much because he didn't. I scrubbed my dungarees in a bucket every night because he did.

Seemed a waste of time to me because by noon of the next day they were dirty again. Still, he said that a good sailor wore clean clothes. I took pride in doing good work, of being able to endure broiling sun and chill winds without complaining because that's the way he was. Today I am very grateful to him. He formed habits in me that have stood me in good stead ever since.

The days passed quickly. Because I didn't stand a watch, Sundays were free. The first Sunday out I wandered midships after breakfast. It was a fine sunny morning and we were about half way across the Atlantic. I could see the third mate up on the bridge, his officer's cap snowy white in the sun.

That's where I'll be some day, I vowed. The decks were deserted, so I summoned my courage and went up the ladder to the bridge. I sidled over to the third mate, Mr. Brown, and ventured a "Good morning." Before he could answer, a roar behind me made me jump.

"Mr. Mate, what's this boy doing on the bridge?"

It was the Old Man himself. I looked for a way to escape, but the captain was blocking the ladder. I stood there not knowing what to do. Mr. Brown saved the day for me.

"He's up here to learn how to steer," he said.

"Humph," grunted the Old Man. "I thought this new generation knew it all. Well, boy, don't stand there. Get into the wheel house and take the wheel. And mind your course."

I was actually being allowed to steer this great ship!

The quartermaster relinquished the spokes to me and explained that the lubber's line on the edge of the compass represented the ship's head. All I had to do was keep the black line on the course. He showed me the one brass spoke on the wheel which, when it was pointing straight up, meant that the rudder was midships. At night the helmsman stood in darkness except for the dim light coming from the compass binnacle. By feeling the brass spoke he could tell where his rudder was.

And so the days went by. The work was hard, but little by little the strangeness wore off. I got to know the rest of the crew – the firemen, the oilers, the cooks. Slowly, they came to accept me. I acquired a nickname, "Slim." Had I not been accepted, it would have been "Skinny."

The ship made Bishop's Rock, the entrance to the English Channel. As we proceeded up the Channel the bosun spent most of his time trying to keep me on the job. The Channel was full of shipping, and instead of working I spent my time staring at the various craft.

"Bosun, what kind of ship is that?" I'd ask.

"That's called an English drifter. Now get back to work."

"Bosun, what's that one just over the port bow?"

"That's a Frenchman, home from The Banks after 12 months fishing for cod."

And so my education proceeded. Every day I learned something more about the sea and ships and of how the ships were sailed. Although he never by the slightest sign admitted it, I think that the bosun had come to like me, too. His gruffness and growling continued unabated, but he went out of his way to teach me the proper way to splice, to sew canvas, to reeve a tackle, or to do whatever else needed doing.

In a day or two we were up to the entrance of the Elbe River. The pilot who would take us up the river came bobbing over in his little boat, rowed by two apprentice pilots. The bosun had warned me that the mate, Mr. Kelly, was very particular about boarding a pilot. The slightest slip-up, anything done in a slipshod way, and there would be no living with him for days. The bosun claimed that when Mr. Kelly went into a rage, all the Indian in him came to the surface and he went on the warpath, scalping everyone in reach.

It was therefore a great source of pride to me that the bosun let me rig the boat rope and stand by the forward end of it. When a pilot's small boat comes alongside a large vessel, it must make contact well forward, near the bow on the lee side. Then an apprentice must boat the oar and grab the boat rope. This rope must be rigged not more than a foot above the water's edge, not so slack that it would lay in the water, and not so high that it couldn't be reached from the small boat.

Chief mate Mr. Kelly, with Red, my fellow deck boy.

After the rowboat comes alongside, the apprentice grabs the rope, gradually slacking the small boat aft until he reaches the Jacob's ladder amidships. The seaman on the ship must stand by the forward end of the boat rope, holding one round turn on a bitt. The seaman leans over the bow, gauging the height of the waves and the size of the boat, slacking off or pulling in as needed. A mistake in judgment necessitates a second try with its resulting delays.

I watched the little boat approach, never taking my eyes off it. By the grace of God I am gifted with side vision. I spied the bosun standing by the Jacob's ladder, frantically signaling me to slack off. I did, promptly. The rowboat made contact, slacked off down to the ladder, and made fast.

When the pilot came aboard, the mate's affable "Secure, Bosun," was music to my ears.

But praise is a forgotten word on a ship. It wasn't the bosun's job to pass on kind words. The bosun and I set about pulling in the ladder and boat rope. Because we were within sight and hearing of the bridge, the bosun had to confine his usual caustic remarks to a whisper. "Dummer! Stupid boy! You will never be a sailor!"

Hamburg has always been a world-famous sailor town. Tales of its attractions, told in the fo'c'sle at night, had inflamed my imagination. Two young German A.B.s offered to take me ashore with them the first night. Figuring they knew their way around, I accepted gratefully.

When the time came, we all lined up midships for a "draw." I drew the great sum of five dollars as an advance on my pay. When the bosun shouted "Knock off!" at 5 o'clock, we all dashed for the messroom. Supper was over in a jiffy. Buckets clattered in the washroom as we scrubbed at the red lead, fish oil, and tar stains. On those old ships we had no such luxury as running water. In fact, it was an exceptionally good ship that allowed as much as two buckets of fresh water a day. Those had to serve for both bathing and washing clothes.

Promptly at 7 we were off. I was a sailor ashore in my first port. Consciously, I adopted a salt sea roll. Before we reached the city I was swaggering along with my hands shoved in my belt, for all the world like Sinbad himself.

I strode along, eagerly anticipating adventurous sights. But the closest we came was a stop at the post office for stamps and a stroll through the beer gardens surrounding beautiful Alster Lake in the center of the city. An orchestra was playing in one of the gardens, so we sat at a little table under the trees and drank a stein of German beer to the strains of Strauss waltzes.

We were back on board before midnight, leaving behind an uneventful and somehow unsatisfying evening. The next night would be different, I decided. Yet if only I had known what tomorrow night would bring, I would instead have made a vow to stay on board until the ship sailed.

I got my memorable night the next evening. I went ashore with one of the firemen and George, the messboy. Both had made several trips to Hamburg and claimed to be real old-timers in St. Pauli, the waterfront district.

First they took me to a cabaret. Except for a few glasses of my grandfather's home brew and the one stein of beer the night before, I had never had a drink. But now I was a sailor, a tough guy. Hadn't all the sailors I'd ever read about always gotten drunk when they went ashore? Well, by golly, what were we waiting for?

Since we didn't have much money, we couldn't afford to buy drinks in such a fancy place. George got the idea of sneaking out and buying a bottle of cheap brandy. Pretending he was looking for someone, he left the table and sauntered out. We ordered three steins of beer.

While we were placing our order, two girls who had been sitting at the next table rose and came over. Very politely, they asked if they could join us. I was overcome with embarrassment. My face crimson, I nodded mutely. My experience with the opposite sex was practically nil, and where I came from young ladies were more decorous. These were pretty, though, and I was flattered beyond words.

They seated themselves and immediately started chattering like magpies in quite good English. Their conversation, sometimes directed at us, more often to each other, sounded like the latest edition of the shipping news. They knew every ship that was in port, who was in the crew, how long they would remain ... everything!

Amazed, I asked them if they worked in a shipping office. They burst into gales of laughter interspersed with machine-gun German. One of them patted me on the head and said it must be my first trip. When I admitted that it was, she moved her chair closer and asked if she could please have a drink. By this time, my head was in the clouds. Here were two beautiful girls falling into our arms. Being a sailor was the life!

Recklessly, I told the waiter to bring them both a beer. The one who had attached herself to me snuggled closer and said that she didn't like beer and couldn't she have a small Grenadine. The other one echoed her. Nodding assent to the waiter, I boldly put my arm around my new friend.

Just then George returned with the cognac. We dumped a dollop into our beers and took big swigs. A third fraulein appeared and latched onto George. He seemed delighted. Between guzzling beer and cognac, he barked away at her in his native Greek, she all the while smiling and bobbing her head, not understanding a word.

Periodically, the waiter brought the girls more little glasses. There was music and noise and confusion. The cognac slowly disappeared into the beer. The mixture burned its way down our foolish gullets.

My memory of events from then on is dim. I recall the waiter totaling our bill by counting the saucers stacked in front of each girl. The amount was staggering. Craftily, I hid one mark from my funds in my pocket, the price of launch fare back to the ship, and laid the rest on the table. My two shipmates did the same. Our girls melted away. More waiters and the bouncer made threatening noises. Everything swirled round and round. I felt as if I was on a gigantic merry-go-round spinning faster and faster, propelling us through the door. Then I was sitting on the sidewalk, my shirt torn, one knee shoved through a hole in my pants leg.

We picked ourselves up and started for the boat landing. There was a launch service that called at all the ships in the harbor, ferrying seamen to and from their ships. Hamburg is, or was then, one of the greatest seaports of the world, sprawling over miles and miles of the Elbe River. The launch would save us hours in getting back.

It was by then very late; the last boat was ready to leave. We stumbled aboard and took the remaining seats. Seamen from half a dozen other ships were returning just as we were: Danes, Japanese, Frenchmen, Hindus – a floating League of Nations. Most were drunk and quarrelsome. In the midst of them, three or four little Japanese sailors sat quietly across from me like little mice, twittering away in their peculiar language.

We had no sooner pulled away from the wharf when my unschooled stomach rebelled vigorously at the beer and cognac diet. Without any warning, I suddenly vomited. The little Japanese were sprayed from head to foot! The one in the middle stood up, squeaked something, and hit me with all his might, right on the nose. In seconds the whole boat looked and sounded like a first-class war. Danes were walloping Frenchmen, Frenchmen were kicking Swedes, and George, the Greek, was rolling around with the three Japanese, cursing and yelling in Greek and English. I felt as if I were being trampled to death. My nose was bleeding and my stomach was retching. What a night!

The launch finally pulled alongside our ship. We crawled up the ladder, barraged by the curses and taunts of the survivors. Making my way aft to the fo'c'sle I fell into my bunk, torn clothes and all. My last thought was, "Guess you're not a tough old salt after all."

So continued my education. Changing from a boy to a man, from a landlubber to a seaman, always learning the hard way. A bloody nose and a hangover taught me that getting drunk was not for me. Henceforth, there would be no more such foolishness. Smashed fingers and an aching back taught me the proper way to do a job. A cuff on the side of the head taught me to listen instead of talk. A plateful of gravy taught me respect for my elders and my superiors. They were hard lessons; I wouldn't forget them.

There would be other ships and other ports through the years, new shipmates, new experiences. From all of them I would learn something. Someday I would be master of my own ship. Everyone's survival might depend on what I had learned to that point. But all that was far in the future. Indeed, my next voyage might well have been my last, with all this knowledge made useless.

At that moment, there was much still to be grasped. From the captain I learned how to keep my own counsel. I also learned from him how to conceal fear and how to adopt the spurious air of unconcern and confidence that becomes infectious to the ship's crew. It had to be this way, for on the attitude as well as the ability of the master may hang the safety of his cargo and the very lives of that crew.

The sea never changes and its works,
for all the talk of men,
are wrapped in mystery.

Joseph Conrad

—5—

A CLOSE CALL IN THE FOG

All the way home from Germany I spent every spare minute at the wheel learning to steer. Practice makes for proficiency, as the saying goes, and I became adept at holding to a course.

I steered in all kinds of weather, always with the mates cursing me. Because of their constant criticism, I *had* to steer well. If I wandered off the course a couple of degrees, their cursing could be heard all the way back to the poop deck. They watched the ship's wake like hawks. The slightest deviation from a creamy wake stretching in a straight, unbroken line as far astern as the eye could see resulted in one of them storming into the wheelhouse roaring, "Damned kids! What in hell is the Merchant Service coming to? Jesus, the Old Man is daft, allowing boys to take the wheel. Godammit, boy, mind your course!"

Finally back in the States, I had a chance to get home for a couple of evenings between voyages. When my mother suggested I take my bicycle on an errand to the grocery store for her, I said, "What? A sailor ride a bike? I'm too grown up for toys. Besides, I'd rather walk." So I walked to the neighborhood store, knowing that on the way I would meet several acquaintances.

Sure enough, I heard, "Hello, Frank, haven't seen you lately. Where've you been?"

"Oh, I've been to sea. Made a trip to Germany. Just home for a couple of days."

Or it was, "My, aren't you brown?"

By the time I reached the store I was swollen with importance. While he filled my mother's order, the storekeeper showed his curiosity. "What's the food like on a ship?"

"Not so good," I told him, "but you get so hungry you don't care. There's never enough."

Home for two nights. Familiar faces and my mother's cooking felt good. But my feet still itched, and I was ready to go the next morning when we cast off, headed for New York by way of Massachusetts Bay, Cape Cod Canal, and Long Island Sound. This route was miles shorter than going outside of Nantucket Shoals. Because it was close quarters, most ships engaged a coast pilot. But our skipper had pilot's endorsements for these waters, so he did his own piloting.

We sailed past many kinds of ships every day. This was a fishing schooner on the Grand Banks. Was her skipper as good as ours? Was her bosun as harsh?

By this time I was standing a watch, the 8 to 12, with a partner. (Two partners always shared a watch on merchant ships, one standing lookout on the bow and the other taking the wheel.) The chief mate had finally decided that I could steer, so he had taken an able seaman off and put me on. This wasn't for my benefit. By putting the A.B. on day work, the mate got a lot more work done than he got from me on the same job.

We quickly ran into real Cape Cod pea soup. The fog around the Cape gets as thick as soft, gray cheese. It slid by us now, closing us in. At 8 o'clock in the morning I relieved the 4 to 8 lookout on the fo'c'sle head. He warned me that the Old Man was on the bridge and to keep a sharp lookout. Then he disappeared in the fog in two steps and I was alone.

I leaned over the bow and strained my ears. Nothing. Only the hissing of the bow wave and the sigh of the damp wind through the forestay. I paced back and forth between the two anchor chains for a few minutes, then stopped to listen again. Was that a bell? Nope. Pace again. Listen. Stare. Nothing but the water rushing by the blunt, rusty bows. I wondered why the Old Man didn't anchor.

Once, way off to starboard, I heard the deep hoot of another steamer. I shouted up to the bridge, pointing my arm in the direction of the whistle. The Old Man was invisible from where I stood, so at my shout he sent the third mate up to the bow to see what I was yelling about. The mate listened with me for four or five minutes, both of us keeping our heads below the bulwarks to keep the wind out of our ears. Grunting a warning at me to keep my ears peeled, he went back to the bridge. I glanced at my watch: a couple of minutes to 10. Time for me to relieve my watch partner at the wheel.

A quiet moment on deck before I knew about the pea soup.

Now came a combination of circumstances that happens every so often. When they do, disaster is close aboard.

I relieved the wheel, repeating the course and glancing at the compass to see if she was on. I noticed that the engine room telegraph was on Stand By, but the thump-thump of the revolution counter pounded out Full Ahead. My partner repeated the course to the third mate, who was standing just outside the open wheel house door. The Old Man was directly in front of me, leaning on the sill of an open window. The telegraph was at his elbow.

After my partner repeated the course, he hesitated for a moment and then asked if it would be all right if he went to the head before he went on lookout.

The mate said, "Not by a damn sight! Take a bucket up on the bow with you."

The Old Man pulled his head in and drawled, "Let him go, Mister. We're all right."

With those words, the stage was set – no lookout on the bow, thick fog, vessel making 11 knots in treacherous waters.

From where I stood at the wheel I could sight over the skipper's shoulder. The fog was so thick nothing could be seen, not even the foremast. Once we tuned out the steady, repetitive thumping of the revolution counter, all was quiet. The mate shifted positions. Though he moved only slightly, the sound seemed loud in the thick, dark morning. The sea was calm enough to keep the ship on course with only a couple of spokes of the wheel. A false sense of security crept into the wheel house. Everything seemed so peaceful and cozy.

As is the custom with all helmsmen, my mind emptied itself of all thoughts. My eyes, fixed on the compass, were slightly glazed. I was like a disembodied spirit. Only one little facet of my mind still functioned, that part of it that had to do with memory. I was back in that cabaret in Hamburg. Oh, why hadn't I been smarter? Why hadn't I asked my newfound friend to take a walk with me? Maybe she would have asked me home with her.

At that point my imagination leaped. I came hurtling back from my fool's paradise. A slight scraping of the Old Man's foot brought my eyes back into focus. Over his shoulder I could see dry land. A black, shelving shoreline was dead ahead, not more than a few ship's lengths away! My heart jumped into my throat.

I stared at the skipper, frozen with terror. I'll never forget the next minute and a half of his actions. The lesson has served me well ever since.

With one motion, he flung the telegraph handle from Stand By to Full Astern. Almost lazily, he flapped a languid hand at me and said, in a remarkably normal tone, "Better put that wheel hard astarboard, boy. Don't break it off, but get it over."

I grabbed the midships spoke and wound her over. Two and a half turns spun under my flying hands. The ship was light and answered promptly. The bow swung faster and faster. The way was off the ship and she was now turning nicely.

At that moment the fog shut in again. Our glimpse of the beach was a freak of the fog. It had opened like a long avenue that showed us a slice of disaster. Then the gray, impenetrable stuff came down again.

After such a close call, the only obvious thing to do was anchor. But of course we didn't. Away we went, full ahead, and the devil take the hindmost. We were due in the next morning to load, and by God we'd better be there or there'd be another skipper on the bridge. Though worse for the wear, we docked on schedule.

Years later, I realized that in that short period in the darkening fog, a lot of thoughts went through the skipper's head. First, he knew to his everlasting shame that he was way off his course. The currents, the tides, had fooled him. Second, he had only seconds to rectify his errors. But third, and to me the most important of all, was that knowing all this, knowing that although he was almost licked, he was still able to say calmly, "Better put that wheel hard astarboard, boy."

As the years went by I sailed with other skippers, some kind, a few cruel and heartless. All of them, with no exceptions, were excellent seamen and shipmasters. They sailed in hard times, in the midst of the country's worst depression. Bottoms were a glut and ocean freight rates had sunk to an all-time low. The fo'c'sles were full of seamen holding second and chief mate's tickets, glad to have a berth. For the three years that I was A.B. on one ship, we had the same three mates and the same skipper. All three of the mates held master's tickets.

Yes, in those days you had to be consistently good to be a master. The owners had their backs to an economic wall. To keep their vessels sailing they had to have officers who could wring the last farthing from a Charter Party, trip after trip. Captains drove their ships and crews unmercifully in fogs and gales. They had to. There were hundreds on the beach ready to take their place if they didn't.

We in the fo'c'sle complained incessantly as all sailors do, but not too seriously. We knew that for each of us there were swarms waiting on the dock in each port to take our berth, too. I remember docking in Baltimore in the early 1930s at daybreak. As soon as the gangway was lowered and Customs had cleared us, a horde of unemployed seamen poured up the ladder. They were so hungry they were perfectly willing to take over the messroom, serve our food, wash the dishes, work on deck – anything to get something to eat.

Those were the times that bred the kind of shipmaster I sailed with. I copied their speech, their manners, their beliefs, for they were my teachers, my idols, my gods.

To be sure, sometimes they took chances against their better judgment. It's easy to say, "Mister, it's getting thick, slow her down," or, "Mister Mate, better drop the pick 'til it clears up." But there was always an owner sitting at a piled-up desk trying to keep that ship employed. She was constantly due to load or discharge on a certain day in a certain port. If she was late, another ship got her cargo.

The skipper of the SS *Culberson* was of that competent, hard-driving breed, making decision after decision to wring the most out of his ship and crew, and always pulling us through. There were times, sailing with him in later years, when I stayed at the wheel all night because it was too wild for anyone to come to the bridge to relieve me. All through those dark hours with the wind screeching through the rigging I felt safe because of that dark form in front of me quietly peering out into the gale, occasionally giving me a soft command to "Ease her a bit, boy."

The day came years after I left his ship when he was driven ashore on the east coast of South America, below Buenos Aires. I was shocked at the pictures I saw in the papers later of his cargo of trucks, driven into the sand and shale of the bleak, forbidding coast north of Cape Horn where the *Culberson* went down. They brought a shuddering thought: if it could happen to him, it could happen to anyone.

To this day, that timeless sea chanty, a holdover from the Liverpool packet sailing ship days, still haunts me: "Drive her, Johnny, drive her."

— 6 —

SAILORING DAYS & MONKEY BUSINESS

Sometimes mischief was done on board. Way back in the early 30s, I was able seaman on the same ship for three years. Not because it was such a good ship, but because the Depression was going full blast. If you quit and paid off, you'd be lucky to get another berth in a year.

This ship was on a regular run, delivering to Boston, New York, Philly, Baltimore, Norfolk, a couple of Carolina ports, then to Jacksonville for a deck load of timber. From there, our first foreign port of call was Pernambuco, Brazil (now called Recife), a backwater port almost on the equator. We went south from there, calling at Rio, Santos, Bahia (now called Salvador), Rio Grande de Sul, Montivedeo, and finally the paradise of South America, Buenos Aires. Our last port before heading for home would often be Para, Brazil, a thousand miles up the Amazon River. We reversed the trip to return home, calling at the same ports, loading for the States.

Because I had been on board for so long, I was on the 8 to 12 watch on these trips. In those days there were only two A.B.s on a watch: one on the wheel and one on bow lookout. Even then, if it were a clear night, the mate would have the lookout overhauling a lifeboat or stacking dunnage in the shelter deck.

All mates in those days were work crazy, working themselves from 4 a.m. to 8 p.m., seven days a week. The mate on this ship even worked all during his bridge watch. He was a marvel with a needle and palm. He'd sit on a stool out on the bridge wing and hand-make lifeboat covers, wire-reel covers, or anything else that needed stitching. His name was Mr. Bang and he was a native of Schleswig-Holstein, which used to be a country between Denmark and Germany.

As I look back, Mr. Bang was the very finest seaman I've ever known. He went to sea on German square-riggers when he was just 12. Down around Cape Horn to Chile he went to load nitrates for Germany. For a year or more I was on his watch, and in the dark, quiet hours he would tell me stories of his young days on those hard-driven windships.

I remember one story in particular. It was his first trip, and he only a child. On the way down to the Horn it kept getting colder. Down in the Roaring Forties the gales were constant. Make sail, reef down, all hands – it never let up. There were only two watches in those days: four hours on, four hours below, interrupted by the constant "All hands!"

To set a reef or furl, the sailors had to climb the ratlines to the crosstrees, then scramble out on the yard while standing on a swaying footrope strung under the yard. Then they had to lay their bellies on the yard and fist the wildly flapping sail. The heavy storm canvas used down in those latitudes was thicker and coarser than any sails seen today. Sometimes the hands spent a whole watch clawing at

Mr. Bang, chief mate of the SS Culberson, the finest seaman I ever knew.

the canvas, only to have it blow out of the gaskets and flap away downwind. No seaman of those days ever had any fingernails. Their fingertips were just calloused balls.

The youngster's ship was way down near Cape Stiff when the cry came: "All hands!" Up went the crew, gale winds tearing at their clothes. The higher they went, the more the movement of the ship they felt. Young Mr. Bang got violently sick and threw up, yet the poor kid stayed up there for the whole watch, fighting the canvas. At last, half dead, the crew made their way back down to the deck. Young Mr. Bang was just about to stagger below when the chief mate fetched him a clout in the head.

"Come with me, boy!" That damned mate flung him down on deck in a frozen puddle of his vomit. "Scratch it up with your fingernails before you go below."

And so he spent his watch on deck, scratching hopelessly with nonexistent fingernails. Only 12 years old!

Ships, in my early days, were largely self-supporting both on deck and in the engine room. All the cargo-handling gear now furnished by the stevedoring companies was made then by the bosun and senior A.B.s. All the wire cargo runners were spliced by the bosun, as were all mooring lines and springs. The black gang also did their own repair work, fabricating many parts on the engine room lathe. Paint was made on ship as well.

There was one voyage when we were due to sail from Buenos Aires at 5 p.m. but couldn't because of low water. By then, everybody had spent all their pesos, of course, and now here we had another night in port. I got up my nerve and decided to hit Mr. Bang up for a loan. I went midships and timidly knocked on his screen door.

"Come in, Slim. What's on your mind?"

"Well, you see, sir, Earl and I would like to go ashore, but we're broke. Could you please, maybe, spare five bucks?"

"Why, I guess so." He opened his desk drawer, rummaged around through an assortment of nails, light bulbs, paint brushes, and God knows what other junk, the accumulation of ten years as mate. "Here we are," said he, pulling out a crumpled five dollar bill.

As I stretched forward to take it, he grabbed me by both shoulders and flung me right through the screen door! I slammed into the steel alleyway bulkhead and slid to the deck with pieces of the door hanging from me.

"That will teach you to take your hat off before you enter a chief mate's cabin. Now fix the door before you go ashore." Never raised his voice, never even got up from his chair. He wasn't mad, either. It was all a matter of discipline and manners.

Food on those old rust buckets, or the lack of it, was the subject of constant bellyaching. Ships were manned by 30 men. The steward was allowed 29¢ a day per man for three meals per day. A boiled mackerel for breakfast was typical – never an egg. Dinner would be old bull liver, tough as shoe leather. Supper was rancid cold cuts and bread. The steward bought his beef in the Argentine: bull necks and a few fore-quarters. Milk for coffee was a half can of condensed milk poured into a gallon pitcher of water.

All of us used to stock up in Jacksonville with cans of sardines, deviled ham, jam, etc. Then the first thing I did on arrival at Pernambuco was to run up the dock and buy a dozen eggs. I could get the dozen eggs and a bushel basket of oranges and papayas for a pack of cigarettes, which cost me six cents from the slop chest. Back on board I'd stick a steam line in a bucket, boil the eggs, and have a feast. I never did figure out why, if I could do it, that damned steward couldn't.

The mate, Mr. Bang, was a nut about the condition of his bowels, so he used to stock up on cornflakes and bran which he kept in the sideboard in the officers' saloon. Being on the 8 to 12 watch, I used to cut through the saloon at 20 minutes to 12 at night to call the second mate for his watch. On the way through, I'd snatch a box of cornflakes and a full can of milk, which I craftily hid on deck. At midnight, when I was relieved, I'd sit out on #5 hatch and eat it all, disposing of the evidence by throwing the empty box and can over the side. For weeks I heard the mate raving about the thief on board and what he was going to do to him when he caught him. He never once suspected his star pupil – me!

Then came my downfall. The saloon messboy told me, in great confidence, that the steward had acquired several gallon cans of strawberry and raspberry jam. He was doling it out very stingily to the officers. Once a day each got a little saucer of it.

Oh boy, jam! My mouth watered. For several nights I searched unsuccessfully through the saloon and the officers' pantry. Finally I got the messboy to tell me where it was: hidden in the galley behind the coal scuttle.

The next night the mate had me greasing cargo runners instead of standing bow lookout. By midnight my dungarees were soaked with dirty black oil. No matter. I stole into the galley. Feeling around in the dark, I found the jam. Armed with an almost full can and a fistful of pilot crackers, I hoisted my backside up onto the cook's scoured-clean chopping block and had a feast scooping out the jam with the crackers. When I could eat no more, I put the jam back behind the coal scuttle and sneaked back to the fo'c'sle. My watch partner smelled a rat, but I told him nothing. I was onto a good thing and wasn't about to share it with him. But I had slipped up badly. I never thought about my oily dungarees. In the dark they had smeared black oil on the cook's chopping block.

The next day the steward, who was no dope, started playing detective, asking questions of the engineers and mates about who had a dirty, oily job the night before. When he got to Mr. Bang, the cat was out of the bag and they set a trap. The galley ran athwartships and had a steel door on each side. The galley was rarely locked at all, and in good weather the doors were hooked open.

The next night I was perched up on the chopping block again, stuffing jam and crackers, when *Clang!*, both doors slammed shut. The steward stood yelling outside the port door with the chief mate bellowing outside the starboard door.

"We caught him! We've got the son-of-a-bitch!"

In they came, their flashlights blinding me. The mate belted me off the chopping block and that belly-robbing steward started kicking me. I kept rolling out of the steward's way 'til he hit his foot on the stove. He only had carpet slippers on, and nearly broke his toe. I scooted out the door like a rat and escaped. Afterward the mate never once said a word, but for a long time he was very cool. He knew damned well that not only was I a jam thief, I was also the skunk who ate up his cornflakes and bran, making him constipated the whole trip.

It was on this ship that I hit on a business venture. An A.B.'s wages were $57.50 a month, not much even then. There were two large pet stores in Boston. I went to them and struck a deal. They'd pay me $5 apiece for

Sitting on #5 hatch with some of the crew: (L to R) Mike Collins; an unidentified oiler; Earl Burch; me; a passenger; and "Filthy McNasty," an ordinary seaman who had an unfortunate aversion to soap and water.

marmoset monkeys, $10 for spider monkeys. I could buy them in Bahia for a pack of cigarettes each.

The next trip I stocked up: six marmosets and three spider monkeys. They didn't make me too popular with the crew. In those days, all eight of the deck gang lived back aft in a fo'c'sle, and that's where I kept my monkeys for the voyage. The monkeys weren't loose; I tied strings around their loins and tied them to the edge of my bunk. Surprisingly, they were quite clean; still, the rest of the crew gave my bunk a wide berth. We had no problems, and made it safely back to Boston that summer.

Thus my first venture in the monkey business was a success. The 60 bucks I received was more than a month's pay. During the next two or three trips, I did pretty well again. However, as winter in the northern latitudes set in, I had troubles with the monkeys getting sick. Monkeys need to be kept warm because they are very susceptible to pneumonia.

At last I hit on a solution. I started keeping them in the steering engine room. The steering engine is a huge steam engine which turns the rudder. Located all the way aft, it was always very warm and steamy. The monkeys seemed to thrive in there, and my shipmates were happy to have them out of the fo'c'sle.

Then disaster struck. One of the black gang decided to get in on my action and make a quick killing of his own. He bought a small ape, about the size of a three-year-old kid. He chained him up in the steering engine room, where he spent all his time trying to get at my little guys.

We started north from Brazil. When we got into the doldrums, just north of the equator, the heat grew fierce. Just about that time the chief engineer ordered the third engineer to do some repair work on the steering engine during his watch below. He stood the 8 to 12 watch, so about 1 in the afternoon back aft he'd come. He hated that little ape with a passion, and would torment him by yanking on his chain.

The heat in that steamy room was getting to him as well, so after a couple of days he showed up with a big oscillating fan which he had unscrewed from the bulkhead in his room. He set it on deck and turned it on. It made a big improvement not only for him, but for the monkeys and the ape, too. That little ape was something to see. He would parade in front of the fan, holding up first one arm and then the other, letting the cool air blow into his armpits.

But the damned engineer was a cruel bastard. He hadn't brought the fan in for the ape's benefit. When the ape started parading, he'd reach over and shut the fan off. Mr. Ape was pretty smart, though, and quickly learned how to throw the switch back on.

The next afternoon that lousy engineer decided to outfox the ape. He wired the switch so the ape would get a hell of a jolt when he tried to turn the fan on. It worked, all right. The electric shock knocked him flat. As soon as he could, the ape picked himself up and walked slowly over to the third, who was on his hands and knees fixing a pipe. Leaning over, the ape opened that great mouth of his and bit the entire calf muscle out of the mate's leg.

We heard the screaming and ran. The engineer was rolling around in agony, bleeding something awful. I ran amidships and got the chief mate, who was a pretty good first-aid man. He tied off the engineer's exposed blood vessels with sail twine and bandaged his leg up. Four of us carried the engineer to his room, from which he never emerged 'til he went down the gangway to the ambulance in Boston.

That was the end of my monkey business. Mr. Bang shot the ape, strangled my monkeys, and threw them all overboard. He made it plain: there would be no more livestock brought aboard this ship, not even so much as a Brazilian canary.

There is many a slip
Twixt the cup and the lip.

English proverb

— 7 —

WHEELING AND DEALING

After my monkey business fizzled out, I cast around for some enterprise to take its place. I was still A.B. on the same ship, running between U.S. East Coast ports and South America. It was 1933 and my $57.50 per month didn't go very far in the flesh pots of Buenos Aires.

Radio had grown by leaps and bounds from the homemade crystal sets of a few years ago. Now, in spite of the Depression, 'most every home had its Philco or Atwater Kent. *Amos 'n Andy* was heard nightly, the *Lucky Strike Hit Parade* kept everyone glued to their sets every Saturday night. The radio stores were doing a land office business in small, cheap sets. The more I pondered, the more it became clear how my fortune would be made.

We had just paid off a four-month voyage. After slop chest deductions and "draws" in various ports, my pockets burned with well over a hundred bucks.

We were docked over in Brooklyn, at the foot of Hamilton Avenue. Right after supper I hustled down the gangway, heading for the Hamilton Avenue ferry to Manhattan. Dropping a hundred-reis Brazilian coin in the hopper, aboard I went.

In those days, Brazil had a strange money system. Their standard was the milreis, or one thousand reis, worth about 12¢, U.S. A hundred-reis coin was the exact size of our nickel and worth a little over one cent. It worked great on the nickel ferries and subways.

Docking in Manhattan, I scooted off and headed for Courtland Street. In those days, Courtland Street was lined with cheap radio stores selling brand names no one ever heard of but which worked for a while. Being very canny, I went in one store after another, comparing prices and sound volume. Volume was important. I wound up buying ten small Dewald radios for 12 bucks apiece. When turned up, they could be heard for blocks: perfect for my as-yet undeveloped market.

Back on the ship, broke but hopeful, I hid the sets under the spare mooring lines up on a shelf near the deck head in the steering engine room. Lying in my bunk that night I mused on the future – it was rosy indeed.

On our southbound voyage we would stop at six or seven Brazilian ports from Pernambuco in the north all the way down to Montevideo. These would be my markets.

The competition in the whorehouses in these ports was fierce. One would get the lion's share of the trade for a while by touting that they had a couple of Chinese girls, only to lose it to another house whose runners were extolling the added attraction of a free bottle of Brazilian beer ... on the way out. Those runners boarded every ship the day she docked. Passing out cards in the fo'c'sle, some with pictures on them, they vied for our trade.

I reasoned that a whorehouse with a radio blaring out Brazilian music would surely grab off a big share of the trade. After a couple of trips, when the radios wore out – repeat business! I couldn't lose. Sinking into untroubled sleep, I was well pleased with my uncanny grasp of supply and demand.

In due course we sailed down our East Coast, loading in Philly, Baltimore, Norfolk, Wilmington, Charleston, Brunswick, Georgetown, and finally Jacksonville for our usual deck load of lumber for Buenos Aires. Then it was south on the Great Circle route for Cape San Roque, the northern bulge of Brazil on the equator. We made a fine summer passage, roasting in the doldrums, then picking up the southeast trade winds. Our fo'c'sle, being aft on the starboard side, was a furnace as usual. But nothing bothered me. The vision of all those milreis I was going to get made it all bearable.

Because I had spent most of my pay on radios, I hadn't had much shore leave in our East Coast ports, but did manage to acquire about a million crab lice in Jacksonville. My crotch was scratched raw, aggravated by the terrible heat.

One night I was at the wheel, all alone in the wheelhouse. The mate was way out on the port wing, draped over the wind dodger and probably fast asleep on his feet. The sea was calm and the ship stayed right on course with only an occasional spoke or two of the wheel. I had my dungarees down on my ankles, and was busy catching crabs by the dim light of the binnacle. Whenever I caught one, I'd crack him with my fingernails and place the corpse on the glass so I could keep score.

I had just dispatched number 20 when a strange, faint sound stole into my consciousness. It couldn't be! Faintly but unmistakably, I was hearing *Amos 'n' Andy*. I craned my head first one way, then the other. Where was it coming from?

The Old Man's quarters were just under the wheelhouse, on the starboard side. Just out of my reach were the three brass speaking tubes. One led to the Old Man's stateroom, one to the engine room, and one to the radio shack back on the boat deck. By God, the sound was coming from one of them.

I let go of the wheel and hobbled over, my pants still down. When I flipped open the Old Man's tube, the sound poured out. He had one of those newfangled short wave radios and here was *Amos 'n' Andy*, plain as day. I stood there, entranced, my ear glued to the tube. I got so interested I forgot the wheel, my pants, crabs, everything.

Suddenly, there was a footstep. There was the Old Man, standing at the wheel, peering into the binnacle at the compass. He reached out with a finger and tentatively poked at the dead crabs. *Holy Smoke!* I eased the cover on the tube, reached for my pants, and sidled over towards the wheel.

He peered at me intently. Then his voice started out quietly. "One of those critters is still alive." By the time he got to the end, his voice had risen to a roar. "Be so kind as to kill it!"

"Yes, sir," I muttered, trying to get the ship back on course while pulling up my pants the rest of the way, simultaneously searching vainly for the live crab. Whew! I got off easier than I deserved on that one.

The very next day the mate switched me to his watch, the 4 to 8. He made no explanation, but obviously he wanted me where he could keep an eye on me. My new watch partner was an old hand by the name of Moody Harrison. He'd been going to sea for 20 years or more. He was a fine seaman, but he had one peculiarity: he hated all skippers. This ship was no exception.

Now unbeknownst to us, the Old Man had made some new friends who were fishing nuts. They had filled him full of tales of trolling in the Gulf Stream for big sailfish and marlins. He decided that the South Equatorial current, through which we were steaming, should be just as good as the Gulf Stream, so afishing we would go.

My watch partner, Moody Harrison, schemed worse than I did.

Right outside his room on the boat deck, starboard side, was a contraption called the deep sea sounding gear, standard on all the old Shipping Board vessels.

The gear consisted of a pedestal riveted to the deck, surmounted by a drum with two cranks and a clutch release, on which was wound about a mile of piano wire. The bottom of its lead was hollowed to hold tallow to which a sample of the bottom would adhere. A graduated, open-bottomed glass tube was spring-clipped onto the side of the lead's shank, coated inside with a chemical that turned brown when exposed to sea water. When it was cranked aboard, the sand, shells, mud, clay, etc. which adhered to the tallow, plus the discoloration in the tube compared to a graduated scale, gave the depth in fathoms and a look at the bottom texture. Comparing that to a chart of the area gave the ship's position.

The Old Man had a better use for it. He got a big S-shaped meat hook from the steward's meat box and fastened it to the piano wire. Then he had the bosun unship the big brass ship's bell from the fo'c'sle head and hang it on the bulkhead right outside his stateroom porthole. Once he'd rigged its clapper to the piano wire, he was ready to go fishing.

Out swung the boom, overboard went the big meat hook with a chunk of salt port lashed to it. The captain released the clutch and settled down to wait for a big one to strike. He waited that way day after day. It took him over an hour to crank in the line against the ship's speed each time he replenished the bait.

Finally, my scheming watch partner came to his aid. He stole two long boat hooks from the lifeboats and lashed them together, doubling their length. Jumping out of his bunk when we were called at 20 minutes to 4 one morning to go on watch, he eased his long pole out of a porthole and snagged the wire trailing astern. Very carefully he pulled it into the port. Grasping it with both hands, he gave it several mighty tugs. We could hear the big bell clanging way up on the boat deck. Carefully releasing the wire, Moody strolled midships and mounted the ladder to the bridge to relieve the man at the wheel. There was the Old Man, naked as a jaybird, cranking away and yelling, "I've got one big son-of-a-bitch!"

Moody worked this stunt for three nights running. After that, the Old Man had the bosun secure the sounding gear and take the bell back to the fo'c'sle head where it belonged. No more fishing for him.

Finally we headed into Pernambuco, a Godforsaken place if ever there was one. The port was mostly artificial, created by man-made breakwaters. A strong current set vessels against the dock. For that reason, a native docking crew boarded us out in the harbor and helped us make fast, fore and aft, to large buoys lying off the dock and parallel to it. All we had to do was slack off on these lines and the current set us alongside. Sailing away was the reverse: let go everything ashore, heave away on the buoy lines, and away.

The heat, as always, was fierce. Those old ships had no air conditioning. Down there on the equator, at times it seemed as if you couldn't breathe. The fo'c'sle was like a furnace. At sea, under way, we could rig windchutes out the portholes. But in port there wasn't a breath of breeze.

Right after we docked, up the gangway came the usual Immigration and Customs ghouls, as usual making a beeline for the Old Man's office to receive their cumshaw. Nobody else could board or leave ship until they departed. As they went down the gangway, up poured the usual horde of bloodsuckers: pimps, a traveling hair cutter (one pack of cigarettes for a fast cut, sitting on #5 hatch), salesmen staggering under a gigantic load of birdcages full of tropical birds of every color. Then came the booze salesmen. They had the best: Johnny Walker Black Label, the very best American ryes, Gordon gin, British rum. The bottles were absolutely authentic. But the contents ...! They all contained a native drink called "Casash," as near as I can spell it. This vile, poisonous stuff was made from fermented sugar cane pulps and God knows what else. It was over 100 proof. It must have held some weird narcotic, too, because it not only made you stinking drunk, but stark raving crazy to boot.

Ignoring the booze salesmen, I singled out one of the pimp runners with whom I had a nodding acquaintance, motioning him to follow me. When no one was looking, we ducked into the steering engine room. With a great show of stealth, I dug out one of the radios and plugged it in. He pretty near fainted with greed.

The haggling began. Whenever he seemed to cool off and stand pat, I'd switch stations. Finally, I agreed to let the radio go for 60 bucks in milries. Whipping out a piece of cord, he made a sling. He hung the radio in it under his armpit beneath his jacket. He sauntered out on deck, slipped down the gangway, and was gone.

Pernambuco was a small place. Not wanting to glut the market, I decided to pull in my horns and be content with selling just one radio this trip. I already had half my investment back, a great fistful of milries notes to exchange for Argentine pesos in Buenos Aires, and still had 11 radios left. Things were looking up!

The first and only night in port I got stuck with the midnight to 8 a.m. gangway watch. Along about 1 o'clock, the crew started to straggle back aboard. I could hear them coming from way up the dock: drunken singing, cussing, arguing, being sick. A normal first evening in port.

The next morning at breakfast, I heard the usual rehashing of their adventures of the previous night. Then a disturbing note crept into the tales. It seems as though most of them had hit what was supposed to be "the" joint. It had an American radio. Trouble was, when they came to pay up, the going price had doubled. When I heard that, I knew I'd have to watch my step. If they ever found out that my radio caused them to have to pay through the nose, I'd be in bad trouble, so I laid low.

We quickly hit all the ports southbound. In Bahia I unloaded two radios. None went in Rio because we lay way out in the road-stead at anchor, discharging into lighters. In Santos, business peaked, but that damned city was almost my downfall.

In quick succession, I sold six radios. Then I made a bad mistake. I put one radio on the shelf next to my bunk to enjoy the Brazilian tangos. A couple of days later, a water tender and an A.B. came into the fo'c'sle and stared intently at the radio.

"Where'd you get that?"

"Courtland Street in New York. Why?"

"Well, we were in the Trocadero last night and they had its twin. And we got way overcharged. Special entertainment, they said. You skinny bastard, you sold it to them!"

The cat was out of the bag. The more I tried to lie my way out, the deeper I buried myself. I hotfooted up to the mate and begged for a day off. I figured I'd better disappear for a day before somebody flattened me.

So four of us, Charlie Wilson, an oiler; Little Joe, a water tender; Bill Welch, an A.B.; and myself went ashore right after breakfast, dressed in our best shore suits. We were headed for the cog railway terminal. Some years before, some very clever German engineers had carved a railway line right up through the mountains to San Paulo, the capitol of Brazil, known as the richest city in South America

What a great experience! And what views! The cars were mostly glass. Up and up we went in those glass cars at about a 45 degree angle. The seats were canted so we were always sitting level. We passed on the edges of gorges thousands of feet deep. We could look way down on the tops of tropical vegetation on one side, and far up the rocky sides on the other. The porter who served us *café con leche* claimed the train to be amongst the engineering wonders of the world. I believed it.

When we arrived, we became true tourists. We visited the snake farm and saw venomous snakes being milked for their venom. We walked for miles, gawking at the breathtaking white buildings. After a fine Brazilian lunch, we even poked our noses into a first-class gambling palace where we shot a few milreis on the chuck-a-luck machines. Late afternoon saw us boarding the cog railroad for the trip back down to Santos. On the way down, we realized why San Paulo was built up in the mountains. It was so cool there! The lower we went, the hotter it got.

Fortunately, by the time I got back, things had cooled off on the ship itself. Spending the day away had probably saved my life. I took stock of my present situation. I still had three radios left. No sense selling any in Montevideo. In those days, Uruguay had a very unfavorable rate of exchange. Since we had to pay 1.10 U.S. for one of their pesos, we never even went ashore.

I managed to peddle one radio in Rio Grande du Sul. That left me with two as we wound our way up the River Plate to Buenos Aires to dock in La Boca and discharge our deck load of lumber.

In Buenos Aires, Customs was the worst. The entire port was completely fenced off – miles and miles of it. This immense area was patrolled

Me, Wilson, Welch, and Little Joe in San Paulo, dressed in our best shore suits.

by "Marineros," uniformed similarly to our Navy sailors. Like the cops in Spain, they always traveled in pairs. They had the authority of God. What was worse, they were absolutely incorruptible. If you *ever* tried to bribe one, they'd hang you!

I made sure the radios were well hidden before we docked. La Boca was the very worst part of Buenos Aires. Life was cheap on its waterfront streets. I decided to stay aboard until the lumber was discharged and the ship shifted to Darsena Sud, near more civilized surroundings. Then I headed for the Avon Bar, a famous hangout for merchant seamen.

At the Avon I got a favorable rate of exchange for a fistful of millreis and settled down with free peanuts and a stein of superb German beer. Buenos Aires, in those days, had a tremendous German population. They ran breweries, restaurants, and God knows what else.

I got to talking with a German at the next table. When I discovered that he worked for Hohner Harmonica, a German company that made and sold high-quality harmonicas and accordians worldwide, my ears pricked right up and my nose twitched at the smell of pesos.

Very casually, I let it slip that I just happened to have two first-class American radios. He bit like a trout in spring. Would I consider selling one? I said I was most reluctant, but would be interested in a trade for harmonicas and/or accordians. But it had to be good because if those Marineros caught me smuggling radios ashore, I wouldn't get a fine; they'd lock me up in their stinking hoosegow and throw away the key. We finally struck a deal: two dozen big harmonicas and two accordians for the two radios, delivery to be made in the Plaza of the Vienticinco de Mayo. Naturally, I didn't trust him and he didn't trust me. I was quite sure he was stealing the stuff from his own company.

The next night after supper, I rigged a sling under my armpit for the radio, put my jacket on over it, stuffed five packs of Lucky Strikes in each sock, and headed up the dock towards the gate. The ten packs of cigarettes were worth five bucks in pesos and would buy me a first-rate dinner in the Imermann Hotel – *bife con huevas* with all the fixings – with enough left over to light up the town 'til the wee hours.

I was pretty shaky going up on the dock. I felt that damn radio getting bigger and bigger, bulging suspiciously out of my jacket. The area was crawling with Marineros. Each time I got near a pair of them, I'd gradually bear to starboard so the radio was on the side away from them. "*Buenas noches*," I'd croak, and they'd put two fingers to their caps as I passed by in a manner I hoped was nonchalant. Apparently it worked.

I jumped on a streetcar and headed for the rendezvous. There was the German, right on time with a big cardboard box containing half the loot: one accordian and 12 beautiful harmonicas. We made the exchange and scheduled a repeat performance for the next night. Despite all my sweating it out, it was all ridiculously easy.

The morning after I finished trading, the bosun announced that there was something wrong with one of the ship's boilers. We were to finish discharging, load for Boston only, and proceed directly home on two boilers. Was I lucky! I'd traded my last radios and was set up for Boston. Being a very cultural town, Boston was full of high-class music stores which would be very happy to take my harmonicas and accordians at a nice fat profit for me.

My only problem would be finding a good hiding place in the steering engine room, because Boston Customs were real Irish bastards. I was also faced with the problem of smuggling my loot ashore. The harmonicas were easy. Stick a few at a time in my pockets. The accordians were going to require some thought. I couldn't just sling them over my shoulders and walk down the gangway ... could I?

Sailing day finally arrived. Pilot aboard, lines singled up, all hands standing by fore and aft. Let go forward, let go aft, Slow Astern. Round she swung and down the River Plate we slogged, maximum speed about six knots.

Buenos Aires to Boston at six knots is one long voyage. The ship wouldn't steer well at that pace, and wallowed along like an old barge. We had watch on, watch off, seven days a week. Lousy food, constant heat – no wonder everybody got cranky and short-tempered. Fights broke out. Almost daily we heard "step out on deck." We had all told and retold our worn anecdotes and were heartily sick of them. We were sick of the sight of each other. Personal habits, once unnoticed, grated on nerves.

All during that long northbound voyage, I wrestled with the problem of smuggling those accordians ashore. My choices narrowed to three. I could declare them and pay the duty, but that ran against my larcenous soul. I could try bribery, but that was too risky. If I picked the wrong man, the consequences could be dire. If the accordians were confiscated, I'd have to pay a fine equal to double the duty, and I could be charged with attempting to bribe a Federal officer.

My third scheme was altogether too crazy even to consider. I would become a blind beggar. Slinging an accordian over my shoulder, hanging a tin cup around my neck, complete with black glasses and white cane, I would stroll down the gangway and out the dockyard gate. Insanity ... ? Or ingeniousness? The Customs rats would never know I was a seaman. They'd figure me for just another itinerant beggar.

As soon as we'd docked, my first option had expired. All foreign purchases had to be declared prior to docking, and I hadn't declared them. Then another knotty problem reared its nasty head. Each accordian was in an expensive fiber case. Carrying one down the gangway in its case would be a dead giveaway. Blind accordian players didn't go around carrying their instruments in expensive cases. Now what? I felt like a rat in a trap.

We were to stay in Boston at least ten days after discharging and loading, shifting ship to a repair yard to have our boiler fixed. Bingo! There was my solution. The repair yard would probably have only one Customs guard, maybe none. I was all set.

I persuaded the bosun to give me the midnight to 8 a.m. gangway watch so I had all day to myself. As soon as my watch was over I had a quick breakfast and turned in. By noon I was up for dinner. One o'clock saw me heading for the streetcar to Boston, three harmonicas stowed safely under my coat. Getting off at South Station, I walked up to the Boylston, Tremont Street area, where all the fine shops were. Several swank music stores displayed baby grand pianos, cellos, and violins in their windows. I picked out the swankiest, drew a deep breath, and sailed through the glass doors. A stuck-up salesman asked if he could help.

"Thank you, but I'd like to see the manager."

"I'm the assistant manager. How may I serve you?"

Boy, he was high-falutin'. Trying to hide my hands so he wouldn't see the broken nails and heavy callouses, I drew out a harmonica and showed it to him.

"Mmm," said he, extending a limp, white hand. He turned the harmonica over and over, blew a few notes. "A Hohner, and a nice one. Where did you get it?"

"Germany," I answered promptly. "I've been studying over there and brought a few home to help pay for my studies."

"Why don't we step into my office and discuss this further."

By Godfrey, before I got out of that little office I had sold all 24 of them for seven bucks apiece, C.O.D. Hurrying back to South Boston, I loaded up on harmonicas. I taped up them up and down both legs and stuffed them in my pockets, my belt, and one up each sleeve. If the wind ever blew up my pants legs, I'd sound like Sousa's brass band passing by.

I was back on board in time for supper, with 164 long green ones in my kick. Then my greedy mind started working. Why did I ever sell them all to the very first store? I should have shopped around. Oh, well. Actually, I did very well for those lean, hungry days.

I spent the next few nights making a blind man's cane out of a piece of dunnage. I painted it white and hung it in the fiddley to dry before daylight. I had the steward buy me black, opaque glasses on one of his trips ashore. Then I was ready. As soon as we shifted to the Bethlehem yards, it was go for broke.

A few days later, I headed uptown again. I had to strike a deal for the accordians before smuggling them ashore. I'd look foolish, if not suspicious, wandering around the swankiest section of Boston with a big piano accordian hung over my shoulder.

This time I bypassed my harmonica customer and checked out the windows of other music stores. By God, in the second or third store, there smack in the middle of the window was an exact duplicate of my accordians! Shiny black, lots of bright nickel, generous inlays of mother-of-pearl. It shone under a spotlight, glittering and gleaming like the stars. Positively beautiful! And so was the sign: "Special – $495."

In I went. The owner himself came to help me. Hiding my hands again, I said I was interested in the accordian in the window. He immediately shut off the spotlight and plucked the instrument off its stand.

"Here, try it. It's the only one I have. They're most difficult to get. Have to import them from Germany, you know, and that chap Hitler is causing us no end of difficulty."

Music to my ears! He kept urging me to try it, to listen to its superb tone, note how responsive the keys were, and on and on. I muttered something about a sprained wrist, still keeping my paws in my pockets.

I'm the world's worst haggler, but I did my best. The price seemed too high, I said.

"My dear young sire, you must realize that with the ocean shipping charges and the exorbitant import duty, that instrument actually cost me $400."

I could hear those angels singing again. How sweet it was! Very gently, I let it be known that I was selling, not buying. I used the same story: studying in Germany, felt it was time to come home ... "That chap Hitler, you know." ... brought two accordians with me, needed the money, etc.

Blessed be the saints that watch over such as me, we struck a bargain: $325 apiece, C.O.D. Now all I had to do was work my blind man stunt twice. The old butterflies started flapping their wings in my stomach. They never stopped until the big day arrived.

The mate and first assistant engineer had hired all the crew replacements now, so the fo'c'sle was full again. I wanted to rehearse my act, but didn't dare to. There was no privacy.

The next morning a tug came alongside to move us for repairs. The usual "All hands, fore and aft," and we shifted over to the ship repair yard. As soon as we docked, I hurried down the gangway to scout for Customs men. I couldn't find a single one, but that didn't mean they weren't lurking around someplace. There were two gates manned by timekeepers checking workmen in and out. Not too bad, I decided. I couldn't delay any longer.

I headed back through the yard to the ship. Ahead of me a workman was trudging along pushing a two-wheeled cart with big wooden wagon wheels. It was piled high with pipefitting tools, pieces of pipe, and God knows what else. As I drew abreast of him, damned if it wasn't Frank Rogier, a Belgian water tender I'd once been shipmates with. I banged him on the back and we shook hands. We'd dumped many a stein of beer together. He was grateful for the cigarette I offered. Apologetically, he said he was reduced to rolling his own. Shipyard pay in the days before unions wasn't too hot.

As we leaned idly against his cart, smoking and reminiscing, all of a sudden a blinding light hit me. "Frank, old buddy, how'd you like to latch on to ten cartons of cigarettes?"

"What have I got to do?"

"I've got two large packages to get off the ship and out the gate. Could you hide them, one today and one tomorrow, under that junk on your cart?"

"Piece of cake, pal. The one Customs guard we have is stinko by 3 in the afternoon."

Boy, oh boy! I could bury the blind man act deep, where it belonged. I'd been nuts even to think of it.

Rogier was working on our ship, which made it even easier. Between noon and 1, while everybody else was eating dinner, he and I scuttled down the gangway with an accordian and buried it in his cart, no sweat. At 3:30 he boldly pushed her right out the gate to where I was waiting with a taxi.

Off I went to Tremont Street, whistling all the way. We repeated the scheme the next day and it was done, easy as that.

There is a sequel to the story of my radio business, one that gave me no end of satisfaction.

One of the A.B.s who shipped over with us was Otto, the same guy who got so mad at me in Santos. This bird was forever making wisecracks about all the dough I must have made with my radios, and what a dirty louse I was to sell cheap junk that would wear out in no time.

Back in New York, I was lying in my bunk reading one night. It was late, and most of the crew were still ashore. I heard footsteps, then a thump.

Out I stole in my bare feet. Peeking around the corner I saw Otto heading up the after deck toward the gangway. Quickly, I ducked into the steering engine room and hid away. There on the deck sat a great big carton with "Philco" stenciled on the side. Ho, ho – so that's what he was up to. I crept behind the engine and waited. Pretty soon back he came, carrying another carton, then a third. Damned if he didn't hide them in the very same place I had used.

While he was bunking them away under the mooring lines, I tried to ease one of my legs out straight. It was becoming cramped. My bare foot grazed a hot steam line. I yelped like a billy goat. Otto shot around the engine and glared down at me.

"What the hell are you doing in here?"

I had no choice but to brazen it out. "Seeing what you're up to, that's what."

"If you ever tell anyone about these radios, I swear I'll stick a knife right through your skinny carcass."

"Otto, I have no intention of telling about your scheme. But why buy such expensive ones?"

"I'll tell you why. I believe in giving fair value, not the junk you were peddling. I paid 45 bucks apiece for these beauties."

Such noble thoughts, I muttered to myself.

Nothing more was said, but I watched him like a hawk in every port. Nothing happened until we got back to Santos. There I saw him in deep conversation with one of the pimp runners. Pretty soon the two of them sneaked into the steering engine room.

We had all been going ashore every night. This night, at supper, Otto guessed he would stay on board. He turned in early. I drew the curtain across my bunk, too, but not to sleep. All was quiet. He and I were the only ones in the fo'c'sle.

It seemed hours before I heard a whistle from out on the dock. I crept up the ladder and stood watching in the dark. Otto lowered the first radio to the dock. A dim form untied it and stuck several milreis notes between the strands of the heaving line, which Otto quickly retrieved and pocketed. As he lowered the third radio, I backed quietly down the ladder and went back to the fo'c'sle.

Pretty soon, in came Otto with a big grin on his square-headed puss. I was sitting on the edge of my bunk, puffing on a cigarette.

"Look at that, you cheap bastard – 800 milries apiece, 96 bucks each. Give 'em quality, that's the secret."

I must say I envied him. There he sat down at the fo'c'sle table, gloating and fingering the brand new, crisp 100-milreis notes.

All of a sudden, he let out a scream of anguish. "Oh, my God! Oh, my God! The dirty bastard!" On and on he went, finally subsiding into incoherent moans.

"Otto, what's the matter? You sound like you're dying."

"Look," he moaned, flinging a note on my bunk. As it landed, one of the zeros fell off the note. They were 10-milreis bills with a zero glued on. Instead of 96 bucks apiece, he'd gotten $9.60. Quality indeed!

Home is the sailor
Home from the sea.

Robert Louis Stevenson

— 8 —

A.B. ON A SHIP TO NOWHERE

I've mentioned before about the old rust buckets I sailed on during the Great Depression of the 30s, and of how bad things were. Our existence was tolerable mainly because we had grown up in that era and didn't know anything different. There was one time, though, that the direct effects of the worldwide economic slump came home to roost.

I was an A.B. (ablebodied seaman) on an old West Coast Shipping Board-built freighter, the SS *West Calumb*, I think it was. She docked in Brooklyn, the cargo was discharged, and the crew paid off. The Chief Mate announced that due to lack of cargo she was to be temporarily laid up. Moody and I were still sailing together, so he offered the job of ship keeper to the two of us. The second mate was to be in charge.

The vessel was shifted to an obscure berth way out in the wilds of Brooklyn. Her boilers were blown down and the black gang paid off. There remained just us two A.B.s and the second mate. It was midwinter, cold and snowing. There was no light or heat, and the deserted foc'sle was like a black tomb. We tried to make do with one kerosene lantern. The second mate, Mr. Brooks, brought his new bride aboard. His room was about the size of a small bathroom, but they, too, made do.

Moody and I were in a hell of a fix. The lack of heat was the worst. We piled on extra blankets swiped from the empty bunks, but my head got so cold I took to sleeping with an old Navy wool watch cap. Our pay had been cut to $40 a month, out of which we had to feed ourselves. The Second's wife had fired up the galley stove, so they were doing pretty good, but she wouldn't let us use it, damn her!

Adding insult to injury, Moody and I had to work on deck 8 a.m. to 5 p.m. six days a week. That damned second mate decided that we would chip rust from underneath the cargo winches. There we were, on our hands and knees in the frozen snow, banging away with chipping hammers. Once an hour Mr. Brooks would leave the warmth of the galley to check on us. After the first few days he separated us, putting one on the forward deck and one on the after deck.

At noon, Moody and I huddled in the crew's mess room aft to eat a couple of cans of sardines and a nine-cent loaf of bread. We had no way to wash, so after a couple of days we were already plastered with rust and dirt. At knock-off time, in the dark and bitter cold, the pair of us would head down the gangway for a cheap, crummy cafeteria. I usually had bacon and eggs with a double order of rancid fried potatoes. That forty bucks had to stretch for a month.

That lousy second decided to let us knock off at noon on Saturday, though not for any consideration of us. It was so he and the new bride could spend the weekend with her folks up in the Bronx. His last words each Saturday would be: "Now, you're not to leave this ship except to eat, and then one at a

Moody and me, clean again.

time!" As soon as he was out of sight, we headed for Manhattan, our dirty clothes in a shopping bag. Since we were both pretty ripe, people on the bus gave us a wide berth.

We headed for 25 South Street – the Seamen's Church Institute, a world-famous place known to seamen everywhere. It was run by the equally-famous Mother Roper. This large, many-storied building housed a multitude of amenities for seamen. A private room cost 35¢. Of course it didn't have a window and was the size of a solitary confinement cell, but it was clean and had plenty of heat.

As soon as we checked in, we headed for the showers, carrying our filthy work clothes. A good half-hour under hot water washed away the grime and eased tired muscles. We scrubbed our clothes, then went to bed in clean sheets. Supper in the cafeteria was great and cost practically nothing. The Library reading room, where we spent the evening, would do credit to a public library, though with the emphasis on maritime topics and religion.

Sunday morning we wandered South Street gawking at the ships tied at the many piers. We had a big Sunday dinner at noon courtesy of Mother Roper. In the late afternoon, we reluctantly headed back to

Brooklyn, knowing we had to get back before Mr. Brooks or he'd have a fit. It was some let-down to crawl back into that black, cold fo'c'sle.

Such was our routine for several weeks: evenings in the greasy spoon, weekends with Mother Roper. We couldn't afford drinking and helling around. Within about three weeks we grew stir crazy. There was nobody to talk to except each other. We were always broke, cold, and hungry.

Then came a small change in the monotony. We were banging away with the chipping hammers in the icy air when the toot-toot of a tow boat caused me to look up. Around the sea end of the pier appeared a decrepit, rusty old stem-winder coal collier pushed by two tow boats. I could just make our her name, almost obscured by the rust caking her bows: *Penobscot*.

As I went over to the side to see better, the skipper hollered over to ask if we would receive her lines. He had orders to tie *Penobscot* to us. "Sure," I said. The second mate took over, shouting all kinds of useless orders. Moody and I went forward to take her lines. As she came alongside, damned if there wasn't a man and woman on her fo'c'sle head, passing the lines down to us. We tied her up forward, then went aft to repeat the performance. There was the same couple, expertly slinging over the heaving lines, then slacking off the big hawsers, moving like a well-trained team.

He was the master of the *Penobscot* and she was his wife. The ship belonged to the Sprague Company, big coal operators. Sprague also operated American Republics Line, to which our vessel belonged. Like us, the *Penobscot* had been laid up for lack of cargo. She was an ancient tub, but beautifully constructed.

As I got to know the couple better, they had me aboard for supper from time to time. The skipper's quarters there were quite sumptuous, just under the wheel house and spanning the entire breadth of the ship. Beautiful dark paneling they had, and lots of gleaming brass, with expensive leather settees for the final touch. It was such a surprise to step from a rust-pitted deck into such opulence. The skipper's wife had installed a small coal-burning stove for cooking. It also kept their quarters toasty warm.

It was such a treat to be invited over. I'd sink into a deep leather chair, listening to the stove rustling quietly. The soft glow of the brass lamps hanging in gimbals, reflecting from the polished wood paneling, created the illusion of being at sea on a posh British ship plying between London and India.

The captain had been everywhere. His Master's ticket was completely covered with pilotage endorsements for every port from Maine to Florida. He would reminisce about his voyages until late at night when his wife shooed Moody and me out.

One cold morning as I crawled between the winches, on hands and knees, chipping hammer in hand, a terrible pain shot through my left knee. It was so bad I felt weak and sick to my stomach.

Mr. Brooks was nowhere in sight. I headed as quickly as I could for the door to the shelter deck. Once inside, I pulled off my jacket, shirt, and pants. Peeling down my long woolen underwear, I peered at my knee and saw a great festering boil, red and purple.

Hauling my clothes back on, I hobbled over to the bulwarks onto the *Penobscot*. The Old Man's wife looked at my leg, fussed around it a while, then applied some tarry-smelling stuff which she said would draw out the pus. A doctor couldn't have bandaged my leg any better.

That night I couldn't sleep. For once it wasn't the cold that kept me awake, it was my leg. I couldn't turn over without hurting my throbbing knee. Sometime during the next morning the boil burst. My faithful nurse bathed my leg and declared I would feel better now, although another boil was developing under the first one. On went the tar again.

There was no way I could work on my knees, so I went midships and told Mr. Brooks my troubles. He wasn't too bad about it, putting me to work in the galley splicing cargo slings out of three-inch manilla. But by the end of the week I was at the end of my rope. There were at least six big boils on my knee and it was agony. I had to cut a hole in the knee of my longjohns to relieve the awful pressure.

Back I went to the skipper's wife, who said she didn't like the look of my leg. All the boils had run together and my entire knee looked like a piece of rotten meat. She declared, "You're for a doctor. There are black streaks on your leg." She and her husband had an old Model A out on the pier. They helped me down the gangway and into the car, and took me to a family doctor somewhere off Columbia Street.

The doctor looked at my knee, talking quietly to himself. He got off his stool and went out. Shortly, he returned with a bowl and a tray of shiny instruments. "Son, try to relax," he said. "I'm going to have to hurt you bad." Swift as lightning his hand reached for the tray and passed twice over my knee. Oh, my God! I thought he had cut my leg off!

The skipper's wife was standing behind me, holding my shoulders. I damned near keeled over, soaking with sweat. I ventured a glance at my knee. He had made two great criss-cross slashes. Now he took tweezers and pulled away the skin. Then he cut it all off with scissors. "Hang on, son," he said. "This will finish it up." And he pulled out the cores of all those boils. Whew! I'd just about had it. I was weak as a newborn kitten.

With my leg heavily bandaged, I tottered out to the car. Back to the ship we went. Somehow, I got back into my longjohns and sweater and turned in. Despite all the ordeal, I felt better.

The next morning, Moody went up to the greasy spoon very early. He brought back a great big breakfast for me, all packed in cardboard containers: oatmeal with real cream, bacon and eggs, home fries, and coffee. It was all stone cold, but I downed every crumb. Pretty nice of him. I owed him a few big ones.

The doctor had given me strict orders to keep the bandages soaked with a weak solution of Epsom salts and hot water. But where to get hot water? We certainly didn't have any. My good nurse solved the problem. She and the skipper lugged jugs of water aboard the *Penobscot* daily for cooking and washing. So she simply kept a dipper of hot water on her little stove so I could help myself whether they were aboard or not. Every couple of hours, I'd make my way over to their ship, carry the dipper out on deck, and pour the hot water over my leg. After a few days, my leg started to heal. No more new infections started, and the pain began going away.

Looking toward the bridge on that old West Coast Shipping Board freighter.

One day the chief mate appeared. The ship would soon be going back in service, he told us. But first, he was hiring about 50 unemployed seamen to chip the rust in the holds and between decks, then red lead and paint these areas. The company was taking on this huge, expensive job only because of the large damage claims coffee importers had made against them. Coffee was our main northbound cargo. As standard loading practice, we used hundreds of straw mats to keep the coffee bags from touching any metal, so rust shouldn't have been a problem. But even with that care, still the claims had been mounting. Since a single bag weighed 100 kilos, if even one was condemned or degraded the cost to the company was substantial.

I hated the air hammers we had to use for the chipping job. Identical to riveting hammers, they had just begun to be used on ships. They sure knocked off rust, but they were hell on the poor soul operating them. To power them, we had air outlets everywhere and a big steam-operated air compressor down in the engine room. The only good part of this was that at least one boiler had to be fired up in order to get the air compressor going so we could use the hammers. With the boiler going, Moody and I had light and heat again.

But shortly after the black gang raised steam and we got heat in the fo'c'sle, the bedbugs came to life. The freezing cold had numbed them even more than us, but now they were eating us alive.

Moody had been reading the story of Count Felix Von Luckner's World War I exploits while in command of the *Seeadler*, a square-rigged armed raider. In it, author Lowell Thomas digresses to Von Luckner's early days as a foremast hand. One shipmate who hated the skipper caught a matchbox full of bedbugs, sneaked into the Old Man's cabin, and turned them loose in his bunk.

Moody, who hated our skipper, decided to do the same. Over several nights he snapped the lights off and on endlessly, flushing out hungry bugs. Like Von Luckner, he put them in a matchbox. I could hear him muttering, "I'll fix the old bastard. I hope they eat him alive! Serves him right. Won't allow the steward enough dough to keep us from starving. Oh, you're going to get it good!"

One morning, sitting in the greasy spoon, I asked Moody how his trapping was going.

"Got the matchbox full. 'Course, every time I slide it open to add more, a few escape. But I'm just about ready."

"Well, how do you propose to get into the Old Man's cabin? It's locked, you know."

"By God, I never thought about that."

He looked crushed. To cheer him up, I told him Mr. Brooks, as the ship's keeper, had all the keys.

"But how can I get them away from him?" he asked. "That bastard probably sleeps with them around his neck."

"You'll figure some way," I told him. "Let's go. It's almost 8:00. If we're one minute late, the keeper of the keys will eat us alive."

And then the idea hit me. "Listen, Moody – why not turn your bugs loose on this lousy second mate? You'll kill two birds – him and that snooty wife of his. What do you think?"

"Slim, that's the best idea you ever had. These bugs are starving. They'll eat them alive."

On the way back to the ship, he made his plans. "Every couple of days, they go ashore to buy groceries. That's when I'll get 'em."

And that's just what he did. The day came when Mr. Brooks and his wife left their cabin unlocked when they went ashore. I stood lookout at the gangway, armed with a chipping hammer to give alarm. Moody slipped into their cabin and turned the bugs loose in their bunk.

The next morning we spied the pair of them coming down the deck toward the gangway, each carrying a suitcase.

"Slim, we're moving ashore until the ship is back in service. I'll expect you and Moody to work hard and no goofing up." He tried to give us a stern look, but the red welts all over his face and neck made him look like a clown instead.

Eventually, the time came for the mate and chief engineer on the SS *West Calumb* to start filling out the crew. I woke up one morning sick as a dog. Flu, I guess. All those freezing cold nights plus a badly infected leg had caught up with me. I managed to get through the day somehow, but by the next morning I was worse: shivering one minute, sweating the next. In desperation I went to see the mate.

After all I'd been through he simply said, "If you're sick and can't work, pay off."

Cold-hearted bastard. But pay off I did, and rode a train back home to Boston. Thanks to my mother, I made a fast recovery.

Once I was better, I swallowed my pride, called the Boston office, and asked for my job back. Two days later I got a postcard from the mate. Scrawled on it were two words: "Come back." Back I went, of course. Jobs were few and far between.

I believe that our Heavenly Father invented man
because he was disappointed in the monkey.

Mark Twain

–9–

SKULLDUGGERY IN THE FO'C'SLE

I suppose it's a sign of old age to compare the good ole days to the present ones. Nowadays, television, movies, novels ... they're all quite explicit about sex, violence, homosexuality. The most intimate and sometimes sordid practices are commonplace in them.

It was all so different back in the 30s when I was a naive young seaman. Even though we thought we were worldly-wise and sophisticated because of sailing to foreign lands and glamorous ports, the truth was that we were abysmally ignorant of the realities of human behavior.

I, for instance, was brought up in a small new England town during the years of Prohibition. Drinking was evil. Sex took place only after marriage. Any deviation, sexual or otherwise, if it existed was swept under the rug, never mentioned.

Thus when I went off to sea at the tender age of 16, I was truly a babe in the woods.

On those old pre-war Shipping Board freighters there were no luxuries. Six able seamen and two ordinaries lived aft in a crowded fo'c'sle. Iron bunks, two high, lined the walls. Small wooden lockers occupied a corner. The deck was concrete, cold to the feet.

I was about 18 and had just gotten my A.B. certificate. I had been to the north European ports several times, and was now on a regular run to the east coast of South America. I fancied myself to be an old sea dog. Hadn't I sampled the fleshpots in dozens of ports, listened to interminable boasts of sexual prowess and endurance?

Broad hints and coarse jokes were told of "wolves," men who preferred boys instead of girls. Being young, and I suppose innocent-looking, I was the butt of many of these jokes. "Watch yourself, Slim. Don't let a wolf catch you in the showers." It was difficult for me to believe that such critters existed, but there must be some truth to it.

On this particular ship, I had a lower bunk parallel to the ship's side. All of us had hung blue denim sheets on a wire along the outside of our bunks to screen out the glare of light bulbs which burned day and night. On the other side of my bunk I had rigged a shelf extending a couple of feet to the ship's side. On it I kept cigarettes, a magazine, a book or two, and a thick, one-gallon clay jug. We used to buy these jugs in Brazil. Such jugs are ideal for water. Being unglazed, they sweat, keeping the water cool. Wide and short, with long necks, they also won't tip over when the ship is rolling or pitching.

Right outside my bunk was a sturdy wooden bench which the occupant of the top bunk stood on to get into his bunk. About three feet from the bench was the bulkhead separating the fo'c'sle from the steering engine room. On this bulkhead was a large steam radiator, our only source of heat in winter.

The sailor whose bunk was above mine was something of a mystery. He was older than most of us, perhaps somewhere in his mid 40s. He was a naturalized Swede with bright red hair: Red Swensen. Having joined the ship in New York, this was his first trip with us. Our ship, like most in those days, had a good sprinkling of Scandinavians. They were damned good seamen, and had learned their trade in sail. Red was no exception. He could splice blindfolded, and could use the palm and needle like a seamstress.

As a first-tripper, he got the unpopular 12 to 4 watch, so we didn't see much of him. The 12 to 4 were always either on watch or trying to sleep.

Red had an odd affectation which led to considerable speculation. He was never seen without a white officer's cap from which the gold band

Taking our departure on a pre-war Shipping Board freighter. Two of the cargo booms on the after deck have been cradled, the others are still up.

had been removed. Rumor had it that he had gotten into some kind of trouble as a mate on tankers.

Our final port of departure was Jacksonville, as usual. Once out of the Saint Johns River, we headed south on the Great Circle course for Cape San Rogue, the northern bulge of Brazil.

The further south we steamed, the hotter it got. There was no such thing as air conditioning then. While underway, we made our own air conditioning of a kind by sewing a denim sheet into a long tube to make a wind chute. Stretched from a porthole to our bunk, it created a nice breeze. In port, of course, it didn't work, and we just sweated it out in those hot, humid Brazilian ports in summer, where the heat hits you on the head like a hammer.

Santos, up a river, was the worst. There we slept stark naked with a pillow between our legs to soak up the sweat. Since we were due to stay in port this trip for three or four days, the Old Man gave a draw. I didn't need one; I had an outlet for Lucky Strikes. The bartender at a waterfront bar had connections with Customs. Instead of me having to run the risk of smuggling cigarettes ashore, he came down to the ship, slipped his friends the usual bribe, and walked boldly back through the gate with a bagful of my smokes under his arm, leaving me with a fistful of Brazilian cabbage.

Being in port wasn't all making money on the side. There was plenty of work to do on board. I spent the first day aloft in the broiling sun in a bosun's chair, and by 5 o'clock I was beat. Dog tired, I made it to the messroom for the usual slop. After supper, everyone else changed clothes to go ashore. I just didn't have the energy to go, so I crawled into the washroom for a shower. Those old ships only had salt water showers, pumped directly from overside. Too tired to think, I stood under the shower and pulled the chain. Dirty, filthy water cascaded all over me. Some kettle of fish! Luckily, I had one bucket of fresh water under my bunk.

After the shower, my spirits perked up a little and I decided to slip ashore. Pulling on clean pants and shirt, I headed for my favorite joint, the one where my friend the bartender held sway. I got a nice table in a corner and settled down with a gin fizz. As soon as it slid down my parched gullet, I called for another. I was feeling better by the minute. Two nice-looking bimbos were eyeing me from the next table. Rather, they were eying the pile of dough I'd lain on the table. I waved them over and ordered gin fizzes all around.

They must have been recent converts to the oldest profession because they didn't speak five words of English. Only Portuguese. We were having a fine time talking a blue streak, nobody understanding a word, when I spotted Red Swensen sitting by himself. I tried to catch his eye to invite him over. The girls realized what I was up to and grabbed my arm, all the while keeping up a torrent of Portuguese. I gave up trying to understand it, but it was soon obvious they wanted no part of Red. Curious as to why, I waved the bartender over to act as interpreter.

"That guy no good; bad, no like girls," he said after listening for a minute.

"Can't be," I muttered to myself. "Who ever heard of a sailor who didn't like girls?" What with the gin fizzes and other distractions, the matter slipped from my mind.

When the bosun yelled "Turn to" the next morning, I was in worse shape than the day before. That damned gin had turned to poison. How I got through that long, hot day I'll never know. "Never again," I vowed, a solemn oath that sailors have been breaking for thousands of years. I kept it for one night, anyway. Wild horses couldn't have dragged me ashore for that night.

I struggled through supper, washed up, and spent the evening sitting under an awning someone had rigged on the poop deck. The sun dropped over the horizon and I went below for some badly needed sleep. Shucking off my dungarees and singlet, I stretched and sighed, "This is more like it. A sensible sailor stays aboard

When the bosun yelled "Turn to," he didn't care what shape we were in.

and saves his money. He doesn't go whoring around those dirty jungle ports."

Even without a stitch on, I thrashed around for a while, fighting the heat. Finally I fell asleep. The fo'c'sle was deserted, and all was quiet and peaceful. About midnight I awoke and peeked out of my curtain. Everything was still deserted. I had a smoke and reflected on how smart I was. All my dopey shipmates were ashore guzzling rotgut booze and chasing whores when they could be peacefully snoozing like me. I stubbed out my cigarette and rolled back in. It was cooling off nicely at last. Off I slid into a sound sleep.

A long time later, something brought me wide awake. I listened. It was Red, weaving around drunkenly and talking to himself on the bench right outside my bunk as he struggled out of his shoes. He was the only one around besides me. I could see the outline of his head and shoulders through my curtain.

Suddenly, Red leaned against my curtain, his head bulging against the cloth. To my horror, I felt his hand creep under the curtain and up my leg. Instantly, I rolled over on my right side, grabbed my big water jug by the neck with both hands, and swung with all my strength. *Blam!* I nailed him on the back of the head and he pitched forward. I tore the curtain aside. There lay Red, blood streaming from his head. What I didn't realize at the time was that as he flew head first off the bench, he dove headlong into the radiator.

My God, he looked dead! I didn't know a thing about first aid. Anyway, he looked far beyond first aid, or fifth aid for that matter. I started to shake. I pulled on my dungarees and ran midships for the mate. Back in those days, the chief mate was a real father figure. He handled all disciplinary problems, deck or engine. He ran the ship singlehanded. The Old Man was a mysterious figure. Seldom seen, he was always there to make decisions or take the rap. But the mate was the man you went to.

I pounded on the mate's door. When he opened up I started shouting, "You'd better come back aft, Mister Mate. I think Swensen is dead!"

"Calm down, Slim. What happened to him?"

He pulled on his pants as I spilled my story. We hurried aft. We both ran into the steel door off the after well deck at the same time. He flung me aside like a dishrag and charged through the door. I picked myself up off the deck and followed close behind.

As we entered the fo'c'sle, we saw Red lying on his back with a drunken oiler and an A.B. squatting over him. They had rolled him over. What a mess! His forehead was caved in. His eyes were half open, showing only the whites. The mate ran his hands over the back of his head where I had hit him with the jug. He raised one of Red's eyelids and peered in. Straightening up, he ordered the two drunks to run up the dock and tell Customs to send an ambulance. As soon as they left, he turned to me and said, "Tell me exactly what happened." I did, leaving nothing out. "Slim, listen carefully to me," he said. "I've known Swensen for a long time. What I know about him will remain unsaid. And all you know is that he fell while climbing into his bunk. Savvy?"

The next morning I had to go up to the mate's room. There were two uniformed policemen there. The mate, who spoke pretty good Portuguese, acted as interpreter. I repeated my story, just as he'd told me to. "I heard a thump, looked out, and there he lay."

The next day we sailed for Montevideo, then Buenos Aires. Northbound, we called at Santos to load coffee for the States. Not a word did we hear, not then or ever.

What happened to Red Swensen I never heard. To me, he was an evil man, possessed by evil forces. I really didn't care what happened to him, as long as I never saw him again.

Honor, Glory, Valor, Duty, Death.
They were all there during The Battle of the Atlantic.

Anonymous

– 10 –

THE NORTH ATLANTIC CONVOYS

Many tales have been written by both British and Americans about the seamen who manned the ships carrying the goods of war across the North Atlantic during World War II.

Most of them portrayed the Merchant Service in its true colors: a vital cog in the machinery of war, its heroes and cowards praised and damned, no better and no worse than any other cog in that vast machine that finally restored peace.

Yet they never told the stories of those who sailed the ships – the welders, shipfitters, and craftsmen of all kinds who forsook their homes and families to go to the ports where the ships were being built. Such men reaped the dubious rewards of overtime and double time (which went home by registered mail) while their kids grew older and their wives grew bitter. I can tell those tales because I lived them. I was one of those men. And here is one of those tales.

About the time of the Sudetenland incident when Germany had stopped rattling her sword and drawn it full length from its scabbard, I had paid off a ship and come home. My son was four years old and I hardly knew him. My wife and I talked for a long time one night. We were trying to buy a little house and the monthly mortgage payments were a heavy burden. We figured that we could hang on to the house if only I could get a job right away. It would mean pulling our belts a notch or two tighter, but at least I'd be home with my family.

Luckily, I got a job within a week as a rigger in one of the local ship repair yards. I mistakenly assumed that the work would be much the same as on board ship: splicing wire and rope, refitting lifeboats, hoisting stores, rigging derricks, and the like. I was dead wrong. That was "fancy rigging" and belonged to the old-time riggers. My next six months were spent deep in the graving dock, up to my ankles in freezing water, dragging heavy tackles and chain hoists through the muck.

The leading rigger was like a bosun, never satisfied.

"Where've you been?" he'd say. "I've been waiting 20 minutes for that tackle."

But the pay was good. I worked almost every Saturday and Sunday, and some weeks a couple of half-nights, too. Best of all, I went home every night to my little New England clapboard house with its old fieldstone fireplace. Banging my lunch box down, I would get out of my dirty overalls, bellowing for Junior to come help me build a fire. While supper was cooking, I'd tell him a sea story about some far-off place I'd visited, or of some ship I'd been on. Outside, the thermometer would drop to 10 and more below zero and I knew I would have to be going down the hill at 5 in the morning, but what the hell. The sailor was home from the sea. No ship could equal this.

It's a good thing we can't look into the future. To me, I was living like a king then. A small, insignificant king, maybe, but my mortgage was going down, all my bills were being paid, and even our little savings account was showing signs of life.

Full summer came. My garden occupied me then. I had shingled the roof and already put by more than a cord of wood for next winter. In my spare time I had even contracted to paint a neighbor's house. The sea was never like this, nor would I ever return to it. Or so I thought that last summer.

One night I came home from work to find an official-looking letter on the mantle. Seamen were becoming scarce. Men holding a ticket were badly needed in the war effort. There followed a long list of benefits to be derived from a job afloat.

"Phooey," I said. "I know all about those benefits."

Still, I couldn't help but notice the wage scales. Mentally, I compared a second mate's pay to my rigger's pay. "Gee, I could pay off the mortgage in one year instead of ten!" But I steeled myself against that. I burned the letter in the fireplace that night and vowed, "Never again."

Then another letter came, this time telling of war bonuses. This was something beyond imagination. While I mucked around that wet dry dock, second mates were being paid like Oriental potentates. I tentatively broached the subject at supper that night. Words were exchanged and the subject became closed. But I couldn't stop thinking, comparing. It seemed to be the chance of a lifetime to get my head above water, to pay for my house and buy all the things we'd never had.

Coming home one night soon afterward, my thoughts fell into place and I reached my decision. Back to sea I would go, and every penny would be well accounted for.

The next few days weren't pleasant ones. My interest in the dry dock waned until it became unbearable. At home, matters reached an impossible state. I was deemed an unfeeling husband and father even to contemplate returning to sea, especially when war seemed imminent. But away I went anyway, third mate on a freighter bound for who-knew-where.

I found a different life at sea than the one I had left the year before. It had been a quiet, well-ordered existence – watch on and watch off, the eternal discussions about either ships or women, the rare sight of another ship to relieve the monotony of the sea's horizon. Now, a man's life belt was always with him. Night watches were no longer spent in peaceful contemplation of the sky and sea. No more did dreams and fancies of home or the lures of the next port whisk the hours by. Merchant shipping had become a grim, deadly business.

The North Atlantic tossing us around.
The gadget at the top of the foremast was for detecting planes. It never worked.

My bridge watch was the 8 to 12. By 7:30 at night, I would be stepping out onto the lee boat deck bundled to the eyes against bitter cold. There I would huddle in pitch blackness, getting my night vision. It takes from 15 to 20 minutes for one's eyes to become accustomed to the darkness. The Coast Guard had furnished us with booklets explaining the intricacies of night vision. They explained that a completely different set of eye cells were used at night, and that when one's eyes were seeing with their night cells, one was truly color blind. If colors could be distinguished, part of the night vision had been lost. Their tests had proved that the mere flare of a match destroyed most of the eye's ability to see in the dark. All this was most important now because our very lives depended on a good lookout.

All through my watch, I prowled from the port wing through the wheel house to the starboard wing, powerful night glasses sweeping the horizon. My life belt hung over the pelorus stand in the starboard wing. Every time I passed it, my mittened hand would steal out to make sure it was still there. In such bitter weather a man started to die when he hit those waters, and would be dead and frozen inside of 20 minutes. Yet man is a tenacious animal and clings to life. He wants even the extra 20 minutes the life belt affords.

The Old Man came prowling the night watches with us, uneasy and apprehensive. Submarines were taking a fearful toll of shipping. Like all the other freighters of those early days, we were virtually defenseless. Our armament consisted of two little machine guns and an antiquated swivel gun on the poop deck, vintage First World War. Our speed was only nine knots at best, so we couldn't run away.

Though the Old Man must have been scared like the rest of us, he kept his fears to himself. He had been chief mate on tankers for many years, retiring 10 years ago. Now almost 70, he found himself pacing the bridge of a worn-out old freighter loaded to the beams with ammunition.

We used to talk in the night about why we were there, he and I. Like me, he had been dazzled by the big pay and fat bonuses. We both disavowed patriotism as a reason for doing this. He snorted that most heroes were dead and that whole chestfuls of medals wouldn't buy a pipeful of tobacco.

Yet I like to think he was covering up his true sentiments as all seamen do. His children were grown and married, and his pension and savings were more than adequate. So why did he come back? Excitement? Adventure? He'd had a lifetime of both. The truth is simply that he was an American and felt himself one. His country was threatened and he didn't want to be left out of defending her. So here he was, this old man who needed his rest, pacing away the nights on the icy North Atlantic, an old rust bucket under him and the lives of 50 men weighing him down and making him older.

Day in and day out we kept slogging along, making our eight or nine knots. Bad weather followed good, followed in turn by worse weather. We made port and discharged, then sailed back across the Atlantic only to repeat the whole thing over again.

Voyage after voyage after voyage we maintained our vigil and our fears. The only enemy we encountered was the weather, yet a scheming brute it was. Like some cunning animal it lay in wait for us or stalked our trail in the darkness, pouncing when it thought we had let down our guard. Tearing at hatch tarps, shrieking 'round the bridge, it sought to destroy us. Trip after trip it pummeled and mauled us, while mile after countless mile rolled under our stern. Though this was the only enemy that actually attacked our ship, there was never a let-up of the fear of being blown out of the water at any second by our enemies, of being catapulted from our bunks into the frigid sea without warning.

Upon our return after the first voyage, the first and second mates signed off and the Old Man offered me the mate's berth. At last I was first mate! I'd clean up this tub, by God, or else we'd have a new crew. It took me a long time to realize that this was war time, and that a sailor's pride in his ship had disappeared. In my enthusiasm to make her "ship shape and Bristol fashion," I neglected to take into account the mental condition of a new crew just signing on. Many of these hands were fresh out of training schools, signing Articles for the first time. The old hands were usually fresh ashore from a sinking, some of them having had two, three, even four ships sunk from under them, spewing them overboard in nothing but their underdrawers.

Experiences like these tended to destroy any sense of permanency. A ship was no longer a home to take pride in and on which one lavished care and affection. It was a floating bomb capable of erupting instantly into a flaming hell. Under these circumstances it was understandable that a sailor's only interest was in getting her there and back. Ships went to wrack and ruin while peacetime mates like me tore their hair out and ranted at a lazy crew. Eventually, we started to feel the same way they did. Then it was wheel and lookout, take care of the cargo-handling gear and lifeboats, and to hell with the rest of the ship.

I made voyage after voyage with the skipper on that ship. The crew changed almost to a man each time we returned. Second and third mates came and went. So did engineers, those strange people who were seen only at mealtimes and then seemed ill at ease, eating their food absentmindedly, caring little what it was or how it was cooked. With eyes fixed on their plates, they were constantly seeing engine, pumps, boilers, condensers, and all the other things that could go wrong and leave a ship wallowing helplessly, sure prey for the submarines that followed each convoy.

We made fun of the black gang, but they had courage. It was bad enough to be on deck, but down there below the waterline, they would be trapped if we were hit. At least we could see what was happening. All they could do was listen and hope and wait, nursing their engines while the minute hand of the big brass engine room clock dragged slowly 'round until the long four hours of their watch were over.

Every half hour I used to whistle down the speaking tube and give the first assistant engineer a brief picture of what was happening topside.

"The convoy is well bunched and the destroyer escorts are patrolling on all sides, astern and ahead." Or, "We've just executed an emergency turn to port. The escorts are converging, flying the black pennant." In Navy language, that means having detected an underwater object. Fancy way to say they were charging down on a submerged submarine, depth charges ready.

When that happened, I would tell the first to standby for the underwater explosions that were coming. A depth charge exploding nearby creates the effect of a gigantic hammer blow on the ship's hull. Up on deck, the explosion had a muted rumbling sound. Deep down in the engine room and fire room, it sounded like the end of the world. I have been below when one went off. Unless one is forewarned, the experience is nerve-shattering. First comes a tremendous crashing thump. The ship lurches. The lights flicker and many of them go out, shattered by the sound waves.

Feelings run raw below with a sudden depth charge explosion. "We've been torpedoed up forward! Are we going down?" "Should we shut the plant down and jump for the ladders?" "Can't do that; the engine room telegraph is still on Full Ahead. We'll stick around a few minutes and see what happens. They can't all be dead up there on the bridge."

Keeping the first assistant informed of what was going on was the least I could do. God knows, the hell of waiting, wondering, guessing down there in the dimly lit, steamy bowels of a freighter would be more than I could stand. To think we ridiculed "those people" – the black gang.

The deck and engine room will never in a thousand years see eye to eye, my eye included. But they must be given their due credit. Those were brave, patient men. They died by the hundreds, never seen, never heard, carried down to a watery grave while the fortunate deck crews often escaped on a life raft. Yet many of the deck crew died as well, yielding to cold, starvation, or the impersonal machine gun bullets of a Nazi fanatic.

This may sound morbid, pessimistic, as if we on the helpless freighters were defeatists, as if we knew because of our circumstances that we were licked, only waiting to be knocked over like sitting ducks, utterly unable to win. Indeed we were sitting ducks, lacking means of defense or escape. But we were men of a peculiar breed, men who always had hopes and dreams. We never truly believed for an instant that our ship would get it, nor did the men of any ship that went down. That's what kept all of us going, trip after trip, year after year. I suppose the same thing was true for our enemy, for they were men, too.

As the war spread, so did our voyages. For a long time, our destination was always the British Isles. Then came the Allied invasion of North Africa. Our old tramp steamer followed trouble like a hound

North Atlantic convoy photographed by a U.S.S. Albemarle (AV-5) plane.
Most of the ships are tankers.

tracking a rabbit. Soon we were cautiously steaming in and out of the Straits of Gibraltar like an old faithful black ferry boat.

The western approaches to the British Isles had become the grave-yard of hundreds of ships. So had our Eastern Seaboard. So, in fact, had the whole western ocean. But the convoy system by then had been brought to a high degree of perfection and the building program of new tonnage was beginning to catch up with the awful losses. Many ships had been torpedoed and sunk while sailing in company with us, but our luck held.

Usually, the unlucky ships would get it just at dusk, although to the Germans any time was a good time. When the pale, wintry sun was dipping low, the escorts would begin surveying our flanks, trimming us into a close-knit group.

"Close up, close up – regain your proper stations. Enemy underwater craft in the vicinity." The Navy signalman on our bridge repeated the messages in a monotone. Word raced through the ship. "Blackout! Check your portholes. No lights!" Naval escorts were not unlike sheep dogs, their blinker lights substituting for the yapping of the dogs as they nipped at the heels of their docile charges, urging them to bunch up for the night.

When full dark came, our senses became more alert. Keeping station in a low-powered convoy was tricky business. Ships were deeply laden and their engines overworked. With a bit of beam sea running, the columns of ships tended to set to leeward, some faster than others. Then would come the windward bridge lookout, shrieking, "Ship on port beam!" A quick glance to starboard through the night glasses would show our starboard companion maybe a dozen ship lengths off. "Right wheel ease the helm ... steady, steady."

While we were easing right, the ship in our wake kept steadily on, not knowing or caring what we were up to. We had to get back in our column, but how? The ship astern by then had speeded up, having lost sight of our stern, and was now occupying our station while we were steaming ourselves right between two columns of ships.

Speed had to be carefully maintained. Yet in convoy, we never used the engine room telegraph. We did it by voice down the speaking tube. "Up two revolutions, First. That should do it." Or, "Down ten, quick, First. We're right on top of the ship ahead."

My watch as mate was the 4 to 8, so I got both dawn and dusk, and more than my share of the black hours. At the very first sign of dawn, the ships of the convoy gradually emerged as the blackness imperceptibly turned to gray. As the sky lightened, more and more ships came into sight, stretched all over the sea. Columns were crooked, ships out of position. Some would be far back, and some mornings some of them would be missing. One signalman would gab by blinker light with our neighbors. "What happened to the Dutch tanker? What about the Canadian?" Most times we never heard. In some convoys, the commodore would announce by signal to all ships that two ships (or perhaps one or three) had straggled and been sunk.

It was also a heartbreaking experience to see a ship break down. In the early days, that meant almost certain death. Naval escort vessels were so few that each convoy was inadequately escorted. None could be spared to stand by a straggler. It was the many versus the few, and the many were too important to leave. The way would fall off a struggling ship as she swung out of her column. Two black balls signifying "Not under command" would appear on her signal halyards. Ship after ship would steam past her till it came our turn. Our Old Man would raise his clasped hands over his head like a prize fighter. The Old Man on the other ship would wave back, his signalman jauntily blinking "farewell" as she dropped swiftly astern. All of us, escorts and all, kept steadily on while the crippled ship vanished astern to certain death. We – and they – were so helpless ...

Slowly, gradually, it got a little better. Instead of queer-looking little wooden cockleshells for escort, there appeared a new type of vessel, the destroyer escort (DE). It was built for the job, and a fine job it did. Toward the end of the war, the little carriers came to travel in our midst. Rescue ships patrolled our wake, ready and able to stand by and defend a poor straggler, or, failing that, to rescue her crew. We steamed in high style then, escorted like princes. But a lot of ships sank and a lot of seamen died before all this came to pass.

I find the medicine worse than the malady.

John Fletcher

– 11 –

A SHIP'S MEDICINE CHEST

Way back before World War II, medical treatment at sea was pretty crude. One chief mate swore he had only two remedies: iodine for the outside, Epsom salts for the inside! A cargo ship in those days was no place to get sick. Every man had to pull his weight. Just one man laid up, not able to stand his watch, put a strain on the rest of us. But every now and then someone did get sick or hurt.

While still in my teens, I developed some bad cavities in my back molars, brought on by neglect. They plagued me off and on. Finally, they really got bad while we were at sea. For over a week I suffered. First one tooth ached, then another.

In desperation, I sought help from the Old Man. I didn't dare see the mate, fearing that he would try to pull them out with a pair of pliers and they'd break off.

The skipper sat me down, peered intently into my mouth, and said, "Ah, yes. Had exactly the same thing when I was your age. Now you just sit still. I'll be right back." Back he came with a small brown bottle with a glass rod in it. I didn't find out until later that the bottle contained sulphuric acid.

"Now then," the skipper said, "we'll just give those two gnashers on the right a drop of this."

There was a pretty good sea running, and the ship was pitching. Just as he poked the glass rod in my mouth, the ship lurched and the drop fell off the rod between my tooth and my cheek. *Holy smoke!* It felt as if he had thrown a lighted match in my mouth! I hollered and danced with pain. Quick as a snake, he flung one strong arm around my neck and aimed more acid onto the bad teeth.

"Come back tomorrow and we'll repeat that," he said.

If there had been any place else to go, I wouldn't have gone back. But I was trapped. It was probably a good thing because after the third day I had a burned yap, but the teeth were gone, eaten away by the acid. Rough, brutal ... but effective.

Rolling in an Atlantic storm – conditions as usual.

On a later trip, we were making the approach to New York. It was February and snowing and blowing a gale. I was on the 8 to 12 watch and was on the wheel. About 8:30 p.m. the Old Man heard the horn on Ambrose Lightship. He was bound and determined that we would find the pilot vessel and pick up a pilot, despite knowing in his heart that no small pilot launch could possibly go out in such weather.

In those days there was a second lightship nearby: Fire Island. The skipper decided to steam back and forth between the two while waiting for the pilot boat.

"Rig the pilot ladder and boat rope on the port side of the forward well deck," he ordered the third mate. Port was then the lee side. The third whistled to summon Charlie Ennis, my watch partner, from his lookout post on the bow. Down he went to work, in the pitch dark and snow.

The Old Man pulled his head in out of the pilot house window and grunted with satisfaction. He had just heard the horn on Fire Island Lightship. Peering into the binnacle, he ordered me to come hard a'starboard. We changed course 180 degrees, heading back for Ambrose. He'd forgotten about Charlie trying to rig the ladder down there in the dark on what was now the weather side.

Just then, green water burst over the forward well deck on the port side. Out of our sight, a boarding wave picked Charlie up and slammed him into the forward shelter deck bulkhead, splitting his forehead wide open.

The lee side pilot house door slid open and in came Charlie, complaining, "Mister Mate, I can't rig the ladder in this weather."

The third mate turned his flashlight on Charlie. God Almighty! He was streaming water and blood, his scalp hanging down over his eyes. He had unbuttoned his oilskins, and the blood had run down his wet clothes until he looked like a real redskin.

The Old Man took one look at him and ordered the third mate to fetch the chief mate. Up he came, the famous Mr. Bang of the Cape Horners, a marvel with palm and needle.

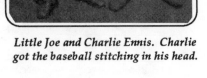

Little Joe and Charlie Ennis. Charlie got the baseball stitching in his head.

"Get down to my cabin, Charlie," he told the injured man. "And for God's sake take a towel. I don't want blood dripping all over my cabin."

When he finished, Mr. Bang came back, rubbing his hands. "Did a first-rate job on him, Captain. Put in some real fancy stitching." He turned to me. "I sent him below, Slim. You're stuck on the wheel by yourself until midnight."

As soon as the 12 to 4 man relieved me, I hurried aft to the fo'c'sle. There was Charlie, sitting on the edge of his bunk, smoking, half drunk.

"How do you feel?" I asked him.

"I'm all right, but my head aches something fierce. Old Bang is okay, though. He gave me a full mug of rum before he went to work on me."

I inspected his bandage. It was bloody already, and slipping over his eye. "Charlie, I'm going to change that bandage. It's a mess." I had two rolls of gauze in my locker. I wrung out a towel in cold water, took off the bandage, and swabbed Charlie's forehead.

Dear God! That damned mate had put in cross stitches that looked like a baseball. And he had done it with a sail needle! Sail needles aren't round like a sewing needle, they're triangular. They made holes in Charlie bigger by far than the coarse black thread that held them together. Charlie was back working the next day. But from that day to this, if he's still living, he's walking around with a perpetual frown on his ugly mug and a baseball seam across his forehead.

Sitting in the shade of a tarp in the South Atlantic. I'm on the right, with Heavy, the oiler, leaning behind me. Next to me is Big Swede, with an engine room wiper behind him. Next come Charlie Wilson, Earl Burch, and a fireman.

Then there was the time a few years after the war when I was master of a ship lying in the port of Dalhousie, New Brunswick, Canada, loading a full cargo of newsprint for New Orleans. We had come in around the Gaspé Peninsula and up the Restigouche.

The second mate and I were lolling over the chart room table discussing our southbound route. We were scheduled to put into Halifax for bunkers. In those days there was a narrow, natural passage between Nova Scotia and Cape Breton Island called the Gut of Canso. It has since been filled in and a causeway bridge built, but then it was open to deep water vessels. It saved many miles over having to go way 'round the island and out of the St. Lawrence estuary by way of Cabot Straits.

Should we take the short route? If the fog caught us in the Gut, we'd have our hands full.

"It's August," I finally reasoned. "We can expect a few clear days. We'll go through the Gut."

"All right, Captain," the mate said.

"We'll have Sparks keep close track of the weather. If fog threatens before we get to the Gut, we'll just haul off and take the long route."

It was a challenging decision. I got great satisfaction from cutting corners if the risk was reasonable. I always figured that part of my obligation to my owners was always to take the shortest route, "having due regard for existing conditions and circumstances," as the International Rules of the Road so aptly put it.

We sailed out of Dalhousie and Sparks commenced feeding me weather reports. Without exception they were good all the way to the Gut, through it, and around to the entrance to Halifax, where we picked up a pilot. When he came on the bridge he asked where we were from.

"Through the Gut," I told him.

"Where's your pilot?"

I was puzzled. "We don't have a pilot. Why do you ask?"

"It isn't mandatory, but vessels running through the Gut always hire a pilot," he said stiffly.

"News to me," I said. If I'd known that, I would undoubtedly have engaged a coast pilot. But because I hadn't, and because I'd made a successful passage, I felt pretty smug.

It took us several hours to bunker. As soon as the fuel hose was uncoupled, we sailed out. Just before we left, the chief engineer told me he had a young oiler who was sick.

"What's the matter with him?" I asked.

"I don't know, but he won't get out of his bunk."

I had wished the thankless job of ship's medicine man on Mr. Butler, the second mate, a big heavyset man with a raucous voice. "Mr. Butler," I said, "slip down there and have a look at that oiler." Then I promptly forgot about it. Later, I wished I hadn't.

We steamed steadily along in fine style day after day, making our usual 10-plus knots. The weather was sunny and fine. The ship was in perfect trim, carrying a homogeneous cargo, taking the mild seas most kindly.

We were a little south of New York when Mr. Butler came up on the bridge one afternoon.

"Captain," he said, "I'm worried about our sick oiler."

"Why? What's the matter with him?"

"I don't know, but he's much worse. He's lost a lot of weight. He's too weak to get up and he won't eat. He says his throat's too sore to swallow."

"Well, as soon as the mate relieves you, we'll go have a look at him."

As soon as the mate came up, down we went. I didn't have a little black bag, and I knew as much about medicine as a quahog clam, but I felt like Dr. Kildare.

"This boy looks awful," I pronounced. He could only whisper. I peered down his throat. The inside of his gullet looked grayish instead of a healthy red. The inside of his throat seemed terribly swollen. He hadn't eaten for two days by then. All he was taking was a little water sipped through a straw.

I took Mr. Butler aside. "Come on up to my room," I said quietly. "I've got a medical book left over from the war. It describes every illness known to man, with symptoms, causes, and cures."

I dug out the book. We started with A, worked through B and C. When we got to D we found it: diphtheria! Every symptom matched the boy's swollen throat, white tissues. Holy smoke! A highly infectious disease, and me with a very young crew. I made up my mind in a hurry and rushed into the radio room.

"Sparks, call up NSS, Annapolis, and tell them we need medical advice. Call me when you get through."

But he didn't get through. Something was wrong with his transmitter.

"Fix it, Sparks. Keep me advised."

"Yes, sir," he said. But the day passed and the radio still was out.

The next morning Mr. Butler rushed into my room. "He's worse!" he said. "The boy's worse. He can't get his wind. I guess his throat is swelling shut."

I knew I had to do something. Back to the radio shack.

"Sparks, what's happening?"

He grinned up at me. "I've got her fixed, Captain. NSS is coming in now." Transmission was by key in those days, not voice radio. NSS sent word that a Navy medical doctor was standing by. We were ordered to transmit symptoms. Sparks tapped them out on his key as fast as I wrote them.

"Stress that the boy is almost suffocating from lack of oxygen," I instructed him.

Back came a question: "Do you have an O.B.A. apparatus aboard?

"Two," I answered. O.B.A. is an Oxygen Breathing Apparatus, a mask into which oxygen is fed from a small cylinder. It's used for fire fighting in an enclosed space.

Back came another question: "Do you have any catheters in your hospital?"

I was stymied. "Mr. Butler, what the hell is a catheter?"

"I know," he said. "I'll go look." Those old Liberty ships had a room set aside as a hospital. In those days it was well stocked with a full line of elaborate hospital equipment. It was supposed to be presided over by a combination purser-pharmacist who had a smattering of medical knowledge from a crash course. By now, though, pursers were long gone.

Mr. Butler hurried back with a handful of slithery rubber tubes about the diameter and consistency of a piece of limp spaghetti.

"Sparks, tell NSS we have catheters."

While Sparks was sending, I asked Mr. Butler what they were used for. His answer gave me the creeps.

"When a man can't pee, you shove one of these up his dink into his bladder to let the urine out."

What in blazes did this Navy doctor have in mind? The boy's problem was on his other end.

Sparks held up his hand for silence; NSS coming in again. Sparks copied the transmission directly on his typewriter. Ripping the copy off his machine, he handed it to me. "This job's for you, Captain."

I quickly glanced over the message. "Come on, Mr. Butler, and bring those damned catheters." We raced down to the main deck. I grabbed one of the O.B.A. suitcases out of its rack near the galley and hurried on to the oiler's room.

"Now then, Butler, open up that suitcase and disconnect the oxygen bottle." The bottle was about seven or eight inches long, about three or four inches in diameter.

I read the message out loud and then gave instructions to Mr. Butler. "Push the catheter up his nose and down his throat. Then I'll tape the other end to the valve on the cylinder, crack the valve, and *Presto!*, he gets oxygen."

"Captain, I'm getting sick to my stomach. You'll have to do it."

"Give me the damned thing!" I grabbed the catheter away from Mr. Butler. Try as I might, though, I couldn't get it up his nose. It was just too floppy. I kept at it, but it was futile. It just wouldn't go. The poor oiler was feebly pushing at my hands, trying to whisper. I gave up and raced back to the radio shack.

"Sparks, get NSS again and tell them it's a no-go. We can't carry out the doctor's suggestion. Tell him things are desperate here."

Sparks started clicking rapidly. Presently, the stand-by signal came over, then a message started coming through: "A Navy destroyer with a doctor on board is en route, Havana to Charleston, South Carolina. Please radio your position."

I ran over to the chart room, grabbed the parallel rulers, advanced my morning sights by our course and speed, and marked our present position on the chart. I copied off the latitude and longitude on a scrap of paper and dashed back to the radio shack.

"Here, Sparks. Send it off."

Orders for our new course came back shortly: "You should rendez-vous with destroyer at approximately 1500 hours."

Immediately after lunch, I went back to the bridge. Mr. Butler was fussing around in the chart room. There has always been an intense rivalry between the Navy and the Merchant Service, each thinking it had the better seamen. In fact, it was more than rivalry. Each disliked the other and never missed a chance to say so. Bar room battles over it were frequent. I could feel every scrap of that rivalry leaking out of every one of Mr. Butler's pores as he prowled around the room.

Ignoring that, I told him to whistle up the bosun and have him strip #1 lifeboat of all unnecessary junk, swing it outboard, rig a boat rope, and have four men stand by to crew it and two to lower it.

"Yes, sir," Mr. Butler said. "We'll show those Navy jerks how it should be done."

About 2:30 p.m., right on schedule, the destroyer poked its nose over the horizon, dead ahead.

"Stop engines, Mr. Butler, and come hard a'port. We'll make a lee on our starboard side."

Up swooped the destroyer, whoop-whooping on her siren, her blinker light clacking furiously. "What's he saying, Mister?"

"He says, 'Heave to, port side a'lee. We will send boat with doctor.'"

"No way, Mister. Tell him we're sending our boat."

The destroyer approached almost alongside, her rail lined with gawking sailors. An officer started yelling through an electric bull horn. "We are launching boat. Make a lee."

I saw the second mate lean out to roar back an insulting remark. I stopped him. "Keep quiet, Mr. Butler. We're looking for help from them. Slow ahead, hard starboard, stop engines. Let them send their damned boat."

They put four crew in their boat and swung it outboard. Pipes twittered: "Lower away." One fall hung up while one lowered away; their boat hung on end. Two of the boat's crew fell off in the drink, the other two clung to the thwarts.

"Haw, haw," roared Butler. "Look at 'em! Seamen, huh? Balls!"

"Shut up," I snarled at him. "We need them."

Finally they got their boat afloat. Oars lifted and fell, and they heaved alongside. Up to the bridge came the doctor, two crew, and their exec. Introductions were exchanged.

"Mr. Butler, please escort the doctor and his crew down to the patient." I turned to the exec and said innocently, "Commander, it was too bad about your boat launching."

He winced, and took a shuddering breath. "It was pretty awful, wasn't it."

"Sure was, but it could have been worse. The boat could have sunk. Or your men drowned." Oh, this was one for the book! I loved slipping the knife in.

The poor exec flushed red as a beet. "Those bastards think they're getting leave in Charleston. Well, I'll keep 'em on board 'til they're ready for retirement!"

Fortunately for him the poor guy was spared further torture by the appearance of the doctor followed by his two crewmen carrying our poor oiler on a stretcher.

"We'll take good care of him," the doctor said.

"We appreciate that."

As soon as their boat was clear, I rang up Full Ahead and we swung back on course. I found out later that my diagnosis was dead wrong. The oiler had septicemia of the throat. With proper treatment in a Charleston hospital, he made a swift and complete recovery. But my mind remained unchanged: it was bad to get sick or hurt on a freighter at sea. The cure was always worse than the ailment.

*I wish to have no connection with any ship that does not sail fast
for I intend to go in harm's way.*

John Paul Jones

– 12 –

A WARTIME TRIP TO MALTA

In a highly irregular move, one day we were sent into Gibraltar for orders. We were bound for some place in North Africa, the actual port as yet unannounced. The Old Man fussed around the bridge growling something about "those damned Limeys" while I went forward to clear away the anchors.

At anchor, there was a great business of British naval launches coming and going. The Old Man's door stayed shut behind various and sundry gentlemen coming and going in fine-fitting uniforms. After the last had gone, the Old Man sent for me.

"Well, what do you think – we're to take our cargo of foodstuffs to Malta. Ever hear of it? These Limeys are nuts!"

Yes, I'd heard of Malta, and recently, too. The Italian and German air forces were determined to bomb it beneath the sea, for it was a sore British naval thorn in their sides. This assignment didn't sound too attractive to me. Our luck had been holding up pretty good; why stretch it? Last voyage, nine ships in our convoy had been sunk, one right on our beam. If she had had ammo on board, we wouldn't be alive here in Gib.

But there we were. And the following night we got underway.

There were only four or five cargo ships. Yet even before we poked our nose out of Gibralter we were surrounded, and outnumbered, by British Navy escorts. At least one was a cruiser, the others appeared to be destroyers. As soon as we were clear they herded us close together for safety.

Our gunnery officer had his 28 gunners at what I call half battle stations, half of them on the guns day and night. They manned 20-millimeter Orlikons plus anti-aircraft guns on the bow and stern.

It was all so unreal. The beautiful blue Mediterranean lay sparkling in the brilliant sunshine. The false sense of security it gave was heightened by the Old Man's absolute conviction that all this war business was way overrated. To him, deliveries were business as usual. His lifetime on peacetime tankers, plus his New England obstinacy, had completely insulated him from the harsh realities in which we now found ourselves. He blamed the Limeys for the whole mess, thought it was a big to-do about nothing. His job, as he saw it, was to take his ship from one port to another, discharge, load, and go on. The gun crews, naval escorts, submarines, and convoys were just obstacles to him, dreamed up by Limeys. We could be in the midst of the most Godawful conditions, but if he felt we were on course, making knots, the weather clear, he'd up and go to bed and sleep like a baby. I envied him.

The morning after we left, the commodore blinked over: "Expect low-flying enemy aircraft, now!" The gunnery officer hit the General Alarm lever. I blew the whistle several times for good measure. Running steps pounded throughout the ship. The Old Man came out, blinking at the morning sun just over the bows.

"What's this all about, Mister? The Limeys making a fuss again?" Quickly, I told him about the signal. "Hrumph. I don't see any aeroplanes."

Swoosh! Two Italian torpedo bombers flashed by at masthead height. I guess they were after the cruiser, for they were gone in an instant. If they dropped any torpedoes, we didn't see them. Frantic signals: "Zigzag plan, now!" Off we went at a 30 degree angle to starboard.

"My God, Mister, did you see those aeroplanes? The damned fools almost ran into our foremast! Guns, how do you know they're Eyetalians?"

The gunner answered, "I've heard people say the Italians were lousy fighters and soldiers. Maybe so, but some of them can sure fly !"

"Ho hum," says the Old Man. "Believe I'll take a nap before lunch."

Don't mistake this. He was a canny, caring shipmaster. He might take a nap now, but he'd be on the bridge all night.

On we went, slogging along at 10 knots, making easting. We were ordered to their port of Valletta. The Skipper and I read up on the place in the Sailing Directions and pored over the Mediterranean chart. We planned as best we could, not that we could do much. We had no detailed charts of Malta. We had no choice but to follow the ship ahead. If something separated us, we had done what we could to be ready.

We got the blinker signal to break off and proced independently to Valletta just at dusk. The Old Man was not in the least upset, but I was. Malta was no place to be, certainly not in a lousy Liberty ship that could barely make 10 knots. The captain and I pored over the chart again. He reckoned we could be off the entrance to Valletta harbor at dawn. He drew the course line, got the compass course from it, and told me to haul out of our little convoy on our new course. I did.

The quartermaster, who was no dummy, raised an expressive eyebrow.

"How do I know?" I told him in answer to his silent question. "Mind your damned course."

The other ships and the escorts disappeared in the darkness, bound for unknown other destinations. We never saw them again.

At dawn, the entrance to Valletta was dead ahead. The Old Man had been on the bridge all night. I found him on the bridge wing, warming his hands on a mug of my coffee.

"Good navigating, Cap."

"What did you expect to see, Coney Island?"

Still, I think he was pleased. A blinker started up ahead of us from what looked to be a tugboat. As we got closer, we saw that a great submarine net was rigged across the entrance to the harbor. One end was fast to either the shore or the breakwater. The other was made fast to the tugboat. To open the contraption, the tugboat steamed around, dragging the net. Our signalman told the Old Man the net was fouled. We couldn't get in for at least two hours. They suggested we steam back and forth while they made repairs.

It was a beautiful Sunday morning, with the blue sea like glass. It was all so peaceful. The war seemed like a faraway bad dream.

"Now then, Mister, there's no sense steaming around wasting fuel. We'll just slip down beyond the harbor a'ways and anchor."

"But Captain, this is a bad place. We'd be a sitting duck for those Italian planes."

"Oh, baloney. Those two the other day were just a fluke. You worry too much. In fact, you're starting to sound like those Limeys back in Gib." Having disposed of me and the Limeys, he leisurely poured himself another mug. I headed for the fo'c'sle head to clear away the anchors.

Though we had no local charts, the Captain took us down the coast a good five miles. I heard him ringing the telegraph for Stop. When the way was almost off the ship, he hollered to let go. I swung my sledge and down she went. I grabbed the big two-handed brake and started to brake her.

Nothing happened.

I wound the brake tighter. Still the big chain kept roaring out. By this time, the ship was going astern to set the hook. I had the brake on as far as it would turn. At least the chain finally stopped paying out. Running over to the side, I was astonished to see the chain leading straight up and down.

By this time the ship had stopped. "His Nibs" had figured that by this time the anchor had taken hold. When I pointed my arm up and down, the skipper blasted at me through the phone. "Dammit mister, you've let out too much chain. We'll have to go astern again."

He rang up Half Astern and backward we went. I kept watching the chain. Still up and down. We must have backed half a mile. The Old Man was hopping up and down by now, yelling at me. Ignoring him, I dropped down the forepeak hatch and peeked into the chain locker. Holy Smoke! All the chain was out. The bitter end was shackled to a big ring bolt in the bulkhead, straining hard against it. Thank God it was. In naval vessels, I'm told, they don't secure the bitter end. Merchant ships do and now I knew why.

Up the ladder I flew and told His Lordship what had happened. Only then did he duck into the chart room and turn on the fathometer. There must have been about a zillion fathoms under us. That's what came of not having a local chart.

It took me quite a while to get all that chain heaved in. Even though I had the carpenter leaning in the chain locker with a chain hook, I had to keep stopping because the chain kept piling up to the hawse pipe. I paced constantly, a nervous wreck. Any time I expected those damned planes to take a slam at us. Maybe the Old Man was lulled by the serenity, but not us.

Just about the time the anchor slammed home a queer-looking launch, some sort of British patrol boat, appeared. Its skipper shouted over that the harbor submarine net was fixed and for us to precede him into the harbor and anchor. Back we went, me still glancing skyward every two minutes. It wasn't just a fairy tale that this island had been under constant seige from the air.

Slowly, we crept in through the opening in the nets. The Old Man backed and filled, muttering to himself. Once more the command came: "Let go!" After the anchor fetched up, I left the fo'c'sle head and headed down the forward deck. The gun crews were still at their guns, joking and laughing. They were a new group. I envied their innocence.

Valletta was a breathtaking sight: snow-white buildings set into steep hillsides. Just as I was climbing the midships ladder to take a better look, the Old Man popped out on the bridge deck above me. "Mister, swing out Number 1 lifeboat."

"Captain, what for?"

"I'm going to Sunday morning Mass, that's what for."

Dear God, he's gone daft! I always knew he was a devout Catholic, but breaking out men to lower a boat with practically all hands off watch standing by to help the gun crew? Well, what the Captain says goes, so I climbed up to the boat deck to release the gripes on #1. I was on my hands and knees, fiddling with the pelican hook, when *Blam!* A great gout of water shot up just off our starboard beam. A damned bomb! Funny, but I never heard a plane, and our guns were silent. Out came "His Nibs" in a rusty black suit and hat.

"What the hell's going on, Mister?"

"That was a big, ugly bomb, Captain, and I think it was aiming right for your cabin. Still want this boat?"

"No, I don't. It's probably too late for church. No telling what hours these foreign churches keep. Besides, it's Sunday and you look tuckered out." Him worried about my health? I didn't believe that for a minute. He was just finally waking up to the fact that there really was a big, nasty war going on.

I shouldn't have been surprised; he was so damned set in his ways. I had known that from my first trip with him when he came out of peacetime retirement into the "Battle of the Atlantic."

We had sailed from Boston in a small convoy to Bedford Basin in Halifax, the main port of departure for eastbound convoys. When the time came one morning,

Me at the helm of the #1 lifeboat.

he went ashore to the Convoy Conference, his very first. When he came back, he made a beeline to the chart room, me right on his tail. Upending a bulging briefcase, he said, "Look at all this foolish stuff. Some Limey spent all afternoon going over and over this junk. Stow it away someplace. Or read it if you'd like. If you can make anything out of it, let me know."

I spent most of the afternoon pawing through convoy diagrams, signals, zigzag plans, emergency signals, various flag hoists and their meanings, on and on until I finally got to the end. When I went down to supper, the Old Man was already there.

"Well," he said, "did you learn anything?"

"Yep. First, we're supposed to sail in an hour."

"I know that! I've already told the chief engineer. Eat your supper. If you hurry, you'll get it down before you go forward to hoist the anchor. Anything else?"

"Well, Captain, it would seem that a dozen or so ships will be sailing with us with a temporary convoy commodore. We're supposed to steam easterly. Then two days or so out we're to meet up with a big convoy coming up from New York. Their commodore will become ours. We have been assigned to a new position, the last ship in the outside port column."

"Fancy that, Mister. Why?"

"Why what, Captain?"

"Why don't they just give us the compass course and leave it to us to keep in sight of each other?" The war really was nonexistent to him.

Right on schedule, out we steamed. The commodore was hoisting one flag after another: "Speed five knots." "Take up your proper station." "Close up."

Our skipper was racing from one side of the bridge to the other. On his way through the wheelhouse he'd shout new steering orders to the quartermaster, bellowing through the engine room phone: "Faster! Slow down!" More often than not, he'd run headlong into the Navy signalman coming with yet another order from "that damned Limey." All ships were blacked out. Night had come on. All we had to steer by was the blue stern light of the ship ahead.

The next day, things were no better. Ships were out of place all over the ocean, out of column, steaming in between columns, the old coal burners sending up clouds of black smoke. It was chaos. And there were only a dozen of us.

At noon the Old Man finally got a pretty fair sun sight from which to work out his position. "I make her to be just about there, Mister. Now let's see. We've got to advance the clocks to our LAT (Local Apparent Time)."

Now, if ever, I had to be diplomatic. "Captain, for the last few years all ships have been sailing on Zone Time."

"What the hell is that? Something the Limeys dreamed up?"

I explained that each 15 degrees of longitude east or west of Greenwich is one hour ahead of or behind Greenwich Civil Time (GCT). As long as a vessel is in that zone, she keeps that zone time. When she crosses the boundary of that zone, she advances or retards her clocks one hour. That way, all vessels in one zone are on the same time.

"Not on this vessel, Mister. I've been sailing all over these oceans for a good many years on Local Apparent Time with no problems. Now set the clocks ahead." The result was that now our clocks were ahead of all the other ships'.

That night the fog came down on us. It was so thick we couldn't see the bow, let alone the ship ahead. Sparks came in with a message to stream fog buoys, wooden contraptions to be towed behind us. They were constructed to jump around and make a big wake. The idea was that the bow lookout on the ship astern could watch it and keep the bridge advised of his leading ship's whereabouts.

We hung the fog buoy over the stern where it promptly disappeared. We knew the ship behind us would never see it. We never saw the one ahead of us, either. Staying in line was going to be very difficult in these conditions. To make matters worse, all merchant ships in those days had only magnetic compasses. The day of the wonderful gyro compasses, perfectly accurate, was far in the future.

Among the gadgets that raised hell with our compasses was the degausser, a great electric cable completely surrounding the hull. It was supposed to neutralize the natural magnetic influence of a steel ship, rendering impotent the new magnetic mines so favored by the Germans. Because of this, all ships were probably steaming on slightly different courses. It didn't matter in clear weather when we just followed the ship ahead. But in thick fog like this, it was a different story. Vessels were gradually getting closer, farther apart, falling astern, or forging ahead like a herd of blind elephants.

"Things couldn't be worse," I thought. But oh yes, they could, and very shortly, too. All ships had to observe constant radio silence, although the commodore could and did transmit in code. Right after supper Sparks handed the Old Man a coded message.

The Old Man turned immediately to me. "Mister, go in the chart room and decode this."

Decoding was a tedious business. A page full of numbers might yield one sentence. I waded through the job and brought the message to the captain in the wheelhouse. The commodore of the main convoy expected to join up with us between 2200 and 2300 hours. At 2300 hours all ships were to change course 40 degrees to port. Holy Moses! That meant 40-odd ships helling along into the 12 of us, and we were all stone blind in the fog. The big convoy was obviously in clear weather, not realizing they had fog ahead of them. In addition, now the Old Man's stubbornness caught up with us. Our clocks were two days' easting ahead of all the other ships. We'd be going hard a'port before them.

The Old Man finished reading the message in the dim light from the binnacle. "Mister, what the hell's this '2200, 2300 hours' mean?"

"Captain, all ships are now using 24-hour time. That means 10 p.m. and 11 p.m."

"By God, Mister, why don't they say so? I'll bet this is another Limey invention. They're not content to drag us into their miserable war. Now they're trying to take over our ships."

About 10 o'clock we could hear ships hooting their fog whistles all around us. The main convoy had arrived and we were in some jam, all right. We could even smell 'em – the stink of big diesel motor ships, the acrid scent of the old coal burners.

The wheelhouse clock rang six bells. The Old Man promptly told the man at the wheel to come left 40 degrees. There we went, plowing through 40-odd ships! How we ever missed colliding, I'll never know, but miss'em we did. I kept the whistle going almost continually. Pretty soon, the only whistle we heard was our own. Daylight came, the fog lifted, and suddenly we were alone on the ocean.

"Mister, where the hell's the convoy?"

"Well, Captain, you know we changed course much sooner than they did, so I guess we're lost."

We hadn't been forgotten, though. Up over the horizon heaved a Canadian corvette, blinking furiously: "Follow me." Docilely, we fell in behind and rejoined the convoy.

From that incident on, the captain learned very very fast what changes the war at sea had wrought.

Finally in Malta, I secured the lifeboat and went below for a mug of coffee. A weasel-faced critter came aboard, then oozed into the saloon inquiring for the chief officer. One of the engineers nodded in my direction. In a heavy Brooklyn accent, he asked to speak privately with me.

"Sure," I said. "Come on up to my room."

He settled himself down at my desk. I didn't like the look of him one bit. He looked like a cheap gangster in the movies. Without any shame, he told me he had been deported from the States for bootlegging during Prohibition.

Then, says he, "You are scheduled to commence discharging tonight as soon as it gets dark. You are to discharge several hundred tons of bagged wheat from #5 hatch into a lighter on the port side. Instead, if you will discharge into my lighter on the starboard side, this is yours."

He opened a sack on my desk, spilling out enough old-fashioned yellow backs to cover it. Before Roosevelt came to office, we were on the gold standard. All bills of $20 and up were gold on one side, green on the other, half again bigger than our present currency. I hadn't seen them since I was a kid. Evidently he had smuggled some of this dough out when he got kicked out.

I must admit, that big pile of cash was fascinating. But I did something then that I'm pretty proud of. Going to the door, I yelled for the bosun and carpenter, two big brutes. Turning to Ratface, I made a patriotic speech. "We've brought this damned cargo halfway 'round the damned world to feed some brave, starving folks, and it's not going into your black market. Bosun, throw this bum off the ship. And I mean *throw!*"

Maybe I should have taken his dough. Or maybe it was no good anyway and couldn't be exchanged. Ah, the hell with it. This war was bad enough without making money from hungry Allied friends. It was a decision I still feel good about.

– 13 –

THE NAVY AT ITS BEST

In spite of the foregoing, I must give due credit to Navy seamanship at its best. On one occasion in particular, it was superb.

I was mate on a Liberty ship. We were in the eastern Mediterranean during the war, steaming west in a small convoy. The second mate, Joe Bandoni, and I had been shipmates before the war as A.B.s. The deck cadet, Tim Pouch, was rotating between watches. At the time of this story he was on Bandoni's watch, the 12 to 4. The Old Man had relieved the third mate from duty and confined him to his room, so he and I shared the 8 to 12 watch. This put me on the bridge from 4 to 10 a.m. and from 4 to 10 p.m. The Old Man took the bridge from 10 to 12, morning and night.

For many weary months we had been slogging around carrying cargo for the British. The long hours and work were taking their toll on me. I was cranky, irritable, and short-tempered.

One morning I crawled up the ladder to the bridge to relieve Bandoni. Full blackout was being observed. With no moon that night, it was pitch black. I entered the lee side door to the wheel house and fell flat over the prostrate body of the second mate.

Before I could get up, Tim came in from the opposite side, called the engine room on the phone, and said, "Down four revolutions. That should do it." He looked into the binnacle and said to the man at the wheel, "Come left five degrees."

"What the hell's going on here? The second mate asleep on the deck and the cadet in full charge? Get up, you lazy bastard."

"He isn't asleep, Mister," Tim said. "He's sick. He just keeled over."

A fine kettle of fish. I risked using my flashlight, shading it through my fingers. His eyes were open, looking right up at me.

"I can't get up," he moaned. "Every joint in my body is on fire."

I blew my whistle for the lookout, and he and Tim carried Joe down to his room. There didn't seem to be much sense in calling the Old Man. There was nothing he could do, and he needed his rest.

When the skipper showed up after breakfast, he was in high spirits. "Mister, Sparks just got a message for us," he said. We're to break off from the convoy and go into Augusta, Sicily. "I'm sure you know what that means."

Indeed I did. Augusta was one of the great natural anchorages. It was used to form up homeward-bound convoys. I told him about the second mate then, and he pooh-poohed the news.

"Probably overtired, though God knows why. He just stands up there drinking coffee eight hours a day. Have a look at him, Mister. We might just be going home."

Leaving the Old Man, I went down to have a look at Bandoni. No question about it: he was sick and in big pain. The working of the ship, even in the fairly good weather, caused him excruciating pain. His joints, from head to foot, were killing him. I got extra pillows and wedged him in against the bulkhead. Then I filled him full of aspirin and arranged with the saloon messman to bring in his meals.

Meanwhile, the Old Man swung us out of the convoy and headed for Augusta. I grabbed a quick bite of breakfast and headed back for the bridge. The Old Man was in the chart room studying the chart for Augusta.

"A perfect anchorage, Mister," he greeted me. "We'll just ease along inside, drop the pick, and be snug as bugs."

"Fine, Captain. But if we get orders to go home, or even if we don't, there's just you and me."

"You're a worry wart, Mister. Bandoni will be up and around in no time. Now stop worrying and get forward and clear away those anchors."

Sicily was dead ahead. The skipper took us through the harbor entrance in fine style. There were a lot of ships anchored, but he slipped right through them and picked a good spot to anchor.

"Let's go, Mister. Three shackles at water's edge."

Often he was a pain in the ass, as all skipper are. But he was a damned good ship handler.

As soon as she fetched up, he told "Flags," our Navy signalman, to start blinking. At last, the long-awaited answer came from shore: "You will join westbound convoy for the States three days hence."

"Now, by God, that's a message!"

The next day I held a boat drill with our motor lifeboat. Actually, I wanted to take a little cruise around this beautiful harbor. I rounded up the bosun, carpenter, two Navy gunners' mates and a couple of A.B.s, and off we went. We had a full tank of gas and not a care in the world. It was like "school's out." We had spent so many months being scared and tired, with practically no chance or desire to go ashore, we were like colts let out to pasture again.

A destroyer escort (DE 145) operates with an escort carrier.

One of the A.B.s pointed out that several ships were making steam. Their funnels were belching smoke and their anchor chains clanked over their windlasses.

"What the hell," I said. "We don't have to worry about that." I put the tiller over and opened the throttle wide. We swung around under the falls. Above us, we saw the Old Man dancing up and down on the boat deck, screeching like a maniac. He had the falls all rigged to the winches. The very minute we hooked on he hollered, "Heave away!" and up we went, still in the boat. As soon as we came even with the deck, the Old Man ordered me to jump out and get my ass forward and heave up the anchor, *fast.*

"What's going on, Captain?"

"Air raid! All ships are to get underway."

I raced up to the fo'c'sle head, grumbling about our short vacation. The carpenter and I got the anchor aweigh. She was just coming into the hawse pipe when I heard the phone jangling. Signaling Chips to shut off the windlass, I answered. It was the Old Man.

"Let the goddammed anchor go, Mister. No air raid!"

I kept looking in on Bandoni as often as I could. If anything, he was worse. He couldn't get up to go to the head and there were no bedpans on these ships. He had to make do with a bucket. He didn't want to eat, and was starting to moan and cry. The poor guy was in bad shape and we couldn't figure out what was the matter with him.

Two days later, we got the orders to raise the hook. Out we steamed, Slow Ahead, ships ahead and astern of us. We formed into columns like the old veterans that we were. As I climbed wearily to the bridge, I allowed as how we had earned a stripe or two.

We were in good company. Instead of British escorts, this time we were being herded by D.E.s and destroyers of the good ole U.S. Navy. The convoy was headed due west for the Straits of Gibraltar and the Atlantic. At the Straits, more ships came out from Gibraltar and joined us. By the time we felt the first long swells of the open Atlantic we were a full-fledged, first-class convoy.

The weather started deteriorating almost immediately. Being light, with no ballast except sea water, our ship began to thrash around. A full westerly gale blew up and soon we were pitching badly. The saloon messman came up to the bridge and begged me to come look at the second mate. I got the Old Man to relieve me and followed him down. Joe was screaming with pain. The pitching of the ship was tearing him apart. I patted him on the shoulder and raced for the bridge.

"Flags, blink over to that destroyer and ask if they have a doctor."

Back came the answer: "Standing by."

I scribbled a message outlining Joe's symptoms as best I could.

Back came their question: "How old is the patient?" A few more questions followed about his condition. Then, an answer: "Your second mate exhibits definite symptoms of rheumatic fever. Administer one-fourth grain morphine sulphate twice a day. When the weather moderates we will attempt transferring the patient to this vessel."

I got the Old Man to open the safe where the narcotics were kept. We had never used any before. The morphine pills were very tiny, fitted one atop the other in a glass bottle the diameter of a straw. We shook one pill out. Because it was a half-grain tablet, we had to cut it in two and return half to the little bottle. The skipper pulled out a big form and laboriously filled it out. Every crumb of this devilish stuff had to be accounted for.

I went back down to Joe, clutching the wee chunk of pill. It seemed so tiny, I wondered if it would do him any good. I pushed it down his throat and settled back to wait. Nothing happened. He went right on moaning and crying. Maybe they were stale, I figured. They'd been in the safe ever since the ship was built. Then, very slowly, Joe began to quiet down and slipped off to sleep. For four days I dragged my weary carcass from the bridge to Joe to the saloon, then to bed for a couple of hours and back to the damned bridge.

The Old Man and I were now standing all the watches, him taking the 8 to 12 and me standing the rest. When I wasn't standing watch or playing nursemaid to Joe, I was trying to bring my inventory books up to date and wrangling with the bosun about what work the crew should be doing.

After four days, it was still howling a gale. Every day I gammed with the doctor by blinker light. Joe was getting worse and I was afraid he was dying. The effect of the pills was wearing off and by now we could hear him yelling way up on the bridge. I reported this to the doctor. He blinked back: "Do you have any codeine sulphate? If so, switch, same dosage." Sure enough, way in the back of the safe was a little glass bottle of codeine sulphate. I started feeding the new pills to Joe, hoping for the best. For a day and a half they worked; then the yelling started again. I was ready to start yelling myself.

I had Flags blink over the bad news. There was some delay before a lengthy message came back:

"Fall out of station to port. Steer 270° true. Maintain exact speed of eight knots. We will steam parallel to you on your port side. We will fire Lyle gun with messenger line across your after well deck. You will pull our line aboard, making it fast to your #4 hatch, cradled booms. We will send over breeches buoy trolly to which you will secure Stokes basket with patient securely lashed in. He will wear a life preserver. Please acknowledge your complete understanding."

We acknowledged and things started to move. The bosun and his crew stood by on the after deck. I went down to get Joe ready. The messman helped me dress him in his warmest clothes and tied a life jacket on him. Then we lashed him in the Stokes stretcher and carried him out to the after deck.

I distrusted this Navy scheme. What if the ships rolled away from each other with the line still made fast between them? The line would part like a thread and Joe would be drowned. It seemed so foolhardy, yet something had to be done and I didn't have a better solution. In my anxiety, I underestimated the U.S. Navy.

By the time we got Joe to the after deck, the destroyer was close to our port beam. The Old Man and Tim were carefully conning our ship, maintaining course and speed. The bosun had rigged a four-legged bridle which he shackled to the rails on the stretcher. We were ready.

Bam! Their Lyle gun fired right over our #4 booms. The bosun and Chips pounced on it. They pulled over the big line with its trolley line and block and made the line fast to the port boom. The trolley block was made fast with a round turn and two half hitches, the bitter end married to the standing part and secured with marlin. Now it was easy to see the destroyer crew's plan. They had fastened a snatch block well up on the midships structure. Their end of the line was rove through it. Twenty sailors were tailed onto its end. As the ships rolled toward and away from each other they ran up and down the deck, keeping a constant tension and preventing the line from parting. *By God,* I thought, *they have one clever bosun's mate over there.*

We lifted Joe and the stretcher up on the bulwarks. Poor Joe looked me in the eye and whispered, "I always knew you didn't like me, but this is a hell of a way to get rid of me!" He was wrong, but I had no time to answer. I waved to the destroyer, and away he went.

The 20 Navy sailors moved up and down the deck, signalled by their chief. Other sailors heaved smartly on the trolly line. As they worked together, Joe sailed through the air for all the world like a passenger on a ski lift. As he neared the destroyer, a big swell swept under him just as the line was slacked. In the next moment, dozens of hands snatched him from the drenching wave and hauled him aboard.

My hat is off to those Navy sailors. They were *real* seamen.

We released their gear and resumed our station in the convoy. The destroyer hauled way out on our beam to resume her escort duties. The weather turned rough and rotten again and stayed like that all the way to New York. But we made it and so did Joe.

Months later I heard that he had recovered except for the permanent damage done to his heart by the rheumatic fever. But we did both make it. And as the log book says, "So ends this day."

On June 6, 1944, there was only one piece of land and water worth concentrating on; and any soldier, sailor, or airman who could not join in was missing an irretrievable moment of history.

THE CRUEL SEA
by Nicholas Monsarrat

– 14 –

THE NORMANDY INVASION:
THE BEST-KEPT SECRET

The role played by merchant ships in the invasion of Normandy in World War II is a story indelibly imprinted in my mind. In fact, it was probably the high point in my seagoing career.

It all began for me this way.

I was mate of the *Cyrus H.K. Curtis*, an American Export Line ship berthed at the company's pier in Jersey City, New Jersey. We had just come in from a long voyage in the Mediterranean where we had been shuttling between North Africa and Italy, carrying supplies to the armies fighting up the Italian peninsula.

One morning I went to the marine superintendent's office at the head of the pier to see if I could get a few days off to go home to Massachusetts. The superintendent, Capt. Blackledge, had had a long career with Export before the war. His natural abilities made him ideal for the important post he now held. Among these talents was that of a master con artist. He hadn't the slightest scruple about telling a few tall ones to fill out a crew. I should have figured that when I came to ask for leave he'd cook up a beaut – but, naively, I didn't suspect a thing.

Turning on all his charm, he sold me on the story that the ship was scheduled to make a short trip straight to Liverpool and back, and if I'd make this one trip it would be a personal favor, look good on my record, blah, blah. As soon as we returned, six weeks at the most, I could have a whole month off. I swallowed it hook, line, and sinker, as he knew I would.

Back to the ship I tramped and set about making up my stores list: wire, rope, shackles, paint – all the things needed for another North Atlantic voyage. Since it was to be such a short trip, my list was fairly short.

Time dragged on. Longshoremen were loading us with the usual wartime cargo: trucks, jeeps, spare parts, foodstuffs. You name it, we loaded it. The ship was in its usual state of bedlam with alleyways full of repairmen, salesmen, runners, God knew who.

Now, Jersey City was nine miles south of nowhere. To get over to New York City took forever on the tubes. Locally, the only attractions were the Jersey City joints. They were real dumps: dark, smelly, dirty. The usual social drink was a double shot and a beer. So most of the other regular officers and I stayed on board playing cards, telling lies, feeling homesick.

Most of the crew had paid off when we docked, so we were short-handed by now. I had only the bosun, the carpenter, and two or three A.B.s.

And of course I had the deck cadet. These cadets were students at King's Point Academy, a fine government school turning out third mates and third assistant engineers. They were required to do six months of sea duty as part of their schooling. Since my cadet, Tim Pouch, had been with me on that long voyage in the Mediterranean, his six months were up and more. He was due to return to the academy. However, he was in bad trouble. Because their sea project involved very difficult tests, the cadets had to do considerable studying during sea duties. I had frequently tried to help Tim with this, but to no avail. He simply wasn't a student. We both knew that as soon as he returned to King's Point he'd be washed out.

However, during the long months at sea Tim had turned out to be a natural seaman. He caught on faster than any sailor I had ever known, and he soon became indispensable to me. Right then I decided to pull a Captain Blackledge stunt on the Academy.

If Blacky could con me into staying aboard for another voyage, I'd do the same with Timmy. Accordingly, when Tim's examining officer called on me a day or two later to fill out his fitness report, I really laid it on, stressing all Tim's accomplishments. At the same time, I insisted that he needed just a little more sea time. It worked! Reluctantly, his officer agreed to let him make one more trip, seeing as it was only to be for six weeks. All during this interview Tim sat in a corner, thankfully with the good sense to keep his trap shut.

When we were alone, I landed on Tim with both feet. "You'll study this voyage, Mister. By God, I just saved your neck, but now it's up to you."

I'm glad I tried, but it didn't work. Though Tim became the best hand on the ship during that voyage, he later washed out of the academy. Despite that, he sat for his third mate's ticket, got it, and went on to become a fine officer and a credit to the Merchant Marine.

But that was still to come. A day or two after being talked into this upcoming trip, my deck stores started arriving. The bosun signed for them from the ship's chandler, checking them off on a copy of my order sheet, stowing them in the forepeak. One afternoon he came up to my cabin. There was a whole barge load of stores alongside, but none from my order list. Up forward I went. Sure enough, there was a big stick lighter lying abreast of #1 hatch, her deck covered with coils of rope, hawsers, wire netting, and dozens of mysterious-looking objects resembling big, long concrete punching bags.

Hollering at the lighter captain, I told him he had the wrong ship, a common occurrence during the war because the ship's names on bows and sterns were painted over, supposedly to confuse enemy spies.

He said, "Is this the *Cyrus H.K. Curtis?*" I said it was. "Then," said he, "these stores belong to you."

Telling him to hold everything, I hurried down the gangway to Captain Blackledge's office. I was teed off. Every chief mate, as a department head, tries to keep his costs down. Such costs are noted in his record and have a bearing on future promotions.

Blacky ambled out of his inner sanctum, purring like a sleek tomcat. "Something bothering you, Mister?" Oh, he was slick, all right.

"You bet there is," I ranted. "There's a whole lighter load of stores alongside that I didn't order, and I'm not accepting them!"

"Ahem," says he, butter melting in his mouth. "Those are special stores consigned to the British Ministry of War Transport. Stow 'em in #1 'tween deck. When you get to Liverpool they'll take them off your hands."

Right then I should have smelled a rat. That story of his was just too pat. These were American stores, and for all of Lend Lease, chief mates of American freighters had never lugged deck stores across the Atlantic to store Limey ships.

But orders are orders. Back I went and told the bosun to hoist the damned stuff aboard and stow it away in #1 TDs. This whole matter stuck in the back of my mind all the way across the ocean, but I never did stumble onto the fact that Captain Blacky had hornswoggled me again.

The next few days just before sailing were typically hectic. A new crew was shipped, last-minute stores arrived, and the new second and third mates reported aboard. The second was a big young Norwegian-American, Bill Ommendson. The third mate was a little, intense young bird by the name of Funk.

When sailing day arrived, the Old Man went ashore for the usual convoy conference. Meanwhile, the shipping commissioner came on board and signed all hands on Articles. As soon as the Old Man hurried back up the gangway, it was hoisted up and off we went, out through the Narrows again, past the old Statue of Liberty. Staten Island and the Quarantine Station slid by on our starboard hand, and it was "Full Ahead" for the pilot boat out at Ambrose Lightship.

It was just coming dusk when we disembarked the pilot and took our departure, course set for Nantucket Lightship. Gradually, dozens of other vessels surrounded us in convoy columns. We were in pitch darkness, no lights showing.

This status was getting "old hat" to the Old Man and me, so I went about my business of securing for sea. I got the anchors dogged down, all booms cradled, hatch tarps wedged tight, and the life boats swung out and griped so they could be lowered instantly if we were torpedoed ... if there were any of us left to lower them.

During the next few days, I got better acquainted with the two junior mates. Before this voyage was over, Bill Ommendson would prove himself to be one solid seaman. His massive physical strength and absolute steadiness, his coolness and suberb seamanship, were a solid anchor to windward.

One night about halfway across the Atlantic, very high seas were running and the ship was rolling heavily. About 3 a.m. Bill sent a sailor to wake me and tell me that six drums of lube oil had broken adrift from their lashings up on the boat deck. I jumped out of my bunk, ran down to the main deck, and broke out the bosun and carpenter.

The boat deck was pitch black. Even after our eyes became accustomed to the darkness, we couldn't see a thing. The wind howling around the lifeboats made it almost impossible to hear ourselves. We certainly couldn't hear the Old Man out on the bridge wing yelling mute orders to us.

Bill was waiting for us. We could hear the oil drums rolling and thrashing around, rocketing from one side to the other as the ship rolled. Each roll sent them shooting outward where they wedged themselves under the two lifeboats hanging over the side. As the ship righted herself, they hurtled back across the deck, bashing the housing. One of them had already ruptured, converting its 30-weight oil into a deck-width liquid skating rink.

Now what?

I hollered up to the Old Man, asking him if he could fall out of our convoy station and head the ship into the wind on a slow bell. With some fancy maneuvering to avoid our sister ships steaming in the pitch blackness all around us, he did it. That lessened the motion of the ship.

When the rolling let up and we were pitching gently, the moment came. We had determined that one drum had flung itself overboard after staving in one lifeboat. The others were now under the boats right at the edge of the deck. Ommendson and the bosun, Frank Ronsani, had made lassos out of 1-inch manilla line. Sliding across the oily deck and under the boats, we each got a drum and slid out on our backsides. We then hauled the drums out, stood them on end, and lashed them to the after boat deck rail. While the carpenter and I were lashing these, Bill and the bosun went back for the last two drums. A couple of minutes later I heard the bosun screaming, "Help! I'm going overboard!"

"What's the matter, Bill?" I called urgently. "Move out of the way. Where's the bosun?"

"I can't move, Mr. Mate," Bill said. "I've got him by the belt."

I could feel Bill on his hands and knees under #1 lifeboat. One of his big arms was over the side, Ronsani clutched firmly in his big paw. God Almighty! I didn't know what to do. Up spoke Bill, calm as you please, and says for me to put a line around him and then for me and the carpenter to pull like hell.

"What about Ronsani?" I croaked.

"Not to worry, Mr. Mate. I'll not let go of him."

All this time the Old Man is yelling at us from up on the bridge, and the bosun is yelling from under us, the black North Atlantic just beneath him.

We did what Bill said and out from under the boat he came, dragging the poor bosun behind him, safe and sound. Ronsani was OK, but I think the fright he suffered stayed with him for a long time. He happened to be wearing a wide, heavy belt of the kind that truckers wear today. Without it, he would have been a goner.

Then there was our young ordinary seaman. Since I've forgotten his name, I'll call him Chad. How he ever got shipped out is a mystery to me. He never told us, and we never found out until much later that he had been in the Navy on a destroyer that was blown out from under him. Anzio, I think it was. As one of a handful of survivors, he received a total disability discharge as a case of something like shell shock. How he managed to lie his way afterward past the U.S. Coast Guard who issued all seamen's papers, through the Seamen's Union, and aboard our ship, no one figured out. But here he was.

Ships' crews can be cruel to someone with obvious flaws, like calling him Fatso for being too fat or Skinny for being too thin. Our crew soon realized that this kid was a nervous wreck. They'd sneak up behind him on deck and drop a sledge hammer, laughing when he flung himself flat on the deck, screaming and crying.

I had two old hands on my watch, first cousins Angus Collins and Scotty Gillis, Gallic-Canadian natives of Prince Edward Island. They had been with me for over two years, so they were senior members of the fo'c'sle. Scotty played the bagpipes till I had to stop him from making that awful noise. He'd stand his lookout watch in the crow's nest and blow his wild, crazy songs on the chanter, the reed and finger hole part of the pipes on which the melody is played. That screeching would sound all over the ship, driving all hands nuts.

I prevailed on those two to stop the rest of the crew from picking on Chad because by then I knew that he actually was mentally sick and belonged in a hospital. It didn't work. Scotty got in a fight about it with

Another of the endless convoys forms up. The box-like object in the foreground is a life raft on the deck of the British cargo ship from which this photo was taken.

a long, rangy Texan, and lost badly. Coming on watch one afternoon with both eyes blackened, speaking out of a split lip, he told me to run my own Ward 8; no more for him.

Ward 8 or no, we continued eastbound on the Great Circle, bound for the western approaches to the British Isles where the Kraut U-boats concentrated. As we approached these waters, the convoy escort vessels scurried around us increasingly. Signals from the commodore of the convoy, flying his flag in a British merchant ship at the head of the middle column of vessels, became more and more frantic, urging us to close up, maintain station, sharpen our lookouts, hold our speed.

On our ship, the Old Man and I didn't have to be told. We'd sailed a lot of convoys in this long war by now: big ones in the Atlantic, little ones in the Mediterranean. Those times we had steamed alone we hadn't like it one bit. So he and I were forever hollering down the engine room speaking tube to either increase or decrease propeller revolutions in order to keep position in our column of ships.

It was about this time that two more psychos developed. The first was a Greek A. B. who wouldn't go to bed on his watch below, and instead took to roaming the decks at all hours of the day and night, carrying his life jacket. Finally, he got so exhausted he took to napping down in the steering engine room, all the way aft, under the Navy gunners' quarters.

He explained to me seriously in broken English that ships never got torpedoed in the stern. Crazy as a bedbug he was. Torpedoes had hit ships from stem to stern time and again.

The other case was the second assistant engineer who stood the 12 to 4 watch. Like the Greek, he had succumbed to fear.

After standing the midnight to 4 a.m. watch down in the engine room he'd come up to the bridge with me, lugging his life jacket, his teeth actually chattering. With daylight coming on I was pretty busy getting the ship back into position, trying to get a couple of star sights, trying to anticipate all the thousand questions the Old Man would ask when he crawled up on the bridge for a cup of my coffee. (It was coffee I had bought and paid for, not that black muck the steward passed off on us.)

Wherever I turned, that damned second was in the way asking fool questions. What did that last signal from the destroyer escort say – submarines? Finally, when he asked if he could have some of my coffee to keep him awake, I yelled, "No! Go below and go to sleep, you nut!" I tried to be patient, realizing how terrified he really was. But finally I got the chief engineer to order him off the bridge. I even suggested he go sleep with the Greek in the steering engine room, whispering to him that ships *never* got it in the stern.

Despite our nut cases, we finally sighted the southern tip of Ireland one fine sunny morning. From there we headed northward up the Irish Sea for the Mersey River. A lot of the convoy kept going, bound for the Channel ports and London. Not one of us had been sunk or attacked on this trip. Things were definitely getting better on the sea lanes. The convoy system had been brought to a peak of perfection, thanks to the British who had been successfully convoying ships since the days of Lord Nelson.

We picked up a pilot and steamed up the Mersey to Liverpool where we made fast to a pier over in Birkenhead on the other side of the river. Even tied up to the dock the crew were giving me a fit. British Customs officers are known the seas over for being bastards. War or no war, they'd tear a ship to pieces looking for undeclared contraband, usually booze and cigarettes.

Chips, the carpenter, who particularly hated Customs officers, had hidden two rat traps in the drawer under his bunk, buried in his skivvies. Sure enough, he caught an official. Damned near took his finger off.

The first I knew of it was from the Old Man hollering from his office. Up I went and there he was, pounding his desk and yelling at Customs's head muckety-muck. Turning on me, he wanted to know what kind of discipline I was maintaining. What kind of mate was I that I couldn't keep my crew honest, especially in this great port of our dear friends and comrades in arms? I started to burn too, and was just about to yell right back at him when one of his eyes dipped in an unmistakable wink. *Ah-hah*, says I to myself. *The old mahoska*. Oh, he was some actor all right.

They took Chips ashore and locked him up, charging him with assault, evading His Majesty's duties, and heaven knew what else. A couple of days later I had to appear in court on his behalf. What a show those Limeys put on! Here was a poor seaman from an Allied ship, his only crime trying to hide a few cartons of cigarettes to smuggle ashore to get enough money to have his back straightened out by one of the plenteous Liverpool whores. Some pompous-looking bird, wearing a silly white wig, started making a long, tiresome speech to Chips berating his dishonesty and patriotism, virtually calling him a traitor.

"Now just a damned minute, your damned holiness," says I, getting out my seat. "You're talking about a fine American ... " That was as far as I got. Two flunkies in monkey suits and brass buttons grabbed me from behind and *Bingo*, I was in the cooler with the carpenter! Fine kettle of fish! There's a first-class war going on and we're locked up. So who's fighting whom?

We sat around in a big tankful of sleazy critters talking like their mouths were full of nuts. Sometime in the late afternoon, "tea" was announced. We got a thick mug with no handle on it, half full of tea, and two slices of bread smeared with ersatz marmalade: the famous Limey supper of "tay and two."

By this time, I was getting worried. The Old Man must have missed me by now. In fact, he had. As though on cue he bustled in, demanding to know what the hell I was doing in here and ordering me to come out at once. I pointed out the obvious: the cage was locked and I couldn't get out.

"Hah!" he snorted. Turning to a jailer (the Limeys called him a turnkey), he proceeded to deliver a soliloquy that sounded like Daniel Webster addressing Parliament. Damned if it didn't work! He paid our fines (mine for contempt, Chips's for everything but treason), and back to the ship we tramped. All the way the Old Man never stopped raving. He sounded like a damned preacher.

The next several days were busy ones, discharging all the stuff we'd brought over. They were also frustrating ones, because no matter how I tried I couldn't get rid of all those stores in #1 'tween decks. I tried the British Ministry of War Transport first. "Right-o," said a very proper Limey voice. "I'll send a chap 'round immediately."

Next morning, a bright, beady-eyed chap arrived at the gangway. "I say," says he. "You're having a spot of trouble about some gear shipped over to us, are you? Let's have a look at it, what?" Those birds all talked a funny brand of English, sort of like a Down Mainer with a sore throat.

Up we went to #1 hatch and down the ladder into the 'tween decks. I shone my flashlight all around while he kicked at the cargo like a buyer kicking the tires of a second-hand car. Finally he pulled a handkerchief out of his sleeve, for God's sake, dusted himself off, and said that he was from the S.T.O. (Sea Transport Office), and that we had a problem.

"No, we don't," I said. "Just get it off my ship. Then it's your problem."

"A slight problem of transport," he amended. "Lorries are quite scarce."

"So what's a lorry?"

"You call them trucks." So why didn't he say trucks? As he went down the gangway, he called back, "Toodleoo. I'll send a lorry soonest." Soonest? *Soonest?*

No lorries ever showed up. Once again there was that big dead rat and I never got a whiff, not even a sniff.

When sailing day arrived we got orders to proceed up the west coast of Scotland to Lock Ewe, a tremendous natural anchorage. It was completely sheltered, had good holding ground, and, like Bedford Basin in Halifax, could hold hundreds of ships. It was a main forming-up place for westbound convoys. Good news! We were homeward bound.

Off we went in a small convoy, seven or eight ships with no escorts. These waters were tough to navigate in. The chart showed islands by the hundreds. All had queer Scottish names: the Little Minches, the North Minches, the Isle of Skye, Isle of Lewis. These were the Hebrides, a godforsaken part of the world.

Unfortunately, just as we dropped the pilot it started to blow half a gale. The rain came down in torrents. Every ship was on its own now. Our Old Man never left the bridge. I napped on and off on the settee in the chart room, trying throughout the night to get an RDF bearing. But the canny Limeys had shut all the RDFs down to avoid giving aid to the enemy. We steamed northward anyway.

Finally, we hauled into Loch Ewe just at dawn. Tim was on the bridge with the skipper, and I was on the fo'c'sle standing by to drop the hook. I was half asleep. The Old Man kept maneuvering around and between ships until we wound up out on the edge of the rows of moored vessels. At last he headed her into the wind, stopped the engines, and hollered to "let go." I belted the big brake handle with a sledge hammer and out she roared. I heard the engine room telegraph jangle for Half Astern to set the anchor. The chain was leading nicely off the starboard bow as she caught the bottom. I pointed my arm in the direction of the chain. The Old Man acknowledged, and I heard the telegraph ring for Stop.

It was a cold, gray, misty morning, and I huddled under the bulwarks trying to light a smoke. Faintly, I heard the cadet yelling from the bridge. As I straightened up, I nearly fell overboard. The ship was drifting backward, heading right for an anchored freighter! I jumped for the bridge telephone. Tim answered.

"For God's sake, Timmy, tell the skipper to come Half Ahead!"

"I can't," he answered. "He's gone to bed."

"Tim, now do what I tell you. Ring up Half Ahead and come starboard, easy."

Tim never rattled. Between us, we got her stopped and then moving again in the right direction. I heaved up the anchor. As soon as I was sure we were clear, I let her go again, and this time she fetched up and held.

Just when we finished, the Old Man came bounding up on the bridge, hollering at Tim, screeching at me over the phone, wanting to know who was the captain, what the hell was going on, and more – most of it unprintable. Finally, he went back to bed and Timmy and I went to breakfast. Tired as we were, the fact that we were bound for home made anything OK.

There we lay in Loch Ewe. Upwards of a week went by. Ships came and departed. We could see the British Navy scurrying around delivering sailing orders to various ships who would make steam and head out, bound for home.

It seemed odd that we were ignored. However, one morning here came the launch. Up the accommodation ladder came two gold-braided Limeys. They disappeared into the Old Man's cabin for over an hour. The word passed through the ship like wildfire: homeward bound! As soon as the Navy left, the Old Man sent for me.

"Well, Mister, heave up the hook. We're on our way."

"Yes, sir!"

"Now hold on," says he. "We have orders to proceed by way of Pentland Firth to Leith."

"Leith, Captain?" I protested. "That's on the east coast of Scotland, away from home. What the hell are we going there for?"

"Don't ask me. All I know is that four or five ships are to sail at once for ports on the East Coast, and we're going to Leith. Now get up on the fo'c'sle and heave up the pick."

Something was rotten in Denmark. Leith is the port for Edinborough. Finally, I was beginning to smell the rat.

Away we went up the coast to Cape Wrath. Rounding the Cape, we headed into Pentland Firth, a dismal hole between the northern tip of Scotland and the Orkney Islands, where the tides run ten knots. Once more it was every ship for herself.

I must say, the Old Man did a fine job of conning her through the narrow, twisting passages. I had been through these waters years ago as a seaman on the Hamburg–Bremen run. I knew full well what a dangerous body of water it was. Yet we shot through in fine style and squared away for the mouth of the long, narrow entrance to Leith.

Once again the Old Man had been up all night and was tuckered out. About 5 in the morning we were off the entrance. No sign of a pilot boat. The skipper slipped into the chart room for a peek at the chart. When he came back, there was still no sign of the pilot boat.

"Mister," says he, "we'll not wait any longer for these damned Limeys. I'm taking her in myself. Half Ahead, and mind your helm." He went out on the starboard wing of the bridge where he could see better. He looked pitiful out there in an old leather jacket, two days' growth of whiskers, an old beat-up cap on his head. This late in the war, age and overwork had taken their toll on the Old Man. Hour after hour, day after day, pacing the wheelhouse was wearing him down. Right near him was Timmy in full regalia: spotless King's Point uniform, pink cheeks, the picture of youth and health.

The contrast was sadly sharp. Yet the Old Man hadn't lost an inch of his touch. In we crept, in strange waters, me hanging out the wheelhouse window using the binoculars, the cadet relaying the Old Man's steering commands to the man at the wheel.

Further and further we went till we could see the piers. It was then I spied a small boat flying the pilot's flag. Hollering, I told the Old Man the pilot boat was dead ahead. He made no answer, nor did he make a move to slow down. We were coming up on the little boat fast. I went over to our master and inquired if we were going to stop and embark the pilot.

"Why should we?" he snarled. "I brought her in, didn't I?" A little later he relented and told Tim to stop the engines.

Up the Jacob's ladder came the pilot. He bustled through the wheelhouse and out on the bridge wing. Brushing right by the Old Man, he grabbed the cadet's hand and boomed out, "Good Morning, Captain!" You're the picture of health this fine morning."

Oh, boy! Timmy tried to disengage his hand, making furtive motions toward the skipper. That did it.

"Mister," said the skipper, "If this Limey or Scotsman, or whatever the hell he is opens his trap just once, you will remove him from my bridge. No, on second thought, I'll do it myself." He strode over to the pilot and demanded, "Now then, what pier are we supposed to dock at?"

Backing away from the irascible, thoroughly aroused Yankee shipmaster, the pilot squeaked, "Quay 8."

"What in the hell is a "key?" If it's a dock, say so. That's all I'll need from you. Get your ass over on the port wing." Damned if he didn't take her alongside beautifully, just like a twin screw yacht. As he and I went below, the Old Man confided, "Can't let these foreigners tromp on us." Made me think of our ensign in the early days of our country. Beneath the picture of a snake it read: "Don't tread on me."

Within minutes of docking, a horde of shipyard workers came steaming up the gangway. I headed for my cabin. At my door was another S.T.O. officer. I invited him in and offered him a snort. He tossed back half a glass, belched, and said, "Your vessel has been chartered by the British Ministry of War Transport, and I'm in charge of converting her to an assault troop transport for about 600 troops."

Holy smoke! And this was to be a six-week's voyage! Now it all became clear. Those "stores" in #1 'tween decks were to be used disembarking troops on some hellish beach.

The days flew by. All the 'tween decks were converted to troop quarters, latrines were built hanging over the sides, all the deck winches and heavy lift derricks were tested and overhauled. Things were moving so fast I didn't know if I was coming or going.

During my few quiet hours I speculated on where we were bound for, and finally became convinced we were going to invade Norway. I remained steadfast in this conviction right up until we sailed from Southend on June 6th.

One morning when the S.T.O. officer had his beak stuck as usual in my booze, he said, "By the way, half your chaps will have to attend gas school this week for three days, and the rest of your crew next week."

"Gas school? For what?"

"There's a good chance Jerry, or whoever, will be giving you a spot of bother with poison gas."

This invasion business was starting to sound serious. Hell, the Old Man and I had had more than our share of luck so far. But gas? Anyway, off I went with half the crew to gas school. The first thing they did was give us a primitive gas mask. Then they told us we'd have dozens of bags of a neutralizing chemical piled up all over the ship. I was told to assign crew members to various parts of the ship and conduct practice drills. We were supposed to run out with the gas masks on, break open the bags (which contained nothing but lime, I suspect), and scatter the contents everywhere. After the second half of the crew had completed the school, I tried to hold the drill. It was a disaster. I ran into the Old Man's room, gave him his gas mask, and told him he was in charge of the bridge.

"OK, Mister, I'll take charge." Out on the bridge he went, muttering to himself. When he got out on the wing he flung the mask overboard, thumbed his nose at it, and told me to get the crew back to work. Later, we threw all the bags overboard, too.

Our stay in Leith was pleasant. Every night we went into Edinborough, truly a beautiful place. The beer was excellent and the Scotch whiskey as smooth as silk. I treated myself to a magnificent British sextant. It was a Huson, costing me 17 pounds and well worth it. I've used it ever since and it's never needed adjusting.

One morning when the nonstop conversion work was almost completed, a British flying officer stuck his head in the door and introduced himself, his eyes glued to the half bottle of Scotch on my desk. Waving him in, I poured him a big dollop. Gratefully, he dumped it down. Pouring him another, I asked how I could help.

"Mr. Mate, actually I'm looking for a bit of a favor. You see, I'm in charge of an Air Force training field nearby, and we're training our chaps to fly out over the ocean and cover you chaps coming to our shores. You see, our chaps need to recognize your vessels instantly. As your ship is a Liberty, and they're coming in such vast numbers, would you please let me bring a group of our flying cadets and give them a close-up look at the type of vessel they'll be protecting?"

"Why, God bless you, Colonel, or Commander, or Leftenant, I'd be proud to have you as my guests."

After setting a date for the following morning. I went down to see our "belly robber" of a steward and told him to figure on 20 or 30 guests for lunch. Such language! He'd have to pay cooks and mess boys overtime, all that extra food, on and on. Finally, I cut him short. "Just do it, you mean old bastard. These guests just might save your worthless hide. And don't you dare scrimp or I'll ... " Before I could finish my threat, he slid by me into his room and locked the door. Well, piss on him.

Next day, down came the cadets. Tim was in his glory. He appointed himself guide and narrator, and he was great. He took them from bow to stern, bridge to fire room. He showed them our deck guns, then rang in the gunnery officer, Lieutenant Blake, who vied with Timmy to show our ship.

I hate to admit it but that damned steward did himself proud, feeding the cadets in relays while their officer in charge dined in style with the skipper and me. Oh, yes, there were good days in those dark days.

The next morning it was raining in buckets. Right after breakfast, one of the hands told me there was a car at the gangway and the driver was asking for me. There at the gangway was a stunning blonde in the blue uniform of a Wren. Wrens were the Navy counterpart of the ATS which were our WACs. They were also Royal Navy. She announced that our guest of the previous day wanted to show his appreciation. He had appointed her to be my guide to really see the sights of Edinborough.

"Well now, how very kind of him. If you'll give me two minutes, I'll be with you." Away we went in the pouring rain. I soon found out she was a full Leftenant in the Wrens and didn't usually do this kind of thing. but had an important job at their flying field. My Boston accent seemed to fascinate her, and she kept urging me to talk.

On the outskirts of the city, she stopped the car. "We walk now," she said.

"In this downpour?"

"Petrol shortage, you know."

Out we got. In an instant my thin topcoat was soaked through, but off we slogged. Somehow, Limeys never seemed to get wet. This girl was striding along, talking a mile a minute, pointing out the famous gardens, buildings, and landmarks. I sloshed along, wringing wet, cold, not enjoying it one bit. After a couple of hours I'd had it. I suggested we stop for a drink and lunch.

"Oh, a hot cup of tea is just what you need."

Yeah, maybe. But a double hooker would suit me better, I thought miserably. We went into a small place which only had tea and cookies. "Well now," I said when we'd finished. "Thanks so much for the great tour, but I must get back to my ship."

"Oh dear, no. You must walk the Royal Mile and climb up to Arthur's Seat." The Royal Mile was an absolute must for tourists, she insisted. Up she stood, dry as a bone while my wet clothes were starting to steam and stink. Grabbing the last cooky, I followed her into the rain.

Off we went, tramping those hard, wet cobblestones up the Royal Mile. When we got to the end, I'd had it. I bleated out that as much as I hated to cut short such a wonderful day, I just must return to the ship. "But you haven't climbed to Arthur's Seat," she protested.

"Where is it?"

Pointing up where bleak, black cliffs disappeared in the mist, she said, "Why, right up there!"

Not me. I was licked and knew it. Putting my wet, sore foot down, I announced: "Allies we are – hands across the seas. Notwithstanding that, I quit."

With a shrug of her perfectly dry shoulders, she murmured, "If you insist, but I do wish you could have seen jolly old Arthur's Seat."

Balls, I muttered to myself. *It could be Arthur's Bare Backside for all of me.*

Finally we steamed out, bound for London, this time with a proper coast pilot on board. Ships slipped up and down this east coast nightly in little groups. German planes and E-Boats were pretty active, and the darkness of a moonless night was most welcome.

By this time we had run out of American food. We had been stored by the British in Leith. Not even our lousy steward could stomach the British stores, but stomach it we did for the next three lousy months.

We sneaked down the coast, protected by darkness, and were soon shoving our rusty snout into the Thames estuary. Up the Thames River we steamed. We were ordered to Tilbury Docks, an enormous complex of piers and warehouses 10 or 15 miles from London.

As soon as the gangway went down, we were buried in shore workers again. Longshoremen swung out the 5-ton derricks at hatches

#1, #3, and #5. The 50-ton derrick at #2 hatch and the 15-tonner at #4 were swung over. Immediately, amphibious ducks, trucks, jeeps, self-propelled guns, everything either wheeled or amphibious, started swinging aboard. Numbers 2 and 4 lower holds filled rapidly with the big, heavy stuff. We were told that when we arrived at our unannounced destination, another freighter would rendezvous with us, carrying a British Army stevedore company. They would board us and discharge the ducks, then load the trucks and jeeps into the ducks.

I asked the S.T.O. officer what I thought was a sensible question. "Why don't the stevedores travel with us?"

The answer was hardly satisfactory. "Decision of the high command, don't you know."

Next day we finished loading the lower holds plus the entire deck, forward and aft. The on-deck stuff was secured with "Spanish windlasses." These were nothing but two parts of wire cable rove through a pad eye welded to the deck. The cable snaked around the chassis of the vehicle, then wire clamps secured the two ends. A stout stick was shoved between the two parts and twisted until the cable was wound drum tight. The ends of the sticks were tied fast with marlin. Simple and crude, but very effective for a short voyage. They could be released in an instant by cutting the marlin, leaving the sticks to whirl around until the cable loosened.

The Old Man and I were sitting in the saloon right after lunch, speculating on our destination.

"Norway," I insisted.

"Bunk," he snorted.

"South of France. I know what I'm talking about. Every piece of evidence points directly to the South of France."

"What evidence? Nobody in this country will even tell you what day it is."

"Nonsense," he shouted. "I know!" Before we could settle this matter we were interrupted by the entrance of a distinguished, commanding figure in immaculate British Army uniform.

"Captain McGirr, I presume. I'm Colonel Mitchell, in command of the troops just now embarking on your fine ship." The captain shook hands with him and introduced me. "Right-o, Mister Mate." We sat down and ordered tea, of course.

The Old Man, about as subtle as a Sherman tank, started prying about our destination. "South of France, of course, Colonel?"

The Colonel deftly fended off our questions with one answer: "All in good time, chaps."

I went out on the deck, midships, by the gangway. British troops in full battle dress and full packs were streaming up, heading fore and aft.

Directing them was an enormous, roaring soldier. As each trooper passed him the trooper instinctively ducked.

I said, "Hello, Sergeant."

"Sergeant Major," he shot back.

"Yes, sir," I squeaked. He looked and acted just like a bigger, uglier Victor McGlauglin. I learned later that a sergeant major in the British Army was far more important in the scheme of things than a whole squad of generals.

The troops immediately set to work brewing their infernal tea. They cooked it in their tin hats, using gasoline poured over sand for heat. The decks were strewn with Jerry cans of gas, hundreds of 'em, under all the vehicles, everywhere. I worried about fire, but the hell with it. Besides, the soldiers were using up all the fire-fighting sand to cook tea with.

Late in the afternoon I heard a hell of a commotion in the crew's mess room. In I went. The crew's mess room and the Navy gun crew's mess room adjoined each other. Both were packed. Peeking over shoulders, I'm damned if I didn't see a Catholic priest, a Jewish rabbi, and a minister all offering their services. Shoving my way to the front, I demanded to know what was going on. One of the clergy informed me that very probably some of these fine young men were going to die quite soon, so they were offering solace to them. Solace, for God's sake!

I said, "I'll make it short and sweet. This whole crew is scared half to death, including and especially me. Now you come aboard and tell us we're all going to get killed. Well, we're not. And you're just making it worse. I'll give you ten minutes, then beat it." All the years since, I've felt guilty about that outburst, but not one of us ever got so much as a scratch. Three of the crew got the clap, though.

Soon afterward, the loonies started acting up again. I was sitting in my room after supper when Bill Ommendson came bursting through the door.

"Come quick, Mr. Mate. That shellshocked crazy kid is going to kill the cook!" Out he bounded with me right behind. He went clattering down the inside stairway to the main deck amidships. At the bottom, there was a door that opened right by the galley. Bill pushed open the door, then started back up the stairs. I tried to push him down, but he wouldn't budge.

"Bill, move down. What's going on?" By pushing right up against his big back, I could peek over his shoulder. *Dear suffering Christ!* That crazy kid had the biggest automatic pistol I ever saw shoved into Bill's belly.

Just as calm as you please, Bill slowly reached out his hand and said, real low, "Give me the gun, Sonny." The kid looked up into Bill's eyes and handed him the gun butt first. Bill and I backed up the stairs to my room. Bill laid the gun on my bunk and leaned against the bulkhead, trembling. I was shaking all over.

"Unload the damned thing, Bill."

"I don't know how, Mr. Mate."

"Well, go get Scotty Gillis. He was in the Canadian Army; he'll know how."

Pretty soon Scotty came up and pulled the clip out of the butt. The gun was empty! It was a German Steyer. I still have it.

I told the Old Man the whole story and urged him to get this nut off the ship. If we ever got into action, there was no knowing what he'd do. He went out on the dock and phoned the War Shipping Administration who came and took him away. They were lucky to get into the dock area because it had been completely sealed off. The longshoremen weren't even allowed to go home. This invasion had gotten to be the best-kept secret of the century.

Shortly, a British pilot came aboard in full uniform. Once again the familiar "Fore and aft, all hands" echoed through the ship. The pilot backed the ship out of her berth and down the river we went. When we got to the mouth we anchored right off the seaside resort town of Southend. We lay there all day, the troops cooking tea and pissing over the side.

About lunchtime, huge swarms of planes started passing overhead, heading east. Flying Forts they were: four-engine bombers. The sky was black with them. All afternoon and far into night they came without stopping. Somebody was sure catching hell, I hoped.

Finally, during supper that evening Colonel Mitchell said he could tell us what it was all about. While I rounded up all the engineers and radio officers, the purser and gunnery officer helped the colonel set up a large, detailed map of the Bay de la Seine. The bay stretched from Le Havre on the left to Cherbourg on the right. With a pointer, the colonel ticked off the code names of the assault landing beaches. "Sword, Gold, Juno" for the British forces. Then, down near Cherbourg, "Omaha, Utah" for the American forces.

Pointing to a seaside village in the Sword area called Gray Sur Mer, he said: "That's where we go ashore. You, Captain, will anchor your vessel as close ashore as depth of water permits. I have proper navigational charts for you and your officers to study."

At last we got the word: Norway, South of France. Weren't we the smart alecks! Then the colonel got down to details, displaying charts showing the narrow mine-swept channels down the coast of England to a point off the cliffs of Dover where we would turn left and head across the Dover Straits to the French coast. From there, we would turn left again, parallel to the coast, to Sword. He emphasized that we would be

SUPREME HEADQUARTERS
ALLIED EXPEDITIONARY FORCE

Soldiers, Sailors and Airmen of the Allied Expeditionary Force!

You are about to embark upon the Great Crusade, toward which we have striven these many months. The eyes of the world are upon you. The hopes and prayers of liberty-loving people everywhere march with you. In company with our brave Allies and brothers-in-arms on other Fronts, you will bring about the destruction of the German war machine, the elimination of Nazi tyranny over the oppressed peoples of Europe, and security for ourselves in a free world.

Your task will not be an easy one. Your enemy is well trained, well equipped and battle-hardened. He will fight savagely.

But this is the year 1944! Much has happened since the Nazi triumphs of 1940-41. The United Nations have inflicted upon the Germans great defeats, in open battle, man-to-man. Our air offensive has seriously reduced their strength in the air and their capacity to wage war on the ground. Our Home Fronts have given us an overwhelming superiority in weapons and munitions of war, and placed at our disposal great reserves of trained fighting men. The tide has turned! The free men of the world are marching together to Victory!

I have full confidence in your courage, devotion to duty and skill in battle. We will accept nothing less than full Victory!

Good Luck! And let us all beseech the blessing of Almighty God upon this great and noble undertaking.

Dwight D Eisenhower

Letter from President Eisenhower to the Allied Expeditionary Force (including merchant seamen) on June 6, 1944.

in the company of some 20 ships in columns of two down to Dover, then in single column going across the narrow, swept channel.

It was a quiet, thoughtful group of men who silently filed out of the saloon. I sat on the edge of my bunk and thought about the days ahead. Things looked grim.

All of a sudden, I jumped halfway out of the door. That Limey pilot was due to get off our ship down by the Dumpston buoy near Dover – and he knew every detail of the invasion of Normandy!

I tore up the stairs to the bridge deck where the colonel was quartered in our one spare cabin and burst out my news. The colonel eyed me for a minute, then said; "Did I understand you to say this chap is leaving us before we go over?"

"Right, Colonel, and if he talks ..." Very quietly, he interrupted me.

"A slight correction to your statement, Mr. Mate. He will not be leaving. We'll carry the nosy bugger right along with us."

Back in my cabin, I reflected on all I had heard that day. I hadn't yet absorbed the full impact of what was happening. None of us had. All we knew then was that we were on the brink of something awesome. It was exciting and frightening at the same time. The constant roar of those Flying Forts still passing in the hundreds gave me a great deal of comfort. We were going to need all the help we could get.

These are the times that try men's souls.

Thomas Paine

– 15 –

THE NORMANDY INVASION: WE HIT THE BEACH

We were to pass through the Straits of Dover during the dark hours, arriving off the beach shortly after daylight. This time there was no feeling of elation as I engaged the windlass and heaved up the anchor.

Down the coast we steamed, two abreast. Not all of us made it. I remember watching one ship in the next column through the binoculars. The jerry cans of gas stored on her forward deck were afire, blazing all around the vehicles. I worried that her ammo might start blowing. She very quickly dropped out of line and disappeared astern. We never heard what became of her.

Soon enough we were south of Dover and reformed into single file, led by a little minesweeper. There were minesweepers on each side of us, too, chugging along, sweeping as they went. They couldn't make much speed with their big sweeps, so we had to slow down to match them. The little temporary marker buoys we threaded through had dim lights on them to guide us. Those Limeys had really done some fine planning for this show.

The slow, dark hours crept by and the tension increased. I stayed on the bridge with the Old Man as the watches changed through the night.

Dawn came early to those June days. At 4 o'clock in the morning, the sky was just beginning to lighten. As the light gradually increased, I looked out the wheelhouse window. Never have I seen, or expect to see again, such a sight!

From one horizon to the other, in front, astern, on both beams, the sea was packed with thousands of ships. Ships with minesweeper escorts stretched on both sides of us for miles. We were all dumbfounded as the vast scope of this undertaking at last sank in. Blinker lights flashed on every side. In this seeming chaos, all was orderly. Ships' masters had done their homework well.

On and on we steamed. With the coming of daylight, that old feeling of being naked and exposed swept over us. What about enemy planes? E-boats? Mines that could rip your bottom out? Yet nothing happened. Peacefully, we turned left and headed up toward Sword.

Out on the port bridge wing we had a British plane spotter. These spotters were civilian volunteers. Ours was a dentist; we called him "Teeth." At training school, the fledgling spotters watched films of Allied and German aircraft at faster and faster speeds as they became increasingly adept. "Teeth" could sing out any type of plane after catching only a split-second glimpse of a wing ducking out of a cloud. He was an excellent example of the admirable English. During these days with their very existence threatened, every man, woman, and child was doing his share.

Slowly, we crept toward the beach, still following our own little minesweeper. At last he swung away. I was on the bow as usual, standing by the anchor. The Old Man was on the bridge, conning her in. The second mate was in the chart room, calling out the depth. Faithful Tim was standing by the engine room telegraph.

Before I expected it, the Old Man hollered, "Let go, Mister." Down rattled the starboard anchor. We were on Normandy Beach facing a determined enemy.

As soon as she fetched up, I headed midships. Colonel Mitchell was waiting for me. "Where's that stevedore ship?" There were ships still a mile or two off in the distance, some anchored, some still steaming about. None were heading our way. "Mr. Mate, they've got 15 minutes. If they don't show up, you'll have to offload my chaps and their gear."

Immediately I sent Tim to break out all hands. Assembling them on the forward deck, I assigned them specific jobs. The deck crew would handle the winches, two oilers would keep them running. The second mate and I would run the winches at the 50-ton derrick at #2 hatch from where I could see the forward deck. The bosun and carpenter would handle the 50-ton guy ropes rove through snatch blocks to the nigger heads on the anchor windlass. They would pull the big derrick out over the side as soon as the lift cleared the hatch coaming. Since I wouldn't be able to see the after deck with its two hatches and 15-ton boom at #4, I put Tim in charge there. Ordinarily, having a kid in charge would cause resentment; this time it didn't because the whole crew knew he was as good a seaman as any of them.

Then the colonel dropped a beaut on me. He announced that all his men would take their places in their vehicles, whether on deck or in the holds. They would release the lashings and rig the hoisting slings.

"My God, Colonel! You want me to hoist this stuff through the air and over the side with men sitting in them? What if we drop one? Or a sling breaks?"

"My men are valuable and I don't want to lose a one," he said. "But we've got a job to do over on that beach, and we're going to do it."

A jeep is lowered from a Coast Guard manned transport into an LCM from the USS Joseph T. Dickman, bound for the beach, June 1944.

"But Colonel," I protested. "They'll be sitting in those vehicles for hours with nothing to eat or drink. Let me rig the scramble nets."

"No. Besides, a stomach wound on an empty stomach has a far better chance of healing." This man was one tough critter. Guess that's why he had the job.

So we got on about it. First, we unloaded the deck cargo. I was running the topping lift winch and Ommendson was on the starboard hoisting winch. The Limeys had furnished us with tin helmets like the ones our troops wore in World War One. Bill looked ridiculous with that silly tin hat perched on his big square head. Mine kept falling down over my eyes, so I flung it overboard.

We hooked onto the big duck abreast of the hatch. Up she swung, with 15 or more men in her, all loaded with rifles, grenades, and machine guns, and draped with belts of ammo. As soon as she cleared the bulwarks, I blew my whistle and the bosun on the windlass flung three turns of the guy line on the spinning nigger head. Over the side she swung. I stopped my topping lift winch and ran to the rail so I could see to signal Bill to lower away. The big duck splashed into the water and away she went. Troops pushed the next one down the deck, and the whole process was repeated until the forward deck was cleared. Meanwhile, the same thing was taking place on the after deck.

Now I found use for some of those "stores" in #1 'tween deck. Those big concrete "punching bags" were designed to be hung over the side at #1 and #5 hatches to act as fenders so the ducks wouldn't drift under the flare of the bow and stern.

While we cleared the upper decks, the poor soldiers in the lower holds were sweating it out. The Old Man was keeping the bridge, hollering orders through a megaphone at Tim and me. We couldn't hear him so we just kept going, hour after hour. The belly robber, bless his miserable soul, kept sending sandwiches and coffee which we gulped while the winches ran.

At last, late in the night, we could do no more. Darkness was setting in and by now the ship was completely blacked out. The colonel pressed us to continue, but I finally convinced him that it was suicide to continue. It was impossible to see down into the holds while hoisting. If a lift got caught on a 'tween deck hatch coaming, we'd not only lose the lift and kill his men, we'd also probably pull the booms down and kill ourselves. Reluctantly, he agreed when I assured him we'd resume at first light.

Bill and I stretched out on the steam guard and dozed. It seemed just minutes later when somebody kicked me. Forgetting where I was, I rolled off the steam guard and onto the deck. I looked up into the faces of the Old Man and the colonel.

"What the hell are you doing, lying on deck?" growled the skipper. "Let's get at it! The quicker we get rid of these damned passengers the quicker we can get away from this damned beach. If we hang around here we could get ourselves killed."

Up spoke the colonel in his upper class English drawl. "I say, Mister Mate, I've brought you a spot of tea. Drink it down quickly, there's a good chap, and give it another go."

Wearily, Bill and I dragged ourselves back to the windlass and resumed hoisting. As the lifts came up out of the hatches, the poor soldiers looked wan and gray. I thought to myself: *Here they should be fit as fiddles, alert and ready to take on anything the Germans have to offer, and instead they're sleepy, hungry, and bedraggled.* My heart really went out to them. We'd be heading back to London shortly, while their moment of truth was dead ahead of them.

Finally, the last lift went over the side. The Old Man was standing alongside me. "Get up forward, Mister, and get that anchor heaved up."

"Wait a minute, Captain. We've got to put all the hatch beams back in, get the hatch covers and tarps on, and secure all the booms for sea."

"Bullshit, Mister. You can do all that underway. Heave her up. I'm going to the bridge and I want to hear anchor chain rattling in the chain locker when I get there!"

Orders being orders, I started heaving up. As soon as I signaled that the chain was up and down, having just broken clear of the bottom, he rang up Full Ahead. Damn him! Our anchors weighed five tons apiece. If one caught on a ledge or some other underwater obstruction, it could pull the damned windlass, or at least part of the chain, right off the deck. He got lucky and so did we; nothing caught.

Now we had several hours of battening down ahead of us. I left all the 'tween deck beams lying in the 'tween decks, putting in only the main deck ones. Hatch covers were flung on, tarps battened down. Then it remained to square the booms, tighten the guys, and heave snug with the cargo runners. At last I crawled wearily into the saloon, dog-tired and filthy.

"What have you got, Messman?"

"Pot roast."

"Not for me. That damned steward's trying to poison us. I'll have bacon and eggs."

"The steward doesn't like special orders, especially when it's so late."

"He doesn't, huh? If I don't get bacon and eggs, you tell him for me I'll come into that galley and fry and eat *him*!"

Damn that steward's soul, back comes the messboy with a watery mess of powdered eggs and raw chunks of Canadian bacon.

"The steward sends his regrets, sir. We're on Limey stores."

Oh, the slippery bastard. *Some day there'll be a reckoning,* I swore. After this sorry meal, I relieved Capt. McGirr so he could go below. There were ships all over the place. The signalman had been blinking to them, trying to get our orders. A minesweeper answered, telling us to fall in behind him, so back across the Straits we headed.

Meanwhile, we found devious ways around the steward's slop. The second mate and cadet soon joined me on the bridge. Each had an armload of illicit tin cans – Heinz, Ltd. canned soup. Bill had craftily hidden them in the flag locker. Those clever Limeys had designed these soup cans with a little cap containing Sterno on the top. Flip off the cap, punch two holes in the top so it wouldn't blow up like a grenade, drop a match down the hole, and *presto!* hot soup in 30 seconds. Boy, they were great. We three practically lived on them for several trips back and forth to the beach.

The trips themselves seemed endless. Back and forth we shuttled without shore leave at all. The memories got blurred, with one trip merging into another: load the troops, hoist their vehicles and our stores aboard, and go again. Fortunately, after that first trip the Army stevedores showed up. They substantially reduced our turnaround, which suited us fine. The quicker we got away from those beaches, the safer we felt.

On one of the early trips, we arrived at one of the beaches just as a piece of real bad weather blew in. We were at anchor, well in shore, waiting for the stevedores who couldn't come out in that gale. The seas were making up pretty good, so the Old Man suggested I go forward and run out another shot of chain. While I was slacking off, the ship started to pound badly. We were aground! The Old Man rang up Full Astern and screeched at me to heave up. We pulled up well off and anchored again with plenty of scope.

By this time we were discharging onto a weird contraption called a rhino ferry. It was a big, flat steel barge about half the size of a football field. On its back end were mounted two outboard motors, each about six feet high. It was a tremendous object, but helpless in a seaway.

Early next morning one of them appeared, drifting down on us in the continuing gale. There were two bedraggled figures on it, waving frantically. *Bang!* She crashed into us. We threw out a couple of lines which they grabbed and tied fast. Then the two scrambled up a Jacob's ladder and stood there, shivering. Damned if they weren't two U.S.

A "rhino" ferry lands vehicles on the beach, June 1944. Note the balloons overhead.

Coast Guard kids. They'd been blown all the way from the American beaches. We fed them and put 'em to bed. When the weather cleared, we moved back to the beach, rhino and all, and offloaded without incident.

On the way back to London, the skipper finally admitted his concern about having run aground.

"I'm worried, Mister. We'll have to go into dry dock and have a look at our bottom. Won't look too good that we were fool enough to let our vessel go aground."

I motioned him out on the bridge wing, out of the hearing of the crew. "Captain, have you written up our grounding in the official log yet?"

"Nope. Planning to do it after we pick up the river pilot."

"Didn't it occur to you that we never ran aground at all? Do you remember that big underwater explosion that went off on my watch that morning? The one we both thought was a magnetic mine?"

"Now look here, Mister. There was no explo ... Oh ho! You'll make a shipmaster yet! Yes. I'll go below right now and write up the log while that ... er ... explosion is fresh in my mind."

Sure enough, as soon as we radioed the War Shipping Administration in London, we were ordered to dry dock. Now, the head of the War Shipping Administration for northwest Europe was one rough, mean critter whose reputation was known throughout the Merchant Marine. Captain Jones Devlin had been master and port captain for years for the United States Line, the cream of American steamship lines. Now he held the biggest job pertaining to shipping in England. We knew he'd personally inspect the ship, and would be tough to fool.

As soon as we were ready in dry dock, Capt. Devlin went straight to the Old Man's room to read the official log.

"Let's get down in the dry dock and have a look at your mine damage," says he.

I trailed along behind the two of them. The Old Man looked decidedly pale. Down we went and crawled under the bottom. Holy Moses! Though there were no fractures and all the welds were intact, from bow to midships the bottom was badly set up between every frame. It looked like a gigantic washboard.

Capt. Devlin, who was no fool, looked thoughtfully at the two of us. "Yes, yes," he said. "That was *some* big mine." He turned abruptly, hurried up the stone stairs, and was away for London. The Old Man and I looked at each other and together, with great relief, gave the thumbs up sign.

At first I was convinced that we had fooled Capt. Devlin. Now, I'm not at all sure. He was just too capable to be hornswoggled by the two of us. Long years later when I had come ashore and gone to work for a large stevedoring firm headquartered in New York, I would meet up with Capt. Devlin from time to time. He was then a vice-president of U.S. Lines. Never once did either of us mention the incident. Maybe he didn't even remember me. Or maybe he'd stood in our shoes once or twice himself.

That evening I decided to go up to London. It was our first chance ashore since Edinborough. Soon I found myself wandering around Piccadilly Circus in the impenetrable blackout. All of a sudden there was a terrible sputtering, roaring sound overhead. Although it predated them by far, years later I realized that it sounded like our modern jet planes. Along with everyone around me, I dove headlong down the subway stairs. The damned whatever-it-was crashed in the street above us and blew up.

It was one of the first German buzz bombs, jet-propelled, filled with high explosives. The British named them Doodle Bugs, and they were something terrible. In the next few weeks they came over by the hundreds. They just ran out of fuel, dropped out of the sky, and exploded on impact. They made a mess out of London and killed a lot of the British.

I guess because of the Doodle Bugs, the British Ministry decided to install a balloon on our afterdeck. They loaded a couple of dozen gas cylinders on deck. Then they bolted a big spool of piano wire onto the nigger head of one of the winches at #4 hatch. They stretched out a big deflated balloon on #4. I made Bill Ommendson our "balloon officer" in charge of these damned things.

Next day we headed down the river again. Bill was aft, happy as a pig in mud, rigging up the balloon. I looked aft from the bridge just before supper and there she flew, way up in the sky. Well, I tell you before we ever got back to the beach that balloon was some pain in the neck. Naval vessels were forever signaling, "Lower your balloon 200 feet." "Raise your balloon." "Stow same on deck." They ran me ragged!

What with fog and changes of orders, by the time we were discharged I hadn't been to bed for two days. Dirty, cranky, full of too many cigarettes and gallons of stale coffee, I was draped over the rail trying to keep my eyes open. A small launch heaved alongside. Up the ladder came a British S.T.O. officer. His uniform was pressed, his cheeks were red, his eyes were sparkling with good health and plenty of sleep.

"I say," he greeted me, "do you know where the chief officer is?"

Peering at him with red-rimmed eyes I said, "You're looking at him."

"Oh, sorry, old chap. Be a good fellow and raise your balloon."

"Why certainly, sir. At once, sir." Aft I went, released the brake, and came midships again.

Mr. S.T.O. said, "I say, that balloon is way too high."

You ain't seen nothing yet.

Just about then the spool ran out. As far as I know, the damned thing is still going.

Sometimes it all seemed unreal. Once, we had just finished loading in London and were standing by fore and aft to let go and sail. It was late at night and dark. As usual, our decks were covered with trucks. We were taking in the lines, me on the bow. The bosun was spooling a 12-inch manila hawser on the nigger head of the windlass. All of a sudden we heard the roar of an approaching Doodle Bug. As it got directly overhead, it shut off.

This is it! I said to myself. Out of the corner of my eye I spied the bosun racing down the deck. Just as I threw myself face down, I saw the bosun launch himself head first under a truck. He didn't quite make it, and crashed head first into its bumper. Thank God the bomb sailed right over our bow, just missing us, and exploded in the next slip. I stood up, shaking like a leaf. I shut off the windlass and hurried down the deck to see about the bosun. He was sitting down, a big flap of his forehead hanging down over his eyes, bleeding like a stuck pig.

Helping him to his feet, I said, "What hit you?"

"Shrapnel," he croaked.

"You're a lying bastard. No damned medal for you. I saw you leave me and dive under that truck. Now get back on the fo'c'sle head and get those lines in. We're sailing away from this cursed place. It's safer over on the beach."

"I can't see, Mr. Mate."

"Well, if you can't see, feel. I'll stitch you up when we get clear."

Back and forth we continued: London to the beach, the beach to London. On one of the London-bound trips we were approaching the cliffs of Dover when, without warning, fog descended. Our little minesweeper escort disappeared. We had no choice but to anchor. The Doodle Bugs were still swarming over from France, and these channels had to be swept every trip. The entire London area and approaches had been festooned with balloons, which were proving effective. The Bugs flew into their mooring cables and fell down before they got to the city.

We heard that the British had trained a squadron of fighter pilots to shoot the Bugs down over the Straits. We were told that these pilots were Belgians who had escaped to England. As we lay there in thick fog we heard the Doodle Bugs approaching from the east. Then we heard the distinctive whine of Spitfires. They were shooting them down, all right, but they didn't know we were right under them! Every so often we heard a bomb splash into the sea and blow up with an awful bang. The Old Man and I hung out the wheelhouse windows, helpless to change or stop any of it.

"Damn it, Mister, I'll be glad to get back to Rhode Island," he admitted. "I'm sick and tired. And, I'll admit it, I'm scared, too."

For all the good it did, I couldn't have said it better.

We made it to London. Generally, we were never in port overnight, so there was no reason for the captain to give the crew a draw on their wages. Consequently, none of us had any money except maybe a few shillings left over from Edinborough.

Damned if the S.T.O. leech didn't inform us this time that we were not due to sail out until the following night. I was broke, having shot the works on my new sextant. Tim and I were drinking coffee, turning over ways and means of getting a few pounds. I was ready to sell one of the anchors. Shore leave really turns a sailor on after so many days and nights of constant work with hardly any sleep. Besides, from eating the steward's slop our taste buds felt like they had rotted off. Food became just fuel on a ship: choke it down and keep going.

All of a sudden Timmy exclaimed, "I've got the answer! Mother and Father have friends here in London. He's attached to the American Embassy. We'll go to town, inquire where they live, and put the bite on them!"

In short order the pair of us were hurrying down the gangway with just enough dough between us to pay for the train fare. When we got to London Station, Tim phoned the embassy and got their address.

Off we went in a bus. When we finally knocked on their door, we received a warm welcome. They assumed ours was purely a social visit, and settled down for an evening's reminiscing. Tim and I squirmed while the conversation droned on and on about mutual friends on Staten Island, the health of Tim's folks, wasn't the war terrible.

The delights of London were fading fast, but Tim was watching very closely for his chance. During a temporary lull he charged right in with his pitch. He had only this one night ashore, no draw, financially embarrassed. Oh, he did a first-rate job. I figured them for at least 50 pounds, which would just about do the trick. I'll be damned if they didn't limit him to five pounds: 20 bucks! And made him sign for it to boot! We beat a hasty retreat to the sidewalk and debated what to do. Like real sailors we put aside one pound for bus and train fare and drank up the rest.

So it went all summer. We felt like a damned ferryboat. Or more like the mythical Flying Dutchman, condemned to sail the seas until Eternity.

Finally, at the end of one trip the Old Man was summoned to the offices of the War Shipping Administration. This was most unusual. With the exception of dry docking, all our dealing had been with either the British Ministry of War Transport, or the Sea Transport Office. We were British in everything but the American flag, which still streamed proudly from our taffrail.

The skipper was gone a long time. I happened to be out on the boat deck after lunch when he came plodding along the quay. I hurried down and met him at the gangway. He had a peculiar look on his sour puss.

"Hello, Captain. Nice time in London?"

"Grumph," he grunted and headed towards his room. Casually, he flung over his shoulder, "Come up when it's convenient."

Convenient? I shot up after him into his office. Settling on his settee, he slowly took off his hat and flung it in a corner. Taking his time, savoring every minute of it, he said, "My compliments to the chief engineer and tell him to make steam. When he's ready, break out all hands, fore and aft. We're shifting to anchor in the stream."

What a letdown! "Captain, I was sure you had good news. We're just shifting anchor so another ship can have our berth?"

"Mr. Mate, maybe I *do* have good news, but you talk so damned much I can't get a word in."

Drag it out, you old devil.

"Now, as I was saying," he continued, "we'll go to anchor this afternoon. Tomorrow morning we'll bunker from a barge alongside. Tomorrow night ... we sail for home!"

Dear God, at last! Though his door had been shut tight throughout this conversation, by the time I reached the main deck the whole crew was cheering. Homeward bound! The damned bulkheads had ears.

Well before supper we were swinging to the hook out in the middle of the Thames. The Old Man and I were trying to choke down the miserable mess the messboy had placed before us.

"Better eat it, Mister. That's what you're going to get till we get back to Jersey City."

By now I'd have given anything for a decent meal. "Captain, would you happen to have any money in the safe?"

"Why, yes. Why?"

"Could you let me have about 50 bucks? Bill Ommendson and I would like to go ashore for the last time."

I ran up on the bridge and told the signalman to hoist the "Launch Wanted" flag, beat Bill to the showers, and we were off to see the Queen. First, we went to a hotel bar and had our fill of Scotches. Then, by continued bribing with good old Yankee money (the Captain had secretly slipped Bill $50, too) we really had a meal. War or no war, American green moved any obstacle.

Feeling no pain and full as two ticks, we ambled out.

"Let's get a taxi and go to one of those private night clubs we've heard about," Bill suggested.

"Right-o, William," I agreed happily.

These private clubs operated illegally all over London. You got in with a membership card the doorman wrote out on the spot for a pound each.

We taxied up to a blank door recommended by our driver. In front stood the doorman, dressed like a Central American general. We paid our two pounds and in we went. It was bedlam. A colored band thundered out jazz and the smoke was so thick you could cut it with a knife.

We'd no sooner settled into a table when over came our waiter.

"We'll have two Scotches," Bill ordered.

"Two, sir? I suggest you start with one."

Then it dawned on us: in these clubs you had to buy a whole bottle.

Sitting at the next table were two young women. In a burst of generosity, Bill went over and got them. We had barely resettled when the Air Raid sirens went off. It was either those damned Doodle Bugs or, worse yet, their successors, the V1s. These new rockets, launched right up into the stratosphere, were far more deadly. But since they traveled faster than sound, if you heard one you were safe.

Lights blinked, the band disappeared. One of the girls suggested we pack up the Scotch and go to her home. Her mother would love to meet two Yanks. Why not? Away we went.

They lived on the top floor of a five-story apartment building. There was no elevator, of course, so we trudged up five flights. We had no sooner met the girl's old lady (who could really soak up the Scotch) when: *Air Raid!* The old lady yelled, "Everybody grab a mattress and down to the cellar."

Down the five flights we stumbled, lugging a mattress apiece into a dark cellar dimly lit by a few flashlights which the Limeys called torches. By the time we got there, the folks from the lower floors had all the space occupied. We had to wedge the mattresses between a chimney foundation and the wall. In we crept. There wasn't room to stretch out, so there we sat with our knees against our chins.

Soon enough the "All Clear" sounded. We picked up our mattresses and climbed back up the five flights. We just got the Scotch going again when: *Air Raid!* Down the five flights again, damned mattresses and all.

The third time it happened Bill balked. "They can blow the damned building to hell and gone, but I'm not going down in that cellar again!"

Nor did we. At dawn's early light, out we stumbled and headed back for the launch, arriving on board just in time for powdered eggs and tea. The coffee had all been used up.

On my way to my cabin, it dawned on me that I had left my nice, expensive topcoat up on that 5th floor. Just then the Old Man stuck his head in. "No more shore leave, Mister." How the hell was I to get that coat back?

A.M.S.I. 40/44

APPRECIATION AND THANKS

The Minister of War Transport has requested that the following message from the Admiral Commanding the Allied Naval Expeditionary Force may be communicated to all officers and mén of the Allied Merchant Navies :—

On relinquishing his command as Naval Commander, Eastern Task Force, and withdrawing from the Assault Area, Rear Admiral Sir Philip Vian has sent me the following message :—

" I would be grateful if an expression of my appreciation could be conveyed to the officers and men of the Merchant Navy who have been operating with me off the French coast.

" By fine disregard of danger, by adherence to orders and by a ready appreciation of the demands of the varying situations that have arisen, the Merchant Fleet has once again proved the staunch and faithful ally of the Royal Navy."

2. It gives me great pleasure to pass on this expression of appreciation from Rear Admiral Vian, and to endorse it most heartily on my own account.

3. All of us who had been associated with the Merchant Navy in past operations in the Mediterranean and elsewhere were confident that the high standard of courage and devotion to duty previously displayed by the officers and men of our sister Service would be fully maintained during this, the greatest amphibious operation ever planned. We have not been disappointed.

4. I would be grateful if, when conveying to the officers and men of the Merchant Navy, Admiral Vian's message, you would add an expression of my thanks and high appreciation of the great service rendered by them to the Allied cause.

(Signed) B. H. RAMSAY,
Admiral.
1 July, 1944

For Posting on Ships' Notice Boards

Letter of appreciation to all British ships and the 26 American ships chartered to the British Ministry of War Transport for the Normandy Invasion.

Spying Tim on deck, I told him to sneak up on the bridge and hoist the "Launch Wanted" flag and for God's sake not to let the Captain see him. I gave him instructions to get dressed and go ashore to get my coat. I gave him the last of my money and off he went.

The hours crept by. No sign of Tim. After lunch the Old Man sent for me. "Mister, all our bunkers are aboard. We'll heave up the anchor and go down the river real slow. Then we'll be able to drop the pilot just at dark and be on our way."

I felt like a rat in a trap. "We can't, Captain."

"What the hell do you mean, we can't? Who's running this ship?"

"Well, sir, the cadet is still ashore."

"What the hell's he doing ashore? Didn't I tell you no shore leave?"

To my everlasting shame, I hid behind Tim. "I don't know why he went, Captain, but I hear the launch coming now."

Out we went. There was Tim, standing in the launch. His blue uniform sparkled in the sun. My brown topcoat looked strange draped over his arm.

"Get aboard this ship," the Old Man snarled at him. "What the hell's that coat for?"

"I found it on the train," Tim lied.

The Old Man chewed him out good, but Tim never flinched and he never implicated me. I have been grateful to him ever since. I'd worn that coat ashore a dozen times with the Old Man and it was hard to believe he hadn't recognized it. Maybe he had.

At last we sailed down the Thames for the last time. Coming out of Southend and proceeding down the coast, we were joined by more and more ships. By the time we reached The Lizard we were a full-sized escorted convoy. We took our departure with The Lizard abeam, seven miles off, and headed southwest on course 247 true towards the Azores and the southern route home.

The bosun and deck crew were busy dismantling and dumping overboard the on-deck latrines and the piles of debris left behind by all those poor, brave soldiers we had transported to an uncertain future.

Arriving home safely felt like an anticlimax, but it was one of the happiest times of my life. I finally got my vacation – a whole five days – and thus ended the chronicle of another voyage.

– 16 –

MURDER IN LE HAVRE

His name was Stanislaus Pulaski, and he was a Pole. Actually, that wasn't his real name. But it's not his real name that's important, it's the story.

When I first met him, he was an able seaman on a Liberty ship. I was the mate. It was wartime and ships were being manned by people of many nationalities. In fact we'd take anyone who could tie a bowline, and quite a few who couldn't.

The bosun assigned Stan to my watch, the 4 to 8. I don't think he knew more than 20 words of English: Yes, no, port, starboard, good, bad. And of course, OK. He was learning amazingly fast, though. He had to, or he'd starve in the crew's mess.

It helped that I had become quite adept at pidgen English. I knew the real basic stuff like, "Baby, you go along me?" "Me hungry, you ketchum fried eggs?" Of course, I could also cuss pretty good in Spanish, French and German. My Arabic was fluent in inconsequentials such as "Effendi, salaam, arrest not me." I even learned a little Chinese from child beggars: "Please, no got mama, papa, no place to sleep." I had perfect Yangtze River dialect.

Unfortunately, I had no Polish. But sailors always manage to communicate, and gradually, as Stan came to accept and trust me, his story came out. Or as much of it as he would tell.

Little by little, in the dark hours in the wheel house, I came to learn of his horrible past. Physically, he was typically Polish: short, broad, extremely powerful. His hair was bright yellow. His face was wide and flat. He eyes were china blue and quite without expression. When he looked at me, those blank, staring eyes gave me the creeps. And well they might. He had lived an extraordinary life in his 25 or so years.

When the Germans poured across the Polish border, Stan was home with his family: mother, father, two sisters. He was a messboy on a Polish ship sailing out of Danzig, home on leave. He and a young shipmate he had brought home with him were out walking around the small farm his father operated. Hearing loud voices, they sneaked up to the back of the house and cautiously peeked through the kitchen window.

Both his father and mother were lying on the floor in a welter of blood. They were dead, bayoneted. His teenage sisters, stripped naked, were being fondled by German soldiers. The boys overheard the soldiers saying the girls would be taken to an Army field brothel. At least they weren't to be killed.

Unarmed and terrified, the boys quickly crawled back through the bushes and hid. Soon they heard the soldiers getting back into their truck. As they drove away, the boys heard the crackle of flames as fire consumed the house and barn.

The two were stunned. Stan vaguely realized that Poland had been invaded, but that was as much of the political situation as he knew. They decided to hole up for the day and travel west by night. Their flight was an incredible story of pure luck. They managed to find just enough raw turnips and other food from kitchen gardens to keep them alive. After two weeks of running and hiding, half starved and with their clothes in tatters, their condition was desperate.

Stan remembered only one thing keeping him going: a vast, all-consuming hatred of the Germans. Night and day, his only thought was: *Some day I'll kill Germans.*

One night they arrived on the banks of a good-sized stream. Now what? After talking it over, the boys decided to swim across. With their shoes hung around their necks, they struck out in darkness. Only Stan made it; he never saw his friend again. Stan crawled up and down the bank until daylight, searching in vain. He couldn't stay. Now sorrow mingled with his hatred as he went on hiding and running, night after night.

God knows how, but he finally arrived safely in France. Kind people took him in, fed him, and sent him on his way. His goal was London. He had no idea of the vast scope of Hitler's ambition, but instinctively knew that he would find safe haven in England. France had not yet been overrun, so he traveled safely to the channel coast and bummed a ride on a cross-channel steamer to Dover.

By stages, he made his way towards London. Since he didn't speak a word of English, he was inevitably arrested. All of England was apprehensive, and a foreigner jabbering in Polish was a prime suspect.

The police sent him under guard to London. It took an interpreter to set matters straight. Through the good offices of the Polish legation, Stan was issued temporary British seaman's papers and found himself an ordinary seaman on a British steamer. He made several trips across the Atlantic and back. Then he was torpedoed off Ireland. He was washed ashore half drowned and repatriated back to England where he promptly shipped in another freighter. Approaching Newfoundland in midwinter, this ship was torpedoed, too. But Stan's luck held. He was picked up by a Canadian corvette and taken to Halifax.

About this time shipping companies in the States were experiencing difficulties filling out crews. Pearl Harbor had come and gone and we, too, were at war. The seamen's unions, Immigration, and the Coast Guard all gave a little, and qualified aliens were allowed to sail on our vessels. That's how I won Stan.

In spite of the gulf existing between fo'c'sle and bridge, he and I became good friends. During the long hours when he was on the wheel, I helped him with his English. He learned fast. Still, there was a mysterious gulf between us. I think he regretted telling me what happened in Poland, preferring to nurse his hatred in private.

The time came when I was transferred to another ship. Despite the union hiring system I managed to take Stan with me, promoting him to bosun. I worked the same stunt twice more. Then, late in the war, I got a fine new Victory troop ship

Me on the bridge, waiting for Stan to come on watch.

built to carry 2500 troops. The only job open for Stan was ship's carpenter, so carpenter he became.

This trooper was the softest job I ever had. She rated four mates, so as chief mate I didn't have to stand a watch. There was no cargo handling gear to maintain. All I had to do was stroll around every day and look wise. We had 27 Army personnel attached to the ship: cooks, nurses, a doctor, and an entertainment staff. The skipper, Captain Paul Mahoney, was an old friend; we got along like brothers.

Off we went. We didn't have orders yet, but we figured we were headed for Le Havre, and that we probably would be loading troops. The trip across the Atlantic was a joy. We had slight seas, good food, plenty of sleep, and got paid to boot.

Sure enough, Le Havre it was. When we got there the troops were not completely assembled, so we were ordered to lay over an extra day. That morning I sent for Stan and asked if he could make a wooden grating for my shower. I had had enough of the slippery tiles.

"Where to get the wood, Mr. Mate?" he asked. His English was coming along just fine.

That posed a problem. For a while, he had me stumped. Then I figured it out.

"Ho, Stan, I've got it." I announced. "Down in #2 'tween decks are all those great feeding ovens for the troops. There are also several warming ovens that have wooden racks in them. Those Army cooks will all be ashore, so you just slip down there and swipe one of those racks. You'll only have to cut it to size."

"You think good, Mr. Mate," he said. "I go."

I guess it's just as well I didn't know what was going to happen down in that deserted 'tween deck. Nobody saw what happened, so I can only speculate.

About half an hour after Stan left, I was sitting at my desk writing a letter to my son. There was no telling when he'd get it, but just writing to him made me feel like I was talking to him. A shadow fell across the page. I looked up and there, to my astonishment, stood Stan. He had come in like a big, silent cat. His blank blue eyes glittered like cold ice. His big, powerful paws were clenching and unclenching like two vises.

"Stan, didn't you ever hear of knocking before entering? What's the matter with you? What are you trembling for?"

All I got was a stream of Polish.

"Slow down. Speak English."

His voice rose to a scream. "I kill German! Dirty dog is dead. I kill him good!"

"Where? Why? When? God Almighty, Stan, you mean it?"

"Yes, Mr. Mate. I reach in oven for wood. Catch leg. German hiding there. I pull him out and I kill him ... so!" He raised those big hands and crushed them together.

Oh, my God! What to do?

"Stan, show me."

"OK, we go."

And down we went. Thank God the ship was deserted. There the German lay beside the oven, his face swollen and contorted.

"Stan, I never saw this. You understand? Stuff him back in the oven. Never mind about the shower rack – and stay out of my sight. Keep your mouth shut. Understand?" At that I left, flinging the last word over my shoulder.

Back in my cabin, the enormity of what I had seen washed over me. All I could do was sit tight and hope that Stan hung onto himself.

I didn't sleep too well that night. I just knew we were both in for big trouble. I was one of those dopes that had never gotten away with anything in my life. To top it off, I was the world's worst liar. Every time I told a lie my face flushed crimson. Even my ears turned red.

The next morning the ship hummed with activity. Two wide gangways had been rigged and troops were pouring up both of them. Our permanent Army staff were racing around, frantically waving clipboards as they directed confused soldiers to their proper hatches. I skipped breakfast and concentrated on making myself as inconspicuous as possible.

About mid-morning the saloon messman found me and told me the Old Man wanted to see me. *Here it comes!* With dread in my heart, I mounted the stairs to his office.

"Come in, Mister. You know Captain Jones, our Special Services Officer. This is his chief cook, Sergeant Smith. (I don't have a record of their names; these will do.)

I nodded and backed into a corner. "Now then, Mister, we've got a problem. The cooks found a dead man in one of their warming ovens. Heard anything about it?"

"News to me, Captain."

He peered at me out of his shrewd, down-Maine eyes. He, too, had sailed as mate for many years. He knew very well that every whisper of gossip or rumor found its way to the mate's sharp ears.

"Hmmm," he said finally. Then, "Well, anyway, I've sent for some shore blokes. Meet them at the gangway and handle things. And make sure they take the body away. These cooks might just fricassee him for supper."

Sick Maine humor, I said to myself as I beat it out on deck.

As I approached the forward gangway, the Army sentry said, "Mr. Mate, a couple of men just came aboard. Told me if I saw you they'd like to see you in #2 'tween decks."

Boy, oh boy, I said to myself. *Here it comes! Now keep your big trap shut. Remember the old Army rule, never volunteer for anything.*

I made my way down through the hatch. Two officers were standing by the oven. A pair of feet, clad in worn-out shoes, were sticking out. The officers introduced themselves: Army intelligence.

"Well now, Mister, what do you know about this ... ah ... incident?"

"Nothing. Only what the captain told me."

"And what was that, please?"

"The Army cook told him there was a dead man in the warming oven."

"And this was the first you heard anything about it?"

"Yes."

"Well, it's all pretty straightforward. Obviously, there were two of them. Stowaways. Only one would fit in the oven. They fought. This one lost and the other one is still hiding on this ship."

"Sounds reasonable to me," I said. *Oh yeah?* "I'll have the ship searched immediately for the missing German."

"German, Mister? Why German?"

Uh-oh! I had slipped up badly. "Well, I just assumed ..."

"We never assume," Captain Jones said sharply. "In our business, it's always facts. And my men will search the ship."

"Yes, sir. Anything you say." Out I went. *Two of them, and they fought. Hah!*

They sent for a bunch of soldiers and searched from the double bottoms to the crow's nest, from the bow to the fantail. Nothing.

Late in the day I saw the body being carried ashore.

After holding up our sailing time six hours, they quit. I met the two spooks at the gangway. They were dirty, dusty, tired, and discouraged. They gave me strict orders that if the missing stowaway turned up I was to radio London.

Just as they turned away, one of them turned back. What he said floored me. "By the way, we searched the body. He was an Estonian. They're stateless, wandering all over the Continent. Poor devils. They're harmless, you know."

An Estonian! Stan had strangled an innocent man. His hatred for Germans had led him to the wrong conclusion.

This affair had turned so tragic. What should I do? I paced the deck the whole night through. I tried to put myself in Stan's shoes, to think as he did. I couldn't, though. I, too, had been through a long war. I, too, hated the Germans, but I didn't hate them personally, like he did. To me, they were faceless, impersonal people, far away. To me, they were either beneath the water in their murderous submarines or specks in the sky, the sun glinting off their wings as they rolled over and went into their dive bombing runs.

Who would I tell? Or should I tell anyone? It was so tempting to wake up Captain Mahoney, spill the whole story, and let him decide what to do. But I didn't. I've kept it to myself all these years, until now.

We never heard another word about it. Death had become commonplace in Europe, even after the war ended. The Underground in France, Communist resistance fighters, were butchering their non-Communist erstwhile brothers for control of France. Corpses were being fished out of the Seine daily.

On the trip home I found myself avoiding Stan. The night before we docked I called him to my room and told him to quit when we paid off. He looked at me with tears running down his cheeks.

"You fire me, Mr. Mate?"

"No, Stan. I just think it's best that we part."

I never saw him again. I did hear later, through the seaman's union, that he quit the sea, applied for American citizenship, married a Polish-American girl, and opened a Polish bakery. I hope he learned to live with his awful past.

It is more blessed to give than to receive.

Acts

— 17 —

BONANZA IN BONE

As a young sailor, I was forever wheeling and dealing. But the best score I ever made took place years later.

I was the mate on a Liberty ship during World War II. We had taken a mixed cargo to North Africa. After we finished discharging, we were to be chartered to the British Ministry of War Transport for an indefinite period.

We lay alongside in Bone, a fleabitten dump on the North African coast. The port and surrounding area were under control of the British Army. The longshoremen were a port battalion who had been recruited from Liverpool, London, Glasgow, and any other Limey ports that had "dockers," as they called them. They were a tough, thieving crew, as longshoremen the world over are.

Christmas Day was just another day. All five hatches were discharging full blast. Number 3 hatch was discharging truck chassis, jeeps, spare parts, etc. from the lower hold. Up in the 'tween decks we had a strong room. Actually, it was a big wire cage with a padlocked door. I had the key. It was full of valuable stuff consigned to NAAFI in another port. NAAFI was the British abbreviation for our Army P.X. We had the usual assortment of toothbrushes, razors, and such. But the huge cage was also piled to the deck with hundreds of cases of Black Horse Canadian Ale. That ale had the kick of a horse, too.

Right after lunch I was making my rounds of the hatches, checking the cargo handling gear. When I got to # 3 hatch I leaned over the hatch coaming, looking down into the lower hold. My God, the crew were all roaring drunk! The winch operators were still running full blast, hoisting a big truck.

Right behind the port winch operator was the big iron door to the mast locker. Inside the locker was a ladder leading down to the 'tween deck. I flung open the door and scrambled down the ladder. What a mess! The strong room door was hanging on one hinge. Cases of ale were strewn all over the place. Two drunken Limeys from # 1 hatch were inside, hoisting cases on their shoulders. I tried to reason with them, but I might as well have saved my breath. They were getting pretty belligerent, so I beat a hasty retreat up the ladder.

Damn! The winch operator had slammed the door shut and dogged it fast. There I was, locked in like a rat in a trap. I banged on the door. "Let me out!" But all I heard were curses.

Right over my head was the trunk to the ventilator for the hatch. This is a great cowl-shaped affair, its round opening covered by heavy mesh. I managed to shinny up inside, and clutched the mesh with my fingers. To anyone on the outside I must have looked like an animal in the zoo, peering out through his cage.

My head was on a level with the forward end of the boat deck. There was the Old Man, all 130 pounds of him, looking down with horror into # 3.

"Capt'n! Capt'n!" I hollered. He looked all around, trying to locate me. "I'm up here, Capt'n." Finally he spotted me.

"What the hell are you doing up in that ventilator? Come down out of there at once. These damn longshoremen are all drunk.'

"I can't, Capt'n. They've got me locked in."

"Well, damn my soul, no Limeys are going to lock up my chief officer. I'll be right down there."

From my vantage point it was like a tragedy unfolding. The captain brushed by the big winch operator and reached for one of the dogs on the door. *Clang!* The winch man swung at his hand with a huge hammer, just missing him. The Old Man danced up and down, screeching like a little tomcat.

"Capt'n,' I pleaded, "don't mess with that big ape. Go get the bosun."

"Shut up, Mr. Mate. I'll handle this."

Damned if he didn't spring onto that big soldier's back. The two of them went stumbling and falling over the steam guard, paying no attention to me up there in the ventilator. Thank God, here came the battalion captain.

" 'Ere, 'ere, chaps. What the 'ell is going on 'ere? Canadian Ale, is it? Almost as good as spirits," said he, taking a long swig of the nearest bottle.

I got out at last, with the Old Man chewing me out all the way up to the deck. As soon as I got away from him I went looking for the Army captain. I made a big speech about this stealing of cargo, getting drunk on the job, how British soldiers in some other port would be deprived of their NAAFI stores. All of it was to no avail. Before the night was over, they had cleaned us out.

"Well, I said to myself, "the hell with them. If they wanted to steal from their own buddies, let 'em. I couldn't stop them anyhow." It was a miracle that the Old Man didn't get hurt, but I was very grateful to him for sticking his neck out for me.

For Christmas supper we had turkey that had first been boiled, a sea cook's clever way of tenderizing an old bird that had probably been frozen back in the 30s. After boiling, it was shoved in the oven for a few minutes for browning.

Nostalgia was ever-present on a ship at Christmas. I remember our radio officer hooking up the loudspeaker in the saloon to his record player. Over pie and coffee, *Silent Night* and Bing Crosby's *White Christmas* poured out, making our thoughts even more sad. Our naval gunnery officer, tears streaming down his cheeks, got in a fight with Sparks, insisting he shut the damned thing off. I settled the matter by sneaking up to the radio shack and turning it off. Merry Christmas, hah!

We spent many a Christmas away from home. This one was in Buenos Aires in 1932.

New Year's rolled around. All the cargo for Bone had been discharged by then. Just a few hundred tons for another port remained. About noon, a fully-loaded British freighter came in through the breakwater. There was no free berth for her, so she was tied up to us.

At supper, the saloon and crew messrooms were deserted. Everybody had gone ashore even though there was no place to go. Mates and engineers went to crash the British Officer's Club. Our crew and the naval gunners headed for the enlisted men's NAAFI. The Old Man and I were left with the bosun and a couple of A.B.s. He and I sat around the saloon table, gazing morosely into our cups of cold coffee. Along about 9, he decided to turn in. I stayed sitting there, feeling sorry for myself. This damned war was going to last forever, or so it seemed.

I came out of my reverie with a start. The wind was howling like a banshee. I ran out on deck right into a North African snowstorm. The wind was gusting pretty high, blowing us right against the dock. As I turned to go in, I heard a weird grinding sound. The lifeboats! I raced up to the boat deck and found a shambles.

During the war, all lifeboats were permanently rigged outboard of the ship, ready for instant lowering. When the Limey tied up to us, we had swung our davits inboard, and he had done the same with his. Even then, they were almost touching. Their ship being deeply laden, and ours being light and high out of the water, were reacting differently to the swells that were rapidly making up. One of their wooden, lap straked lifeboats had ground itself to splinters against our davits, and their other one was fast following suit. Our lifeboats were metal. That plus the position of our davits had protected them from all but a little denting.

I was quickly soaked to the hide, my teeth chattering from the cold. I couldn't see in the pitch dark, so I ducked into my room for oilskins and a flashlight. Then out I went again, jumping over onto the Limey, intending to wake up her chief mate. I met him in the alleyway on his way out.

We stood on his boat deck assessing the damage. There wasn't much we could do. Neither of us had any fenders big enough to do any good. Even if we had had them, there was no way to get them between the two big ships now pressed tightly together by the gale.

As we stood there, a thump came from up forward. The Limey's mooring lines were made fast to our bitts, and one had just parted. I yelled at him to break out his crew, shouting that I'd round up what men I could. If his ship went adrift in this storm, God knew where she'd wind up. What he said floored me: all his crew were ashore. All he had was one apprentice.

"Well, get him," I shouted. "I'll be right back."

I raced through the crew's quarters and dragged the bosun out of his bunk. He rounded up a couple of Navy gunners, one cook, an oiler, and two A.B.s. By the time we got back on deck, another line had parted.

I sent half my gang on board the Limey and we went to work. As fast as new lines were made fast, old ones parted. We toiled on in the dark and snow. The Limey mate shouted that he had no more lines. We kept running forward to aft, using the shipboard end of our lines. We were nearly literally at the end of our rope.

At long last the wind started to die and the crisis was over. I dismissed my faithful volunteers and wearily slumped on the edge of my bunk, too damned tired to pull off my wet clothes. Some New Year's Eve!

A knock came on my door. I opened it, surprised to see the Limey chief mate standing there with a wooden case on his shoulder.

"Right-o, stand aside, there's a good chap." Pushing past me, he set the case down. Right behind him came his apprentice with another case. Behind him came one of his cooks carrying another case. "There you are, old boy. Shipmates, what? Hands across the sea, hey? Cheerio – we'll be back in a jif."

I looked down. Dear God, Black and White Scotch whiskey!

Back and forth they trooped, dumping their loads, departing, then returning again. My room was filling up to the deckhead, my bunk covered three deep in cases.

On one trip the mate said, "Got to double up, old chap. Daylight's not far away, what?"

"Please stop," I begged. "What'll I do with all this booze?"

"Drink it, of course. You did me some big favor. Besides, this stuff is for NAAFI, and those Army blokes never appreciate good Scotch like us merchant men do, right, old boy? We'll be back in 'arf a mo!"

What to do? if the S.T.O. officer came aboard after breakfast and saw what filled my room, I'd probably be shot. In desperation I went up and pounded on the Old Man's door.

"Go away, Mister. Take care of your own problems. Let an old man rest."

"You've got to come out, Captain. Right away."

He opened the door and stood there, blinking, in his underdrawers. "Now what is it, mister? It'd better be good. I don't like being waked up in port."

"I haven't time to explain, Capt'n. You wouldn't believe me anyway. come on down to my room." He padded after me in his bare feet. Dramatically, I flung open my door. *"Voila, mon Capitaine."*

He peered around my shoulder, his little eyes bugging out like a mongoose's.

"I'll explain later, Capt'n. We've got to get this booze hidden in your stateroom before breakfast. Fifty-fifty partners – have we got a deal?"

Wiping the saliva off his chin, he being a Scotsman, he said, "Done! Carry two, Mister."

We filled his shower and bath chock-a-block full, then used up half or more of his stateroom with the rest.

"I'll have to sleep on the settee in my office, Mister," he moaned.

"Take my room and I'll sleep on your settee."

"No, that wouldn't look right. The crew would get to talking. Besides, anyone going through my stateroom door will only do so over my dead body."

This little tale has a very happy ending. We started shuttling to Italy. There, between the Old Man and me, we made contact with a few American flyboys who had money coming out of their pores. They passed the word: a full quart of Black and White, price $125 a quart. Even though the Old Man shortchanged me on two cases which he kept for himself, we did very well indeed.

– 18 –

FANCY NAVIGATING

I was mate on a new Liberty ship once early in the war. The Old Man was a cantankerous, irascible, tired old New Englander, but he and I were good friends. I guess it was mainly because we were both "peacetime sailors," men who had been sailing since before the war.

We had just returned from yet another North Atlantic trip. It had been a lousy, miserable voyage, like they were all becoming. Fearful storms hounded us all the way. The only thing that made it bearable was the solace of knowing that the submarines lurking in our path found it just as intolerable.

Most of the crew paid off and went seeking nonexistent greener pastures. I called the union hiring hall for replacements. From bitter experience, I had not ordered a bosun. Instead, I intended to look over the A.B.s and make my own choice. A good bosun was prized above gold. A bad one could make life miserable for a tired, harassed chief mate. I draped myself over the bulwarks at the gangway, waiting to see who the union would send.

The sound of steps on the gangway roused me from my musing. A snow white officer's cap appeared first, then a gorgeous, tailor-made, form-fitting uniform. One-and-a-half gold stripes glittered in the sunlight. The face beneath the cap was a match for the uniform: perfect features, a pencil thin moustache, and even, blinding white teeth. By Godfrey, he looked just like Errol Flynn!

Painfully conscious of my wrinkled old khakis and battered, salt-stained cap, I straightened up.

"Good morning," he said. "I'm the new second mate, Joe Bandoni. Is the captain aboard?"

"Sure is. I'm the mate."

After shaking hands, I showed him his cabin and escorted him up to the Old Man's quarters. The captain answered my knock clad in nothing but a tattered old bathrobe.

"Well, Mr. Mate," he said. "What have we here, an actor?"

Knowing the old devil pretty well by now, I knew things weren't starting too well for our new second mate. In peacetime, officers wore only a uniform cap with the company's house flag as its insignia. This poor guy must have looked like Lord Nelson to the Old Man, who had only one rusty suit to his name, same as me.

"Well, don't just stand there," the skipper said, "come on in. You too, Mister." He flopped down at his desk and motioned us to the settee. "Now then. You're our new second officer, are you? Tell me, what experience have you had?"

Bandoni reluctantly admitted this was his first job as an officer. He then told us something neither the Old Man nor I had known. New construction was sliding off the ship ways so fast that crews couldn't be found for them. There were just so many of us prewar men, a number that had been substantially reduced by German submarines. To fill the need, the U.S. Maritime Commission opened schools for both officers and seamen. They also cut in half the time required for an original license. Before, an able seaman had to show three years' discharges to sit for a third mate's ticket. Now he needed only 18 months. By showing 2-1/2 years instead of the usual five, he could sit for an original second mate's ticket.

We had heard that the officers' school was located in New London, Connecticut. We found out later that the only reason for this school's existence was to turn out third mates as fast as possible. Never mind all those tedious logarithms, solving the spherical triangles, astronomy, etc. The school just started with pretty capable seamen and taught them how to use a sextant and a new book of tables called *Ageton*, and figured that was all they needed.

The Old Man ran out of questions and dismissed us. As we walked away, Bandoni asked me where we kept the ship's sextant.

"Ship's sextant?" I had never heard of such a thing. "Mine's up in the chart room, right along with the captain's."

"Strange," he said. "They told us at school that the government was supplying each new ship with a Navy Mark something-or-other, because you can't buy one any more."

"Well, I'll be damned. Let me ask His Lordship." I banged on the skipper's door again. This time all he had on was his skivvies.

"What now?" he snarled.

"Captain, do we have a ship's sextant?"

"Who wants to know?"

"The new second mate," I said, explaining what Bandoni had just told me.

"Well, yes we do, as a matter of fact. It's over there in that bookcase. But you tell that young squirt I'll skin him alive if anything happens to it."

In all the hustle and bustle of loading cargo, shipping a new crew, and storing ship, I set the third mate to checking all the lifeboat gear, rafts, and fire extinguishers. I also had him making sure every man in the crew had his life jacket and knew his Fire and Abandon Ship station.

I put Bandoni to work rearranging all the charts that were crammed into and spilling out of drawers. Because you never knew where you might be going in wartime, the captain had really stocked up. I didn't know how big a mistake that was. The Old Man had stuffed them into the chart table drawers helter skelter. Only he knew where they were. I popped into the chart room one morning and was pleasantly surprised. All the charts had been sorted geographically. A neatly typewritten label was affixed to each drawer, listing its contents.

"Damned good work, Bandoni," I said happily. "Now we can put our hands on practically any chart in the world at a minute's notice."

He beamed.

"I mean it," I said. "That's a job that needed doing. Now I'll tell you what. I've asked the gunnery officer to stop at the Hydrographic Office while he's ashore today, and pick up all the latest Notices to Mariners. You can post all those when he brings them." At last we were going to have some order around here, someone to do things right.

In due time, the ship was fully loaded. I had picked up a middle-aged Norwegian as bosun, and he was proving out very well. As soon as the longshoremen finished a hatch and dropped the main deck hatch beams in place, he was right there with his crew, spreading the three tarpaulins, wedging the battens tight, securing the cross hatch battens, and lowering the booms.

I posted the sailing time at the gangway and in the mess rooms. Sea watches were set and we were standing by, waiting for the deck cargo to be secured. The bosun had two men standing by the gangway, ready to hoist it up as soon as the last carpenter went ashore.

The Old Man and his usual retinue – Sparks and the gunnery officer – returned from the routine convoy conference, striding down the pier in strict order of rank, Sparks last. They were following a rigid, unwritten protocol that governs life on a merchant ship. Sailors learn about this by some sort of osmosis, absorbing it through their pores. It's different from the written protocol of a Navy ship. For example, if a Navy A.B. had to go up to the bridge, he would pause with his head just above the top step of the lee ladder and ask, "Permission to come on the bridge, Sir." Our man would remain silent. The mate on watch, spotting him immediately, would growl, "Well, well, come on. Speak up. What do you want this time?" Frequently he would be deflated when the A.B. would drawl, "The messman just made fresh coffee. Want some, Sir?" It was different, all right, but it was just as important to us as it was to the Navy. And the consequences of violating it were just as dire.

The business of getting underway on this voyage sent us through a typical drill. The captain, pilot, third mate, and quartermaster posted themselves on the bridge. I took the bow with half of the deck gang, the second mate took on the stern with the other half.

"Single up, Mister," the captain shouted to me. Turning aft, he repeated the order. We pounced on the offshore line, flinging it off the bitts, throwing three round turns on the windlass nigger head. A shore crew released the end, letting it splash into the water.

"Heave away, bosun," I shouted, and he fed steam to the windlass. Aboard came the first line, all hands faking down. We raced to beat the gang back aft at the same time they were trying to beat us. Finally, both wire spring lines were aboard and only two lines held us to the dock.

"Let go aft, hold for'ard!" The Old Man watched the aft activity intently. He couldn't use the engine until the last stern line was aboard because of the danger of entangling it in the propeller.

The second mate threw his arms up like a football umpire signalling a touchdown. "All clear aft!" he shouted.

"Slow ahead. Let go for'ard," the captain announced. Then, "She's all yours, pilot." Only then the captain stuffed his pipe and leisurely lit it. I joined him on the bridge as usual, reassuring him that all hatches were battened down, the deck lashings taut, all mooring lines and loose gear being stowed below. If it had been wintertime, I would also have assured him that all ventilators were being unshipped and lashed fast.

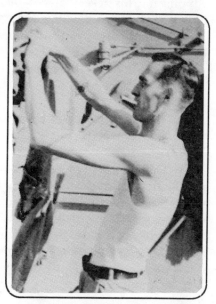

As mate, clothespin in my mouth, somewhere in the Mediterranean.

And so we were off on yet another convoy to an unknown port. The skipper remained on board until the pilot was dropped and the convoy was formed up and we were in our assigned position. As usual, this took several hours. Then he went into the chart room and wrote up his night orders: "Call me at once if the weather thickens." "Call me for any emergency signals." "Call me at once if you have any doubts."

The Old Man stood Bandoni's first midnight to 4 a.m. watch with him. It wasn't a matter of not trusting him. He just didn't know what the mate could do. Being the prudent shipmaster that he was, he had to be shown. After all, he couldn't just go to bed and leave his ship in the hands of a perfect stranger young enough to be his son, or maybe his grandson.

I was heartened to hear the Old Man remark, "Kid seems to know what he's doing. Where the hell did he learn?"

"Well, Captain, he's been an A.B. for a long time. He's stood many a wheel watch in convoy, and he's got sharp eyes and ears."

"Mmmm. Maybe you're right, but does he have to wear that fool uniform in the middle of the night? You'd think he was going to a wedding or something."

As tactfully as I could, I reminded him of an inflexible rule that existed before the war, though it had now gone by the wayside. No matter how crummy a rust tub it was, the rule held that all officers, both deck and engine, were to wear a jacket in the saloon. These were khaki drill jackets, bought and worn for that one purpose. They were never seen anywhere except in the saloons of freighters. They didn't have lapels like present-day uniforms. Instead, they had little stand-up collars, two breast pockets, and brass buttons. An engineer coming straight from a sooty boiler, stripped to the waist and plastered with sweat, soot, and grease, would no more come into the saloon for the noonday meal without slipping into his jacket than he would go down the gangway stark naked. No matter that he was filthy and stank like a polecat, it was the rule.

"Well, Mister, you have a point. But he's so young! I'm going to bed. An old man needs his rest."

Balls! I've seen him keep the bridge for days, his head nodding on his chest while the convoy escorts raced hither and yon, trying to keep us afloat and alive.

With his praises now being sung by the captain, I thought Bandoni was out of the woods. But it was not to be.

Sailing in convoy had become second nature, a way of life. Slogging alone back in peacetime days was but a dim memory. Now, all hands on the bridge always had one eye on the convoy commodore's ship. The commodore was invariably a British admiral, dragged out of retirement to do his bit. I shouldn't say "dragged." Knowing the British as I do, it's very safe to say that those old admirals leaped at the chance. They sure knew their business. Thirty or 40 years under the white ensign couldn't help but produce a superlative seaman, and they were the living proof of it.

The commodore, charged with the internal organization of the convoy, always traveled with the lead ship in the center column. He was accompanied by a large staff of British Navy signalmen, radio operators, and navigators. All orders emanated from him. In daylight his signals came by flag hoist or blinker. At night they came from a hooded Aldis lamp, colored lights, or occasionally by radio.

It was the commodore's habit in all convoys to hoist his noon position. As soon as the flags fluttered out, every ship in the convoy hoisted its position. There was intense rivalry throughout the convoy to see how quickly each ship's position was raised. There was some mild cheating, too. A scene-stealing master would train his binoculars on the commodore's bridge. The second he read the commodore's flags, he subtracted or added a minute or two, then up would go his position. That was a small satisfaction, not one to be stooped to by our doughty skipper.

Still, we were usually among the last to hoist our position. I know our laggard response was rankling in the Old Man's mind just as it was in mine. The trouble was, both the skipper and I were old fashioned, still struggling with five decimal place logarithms out of Bowditch. But that's the way we did it. It was this that became the second mate's Waterloo. He was struck down in the flower of manhood, never to rise again because of one of those age-old unwritten protocols.

On most ships, the shooting of the sun was a solemn – nay, hallowed – tradition. On our ship it was no different. Present was the Old Man, always the second mate, most times the third mate, and sometimes the chief mate. All gathered out on the lee bridge wing with their sextants in their hand. In measured order, they reversed their caps so the visor wouldn't interfere with their sighting. A certain amount of fussing with the sextant shade for show came next. Then it was time for the sighting.

The Old Man peered intently into his scope. He grunted something like, "Good. Sharp horizon." Ever so carefully, each man followed the sun up on its journey to the zenith. In unison, their hands stopped turning the verniers just when the sun was "hanging" for a few seconds before starting down and westward. Then the Old Man announced, "Local apparent noon, gentlemen," and they would all parade into the chart room in descending order of rank. The captain and first mate draped themselves over the chart room table. Lesser ranks made do on the settee.

All set to work reducing their sextant sights to the sought-after result: latitude. The Bowditch tables were exchanged, again in strict order of rank. Now came the tricky part. No matter that one of the other mates finished his computations well before the captain, rank ruled. After the captain, one by one the first mate, then the second, and lastly the third mate put their positions on the chart. There was method as well as tradition in this exercise. Anyone, even His Holiness the master, could make a mistake. Double checking was only prudent.

If all the positions were clustered closely, the skipper's was noted in the log book. If his was way away from the others, as sometimes happened, with very good grace he picked one of the others as the official noon position. Usually, just to save face, he would mutter something like, "Must have been some dirt on my horizon mirror," before hurrying below for dinner. But the important thing is that the captain's position was marked first.

Our second day dawned bright and clear. Finishing inspection rounds with the bosun, I glanced up toward the bridge. Lo, there was our new second mate, hat on backward, peering through the Navy sextant. All of a sudden he started walking toward the wheel house and chart room. Was he reciting poetry? Then I heard, "One chimpanzee, two chimpanzees, three chimpanzees." *Hmmm*, I thought. *He's counting seconds from the time of sight until he can reach the ship's chronometers. Smart boy.* He must have picked that up from some mate while standing wheel watch. Taking morning sights would give him a very good noon longitude as well as latitude. *This kid is going to be all right.*

Out loud I said, "Well, Bosun, let's check the deck cargo lashings." We finished up well before noon, so I decided to join His Nibs in the time-honored ritual of noon sight. Later, I wished I hadn't. The time bomb that would blast that poor young second mate to smithereens was ticking loud and clear. I just didn't hear it. And neither did he.

The third mate didn't have a sextant, so he was relieved and sent below. The three of us paraded out on the bridge wing: the captain, the second mate, and me. Bandoni broke tradition by leaving his cap in the chart room, but no matter. The reversing of caps ritual was a minor rule. The performance began. Up, up, slowly ... hang! The Old Man lowered his sextant and squinted at the second mate's back, already disappearing into the chart room.

"Mister, that boy seems too eager, wouldn't you agree?"

Not wanting to take sides, I only grunted. When we got to the chart room, there was Bandoni, sprawled over the chart table. Bad form! A slight chill crept into the air. The skipper busied himself putting his sextant back into its box. I did the same. The old man laid his little slip of paper with his sextant altitude on the chart table and reached for the *Nautical Almanac*. He couldn't reach it because the second was in his way.

Softly, too softly, the Old Man whispered, "Excuse me, Mister."

"Just a second, Cap," Bandoni replied.

Cap? The countdown was approaching blast-off.

"I make her to be right there, Cap," Bandoni said, snapping shut a small, thin black book.

"You do, do you? And how did you arrive at that position, may I ask?"

"Nothing to it, Cap. This little book does all the work."

"Does it now?"

"Yep. It's called *Ageton*. I heard that Ageton was a Naval officer, and that he put those tables together just to save us all that work you're about to do."

The countdown had reached zero.

"A Navy man, you say? Those overdressed dopes can't find their way out of the shower room. Let me see that book."

Ignition. *Blast-off!*

The Old Man picked up the little book by thumb and forefinger. Holding it well away from him in an exaggerated parody of carrying a dead skunk, he walked to the porthole, undogged it, and flung the book into the sea. Turning to me, he said, "Mister Mate, it's time for dinner. Coming?"

This whole sad episode was really a tragedy. That young man was most able, and showed all the promise of becoming a fine deck officer. The captain, however, was tightly bound by a lifetime of inflexible tradition. This was the new generation taking over from the old. It was an uneasy time, but take over it did.

The rest of the voyage was uncomfortable, to say the least. The poor second mate's navigation activities ground to a standstill. *Ageton* was all he knew. He stood his watches well, kept the ship exactly in her proper station, and was absolutely correct in all his dealings with the captain. But it was all for naught. The captain remained distant and cold toward him. Except for necessary ship's business, he ignored him completely.

When I relieved Bandoni, he hung around, rehashing the whole business. "Where did I go wrong? How can I make amends?"

All my sympathies were with him, but I had to tell him the brutal truth. "The Old Man is what he is. He's never going to change, and that's sad. But he is master of this vessel. You have only one course open to you. When we get back, pay off and get another ship."

That's just what he did. I never saw or heard from him again, but I know he did well.

As for me, the very day we docked I slipped ashore and bought an *Ageton*. The next voyage, the Old Man caught me using it.

The next day, I caught him.

– 19 –

WARTIME GADGETS
(BAD ONES)

In the early days of the war, German submarines took a fearful toll on our merchant ships. Our East Coast from New York to Miami was the graveyard for hundreds of ships, mostly tankers coming up from Gulf ports or the Caribbean.

Southbound ships were diverted from their regular route (Hatteras to the Northern tip of the Bahamas, outside of the north-setting Gulf Stream) to inside the Stream, right along the coast in shoal water. Northbound vessels continued to ride the Gulf Stream from Key West to Hatteras. In both directions, they'd be safer close to shore, or so the thinking went. But not so. Tankers were blown up and sunk every night. From Hatteras south, their masts stuck out of the water like telephone poles. People sunning themselves on the beach at Miami had a ringside seat. Ships were torpedoed right in front of them. Men were burned alive and drowned while they watched in the balmy sunshine.

The same thing was happening on the tanker route from Venezuela and the Aruba refineries to the Florida Straits. The North Atlantic from Nova Scotia to the western approaches to the British Isles was equally bad. Hundreds of thousands of tons of shipping were being sent to the bottom every month. It was a black time.

Finally, at first a trickle and then a flood of new ships came sliding down the ways. Shipyards on both coasts and along the Gulf launched them daily. Foremost among these were the Liberty ships – slow, ugly tubs that saved our necks, or at least contributed a major share to the total war effort. I sailed on nine of them, four as master. I came to know them as I know the palm of my hand, good points and bad.

Far and away their major drawback was their lack of power. Each Liberty ship was powered by an old-fashioned triple expansion steam engine of only 2,500 horsepower. There was a far more efficient and powerful steam turbine being made, but it had been reserved for the mammoth Naval Vessel Construction Program. To solve the power problem, the planners for new construction modified a British hull design by placing three hatches forward of the midships house, and two aft, and placed the steam triple expansion engine in that. The resulting ship had 10,500 dead weight tonnage (the combined weight of its fuel, stores, and maximum cargo). This meant it could carry up to 9,500 tons of cargo in 475,000 cubic feet of actual cargo space. Because most of these ships would be coming home empty, with little or no ballast, they were constructed with double hulls (called double bottoms) for the storage of bunker oil. This placed the ship's center of gravity very low, making them very stiff and providing them with tremendous righting ability. These ships could, and did, roll 35 degrees with no danger. The pendulum effect of the low center of gravity snapped the ships back upright. This made them good sea keeping ships in a heavy sea, but it also made them uncomfortable. It was said that "they'd roll in a heavy dew."

As the submarine sinking intensified, and as more and more ships were launched to be thrown into the breech, the planners intensified their efforts to combat the attacks. A slew of contraptions appeared on the Liberties. I had the misfortune of being shipmate with several of them.

The first of these nightmares to come my way was Mark 29, an innocuous name for a full-blown disaster.

I was assigned to a Liberty being built at the South Portland Shipyard in Maine. After the usual sea trials, we sailed her south to Boston with the usual complement of 28 Navy gunners on board. The gunnery officer told us he expected several more Navy ratings aboard, trained to handle the Mark 29 gear which was going to be installed. He had no idea what this new device was, but expected further instructions.

The next morning a horde of civilian Navy Yard workers came aboard and set to work on the forward deck. Right up on the bows, on either side, they welded a weird pair of frames above the bulwarks. I learned later that they were similar to those installed on mine sweepers. Enormous reels were welded to both sides of the forward deck, fairleads and chocks were burned in the bulwarks, and wire cables were run everywhere. The whole apparatus was utterly confusing.

All this took a couple of days. The next day a big Navy barge pulled alongside. Two strange-looking objects called paravanes were hoisted aboard first. They looked like torpedoes. Each paravane was suspended from one of the frames on either side of the bow. Then came great rubberized cables, four or five inches in diameter. These were wound around and around the big reels, filling them completely.

The next day back came the gunnery officer with his additional men. As he and I sat in the saloon after supper, he explained the working of this diabolical assembly as he understood it.

With the ship sailing at full speed in the open sea, he said, the paravanes would be launched straight out from both bows, at right angles to the ship, tethered on long, stout cables.

"We'll haul the big rubber cables out, making one end fast to the tether holding each paravane," he said. "That will give us four cables on each side of the ship. "They'll be equidistant, and they'll run the full length of the ship."

"That's impossible under sea conditions," I protested. But I hadn't heard the worst of it yet.

"The outer cables on each side are full of sensitive microphones," he told me. "The next two are full of high explosives."

"What about the one nearest the ship?"

"They act as stabilizers to keep the cables in place just beneath the water at a depth I preset," he finished up proudly.

I threw my hands up. Whoever dreamed up this monstrosity had never sailed the North Atlantic in winter. In fact, I don't believe he ever saw salt water in his entire life.

The idea was that a torpedo would pass close to the outside cable. The microphones would hear it and somehow cock the trigger on the next two cables. When the torpedo passed near the first cable, it would explode, blowing up the torpedo and saving the ship. The second explosive cable was there to do the same for a second torpedo.

I sat there, speechless. Finally I asked, "Lieutenant, is this your first trip to sea?"

"Why, yes. I was a school teacher in Ohio."

"Well, you've got your hands full this time. This is absolute madness."

"I wouldn't be too hasty in your condemnation," he said. "The Navy has assured me that this has been thoroughly tested. It will definitely protect us from torpedoes, two on each side."

Unable to get through to him, I let it go. The following day we sailed for Halifax, as usual. We slipped up the coast with a few ships and arrived at anchor in Bedford Basin to await the formation of a convoy to England. In due time we got our convoy orders. Along with another Mark 29-equipped Liberty we were assigned to "Coffin Corner," the last ship in the outside column. I think we were the guinea pigs, set up to attract a U-boat to take a shot at us just to see if the damn thing would work!

Next day the inevitable signal came: "Stream Mark 29." The gunnery officer ran frantically from one side of the deck to the other, yelling orders. He clutched a thick, bound notebook under his arm. Every few minutes he'd consult it and race around with new orders. His crew pulled run our cargo runners off the winches and rigged up their own cables to them. Steam hissed, winches clattered, and the paravanes went over the side.

The Old Man and I stayed clear of the whole show. We retreated to the flying bridge, making uncomplimentary remarks, deliberately letting the Navy signalman overhear us. We knew he'd spread the word the minute his watch below came.

We were so intent watching the action on deck that the Old Man had forgotten to keep proper station in the convoy. We had drifted a mile astern! He flew into the wheelhouse, grabbed the engine room phone, and chewed out the engineer on watch.

"What the hell's the matter down there? Get back on Full Ahead!"

When the first assistant could finally get a word in, he shouted back, "We *are* going Full Ahead – 66 revolutions!"

Then the light dawned. Those damned rubber cables were making enough drag to cut our speed. We were fast falling astern despite all we could do. Sure enough, here came an escort vessel blinking frantically at us and shouting through his bullhorn: "Regain station. Close up immediately."

More cursing and yelling between bridge and engine room. Right on cue, up came the poor gunnery officer, grease all over his nice uniform. The Old Man immediately turned his wrath on him. The whole crew, mine and the Navy, ate it up.

Right in the middle of the confrontation the signalman said to the gunnery officer, "Sir, look over the side." All those big black cables were ripping along on the surface like long black sea serpents. The gunnery officer was off like a shot, tearing along the foredeck. Despite all the yelling, dial twisting, and switch snapping, those flapping cables refused to submerge.

By this time it was sunset, or would have been if there had been any sun. The sky was dirty gray, the wind was making up out of the northwest, and the ship was starting to roll and pitch. We were in for another North Atlantic gale.

Black night enveloped us. The wind moaned in the rigging. We knew we were in for it. There we were, all alone, the convoy somewhere up ahead. It was a miserable feeling. I came off watch at 8 p.m. Before going below, I took a turn about the decks, checking the hatch tarps, lashings, and lifeboats. Feeling uneasy, I stepped into the saloon for coffee. The gunnery officer was in there forlornly poring over his Mark 29 manual.

"I can't find the reason they won't release, Mr. Mate," he said mournfully. "Those cables should be slipping along well beneath the surface."

"Cheer up, Lieutenant," I said with encouragement I didn't feel. "It will come to you."

My uneasiness persisted even after I retired to my quarters later. I sat on my bunk thinking, *There must be a better way to make a living.*

Fully clothed, I dozed off. A furious pounding on my door brought me to my feet. The second mate burst in, his oilskins streaming. "Better come look at the port lifeboats, sir. You'll need your oilskins. It's howling a full gale."

Struggling into my oilskins, I lurched out on the starboard side. The ship was rolling fiercely and it was as black as the inside of a sheep's stomach. I crawled aft on the boat deck. As I groped my way around the corner, the full force of the gale took my breath away. I crawled along, hanging onto the railing welded to the midships house. Abreast of the port boats I bumped into the second mate.

"What the hell's the matter, Mister?" I yelled.

"Sir, I'd better let the gunnery officer tell you."

"What's happened, Lieutenant? What's the matter?"

"It's difficult to explain why, sir," the Lieutenant shouted, "but all four rubber cables have been washed aboard and are draped all over the two lifeboats. But there's really no need to be alarmed. I'm pretty sure they're disarmed. I've pushed all the correct buttons."

A dim form bashed into me. The Old Man!

"Mister," he yelled at me, "get those things off this boat! Quickly, now."

"But Captain," the Lieutenant shouted to him over the scream of the gale, "those things are full of high explosives."

"Quite so, Lieutenant," the captain screamed back. "*You* get them off. We'll be over there on the lee side just in case they blow up and kill you."

I'll give the gunnery officer his due: though it was to no avail, he and his men toiled all through that long, miserable night. Those cables were just too heavy and too tangled in the boats and davits for anyone to release. When dawn broke, gray and gloomy, we were all alone on the sea. There wasn't a mast in sight. The shrieking gale was whisking the tops of the waves off into scud.

The Old Man huddled on the bridge with me. "Mister, we're in some hell of a mess," he said. "If this storm ever blows itself out, some damn fool German is going to come along in a submarine and sink us to hell and gone. Send for the lieutenant."

Up crawled the gunnery officer. He was not only tired, discouraged, and scared, he was miserably seasick.

"Now, Guns," says the Old Man, in a surprisingly kind, gentle tone, "it's not your fault. You just have a jerk for a boss. He's probably sucking up martinis in some plush admiral's club this very minute. But we do have a problem. I don't care how you do it, but I want those cables on the starboard side jettisoned ... immediately!"

Guns was halfway down the ladder before the Old Man finished yelling. He backed up the ladder and said sheepishly, "Please, Captain, what does 'jettison' mean?"

"It means throw the damned things overboard, landlubber!"

How he did it I'll never know, but do it he did. I know I saw sledge hammers and big cold chisels. And I know that at last the whole contraption was cut adrift and sunk forever. Without the drag, we were able to make up knots. At last we spotted the tail of the convoy on the horizon; soon afterward we took up our position in the "coffin corner." When we reached England, naval demolition experts came aboard and untangled the mess on the port boats. It couldn't happen fast enough to suit me.

This British Liberty ship shows its anti-torpedo nets deployed while underway.

The next unholy invention we got, a torpedo net, was only a tiny improvement over the Mark 29. Here's how that worked.

Our regular cargo booms were cradled fore and aft, two to a hatch. To accommodate the torpedo nets, four more booms were added, two adjacent to the foremast and two aft at the mizzenmast.

Now, masts on these Liberty ships were massive steel things. Way up at the top, running athwartships, they were capped by a well braced fore, main, and mizzen crosstrees. The new booms, much longer and heavier than the already-large cargo booms, were pinned to the deck on either side of the masts. They stuck way above the crosstrees, secured in big iron collars welded to the ends. Topping lifts were attached to the heads, leading down to our deck winches. To go with this jungle, a big pile of steel cable netting was stowed on each side of the foredeck.

To rig this nightmare ("stream torpedo nets," in Navy parlance), a man sitting in each crosstree would release the collars, giving the boom a push with his foot while holding on for dear life. If he timed it just right, when the ship rolled and the man on the winch slacked off right with him, the big boom would commence lowering over the side. When the tip was just over the bulwarks, another winch on the forward deck would heave the bunched net to the end of the boom. While this was going on forward, the same thing was happening aft. All of it was happening while we were under full steam.

The next step was to start heaving on an aft winch. Theoretically, this drew the net along a cable stretched between the two booms. *Presto!*, we would be instantly safe, protected on both sides by the two nets hanging well below the surface.

Good theory? Try this. Let's say we're steaming along in fine style and along comes a submarine hungry for a kill. Its crew takes careful aim: Fire one! That nasty torpedo leaps from its tube, heads straight for our beam, and, *surprise!* it's snared by the net. Since it's set for impact, it won't explode. So there we are with a loaded torpedo snagged alongside our ship. What next?

On page six, paragraph five, is the neat solution. Welded to each boom, within easy reach of the deck crew, are two long, securely latched levers. A crew member releases the latches, pulls the levers, and drops the net-entangled torpedo to the bottom.

The catch was, it didn't quite work that way. We heard more than one tale of a ship coming into port with a live torpedo hanging in her net. Not being exactly welcome, she was usually banished to a remote anchorage while demolition experts gingerly extracted the torpedo.

I had a little different experience with this clever device. For some unknown reason, we didn't get orders to use our submarine net on our outbound voyage to North Africa. However, as soon as we passed through the Straits of Gibraltar, homeward bound, the convoy commodore blinked over: "Stream torpedo nets." We got them overboard, all right, but just as with the Mark 29, they produced so much drag we fell behind the convoy again.

Just before dusk an escort came back to us and told us to "retrieve the nets." Fat chance. The wind had freshened considerably. We were in ballast and rolling heavily. The ends of the booms were dipping into the waves. Naturally the manual had the answer. As sort of an afterthought, a minor footnote, it said: "Booms and nets should not be streamed nor retrieved if the vessel's roll exceeds x degrees."

As we were already exceeding the limit, we were stuck. If we tried to retrieve them now, by the time they got halfway up the reverse roll of the ship would send them crashing against the mast, probably flinging the man up on the crosstrees overboard or crushing him to death.

I solved the problem without the manual. I ordered a good yank on those long levers and away went the nets to Davy Jones's locker. Good thing, too. It was three days later before we could hoist the booms.

As though we hadn't yet had enough, next we were blessed with submarine detecting apparatus. This one was a real beaut! The way I figure it, the planners cooked this one up with one hand tied behind their backs, just to keep their hands in, or maybe to meet a desperate quota of inventions.

Two big microphones were welded to the ship's hull well below the waterline, one on each side forward of midships. Wires ran from them to a fancy control box in the wheelhouse. Two great gongs were installed, one on the each side of the wheelhouse bulkhead.

The way it was supposed to work sounded great. The port side microphone would pick up the sound of a submarine's engines. The gong on that side would go off with a sound to wake the dead, whereupon the mate on watch would take "evasive action." What was he supposed to do? Turn port? Starboard? Mess his drawers?

The damned things were overly sensitive. If the bosun dropped a sledgehammer on the forward deck, both gongs went off. Of course, the planners had anticipated this: there was a sensitivity dial for just such an event. Naturally, it never worked. We fixed it by plucking a handful of wires out of the black box.

What we really could have used was a really good gyrocompass. Or that greatest of all contraptions since the Chinese invented the compass: radar. That would have kept ships from wandering off course, slamming ashore with good seamen drowned and good cargoes lost, would have kept them from bashing into each other in fogbound convoys.

Somehow I wonder how we ever won the war. I wonder, too about what kind of jobs those planners returned to. If it was driving cabs in Brooklyn, they were probably overrated.

The good seaman is better in bad weather.

Anonymous

– 20 –
WARTIME GADGETS
(THE GOOD ONES)

After scoffing at the crazy gadgets tried out on wartime Liberty ships, it's only fair to tell of two great ones. When used together, they were and are absolutely the greatest aids to navigation since the compass, sextant, and chronometer: radar and the gyrocompass.

Late in the war I was assigned to a Victory ship being built in the shipyard at Baltimore. The Victorys, just coming off the ways, were a great improvement over the Libertys. Although they had the same basic hull design, dead weight, and cargo capacity, there the similarity ended.

First, they had a raised fo'c'sle head which tended to make them drier. Steel pontoon hatch covers on the main deck made them safer. Modern, powerful, fast, electric cargo winches made cargo handling more efficient. And last, God bless them, they had a 6500 horsepower steam turbine which scooted them along at 16 knots! Now here was a ship!

I spent every day during her construction learning everything I could about her. At last she was launched: the SS *Smith Victory*. We went out on her sea trials. After those Libertys, she felt like a yacht. Why, we'd go to sea like bloody potentates!

Then we received most peculiar orders. We were to proceed in ballast to Savannah, Georgia, to be converted to a troop carrier for 2500 troops. I wondered why this wasn't done while she was being built. Much later, I realized that the war in Europe was fast coming to an end. We were being converted to carry troops from Europe to the Far East for the invasion of Japan.

Off we went down Chesapeake Bay, out the Virginia Capes to the lightship, heading south for Hatteras and Savannah. There was just one small fly in the chowder: we still had a magnetic compass. With everything else on the ship so fine and modern, I would have thought we would have a gyro. No dice.

We arrived at the Savannah Lightship, picked up a pilot, and proceeded up the river to Mingledorf's Shipyard. We went promptly into dry dock, remaining there for about two months. Once more shipyard workers swarmed all over us, tearing the ship apart. All the lower holds were made into troop quarters. In the 'tween decks, great kitchens were built. A hospital, doctor and nurse quarters, officer quarters, and quarters for 27 permanent Army staff were added as well. They even put a piano aboard!

We had a fine time in Savannah while this was going on, swimming at Tybee Beach, eating marvelous Southern cooking. It was a welcome interlude after all those North Atlantic convoys.

The conversion work seemed to drag. Then one fine day the war in Europe was over! The work force was doubled, three shifts were put on, and things started to fly. One morning the second mate pointed out a bunch of workmen on the bridge.

"That's funny," I said. "We don't need any changes there to carry troops. Let's go up and have a look."

Glory be, they were installing a gyro! The master compass was housed in the chart room, with a repeater on each bridge wing and another at the wheel for the quartermaster. I was so happy I danced!

Two days later, the second mate told me another gadget was being installed in the wheelhouse. Up we went again. Just to the left of the wheel stood a large, strange-looking console. It had numerous switches and a round glass face set into it.

"Say, Mr. Foreman," the second mate said. "What's this thing?"

"Why, Mr. Mate, I'm surprised at you. This here is the latest model radar."

Another useless gadget dreamed up by those mysterious planners in their ivory towers, I thought. I had vaguely heard about the Navy's radar, but had never seen it or talked with anyone who had. Even when the second mate announced that the manufacturer's representative would come to the ship the next morning to instruct us in its use, I snorted, "You go listen to him. Not me." And so I didn't go.

Sailing day arrived. We were ordered to proceed at full speed to Antwerp to load 2500 troops for the Orient via the Panama Canal. Because of the extensive alterations to the ship, the magnetic compasses would have to be adjusted. This was a common procedure and would be accomplished by steaming in a slow circle around the Savannah Lightship.

A mate would be stationed at the pelorus (a special dummy compass) on the bridge wing. As the ship steamed slowly around the lightship, the mate would call out the lightship's bearings to the compass adjuster who was stationed at our master magnetic compass. The adjuster would add or subtract magnets in the base of the binnacle to make the needed corrections. It was a straightforward, simple piece of business.

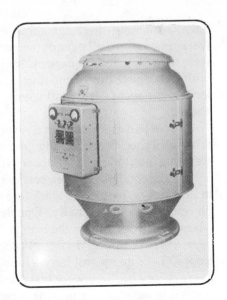

Those early gyros were a wonder, keeping us oriented to true north without fail. At the immediate right is a typical World War II master gyro in its casing. The next picture is a cutaway view – the big door has been taken off of the housing. The photo at the far right shows the guts of the thing, the heavy contraption that spins and actually points toward the right direction. Typically, the master was housed in the chart room. Repeaters located in strategic parts of the ship gave us remote readings where we needed 'em.

As soon as we raised the lightship we started circling. Before we got halfway around, the sky got black as night and we were hit by one of those fierce summer thundershowers. The poor third mate out on the bridge wing was soaked to the hide in an instant. The compass adjuster called him into the wheel house.

"He won't melt," I growled.

"No, but he can't get proper bearings, either," the adjuster said. "He can't even see the lightship. I'll flip on the radar and use it to take the bearings."

"You'll what? Use that gadget? This I've got to see."

Well, I saw. My eyes pretty near popped out of my head. Built into the radar scope was still another gyro repeater, so he was getting true bearings of the lightship all the time. Each time the lighted sweep revolved, it left a lingering blip on the scope. The circumference of the scope was the gyro repeater from which a true bearing was obtained. There was even a little crank which, when turned, propelled a tiny white light out along the sweep. When the light reached the blip, a glance at the indicator above the crank gave off the distance accurately in yards. *Wow!* Was I converted to the true faith! This was no useless gadget. It was a miracle, come to rest on the bridge of this fine ship.

The storm passed. The adjuster and pilot left, and we headed for the Great Circle Route to Bishop's Rock, the southern entrance to the English Channel.

I spent the whole trip camped at that radar set. Every day, every night I looked for ships to take bearings on. We made Bishop's ahead of schedule and I got a good bearing. Then the fog set in. We couldn't see

beyond the bows. No matter; we had the gadget to end all gadgets, and away we went at 16 knots.

A radio message told us to anchor inside the Goodwin Sands for further orders. The Goodwin Sands, in the English Channel, had the same dismal reputation as Nantucket Shoals and Diamond Shoals at Hatteras: a graveyard of ships. Nonetheless, we did ourselves proud. We crept into a perfect anchorage, thanks to our new radar.

After that fine start, loading 2500 troops at Antwerp was a cinch. After picking them up we headed for the Panama Canal. Halfway there, the atom bombs were dropped and hostilities were at long last at an end. We were ordered to turn north to New York to disembark the troops.

Through all of this I acquired an unhealthy dependency on my new toys, so much so that I became lax in the exercise of good seamanship. My snoot was constantly stuck in the radar hood to the exclusion of almost ever looking out the pilot house windows. I relied too much on mechanical devices. Later, it almost proved my undoing.

Peacetime came and we were back in the straight merchant marine business. We had just finished discharging grain in a North European port on another Liberty with a brand new radar. We were ordered to Fowey, England, to load a part cargo of china clay for Philadelphia. I had never been there before.

Fowey is a small yachting harbor in Cornwall on the southeast coast. The weather was lousy but usual for the English Channel: rainy, misty, poor visibility. We were sailing on dead reckoning, heading for the mouth of the Fowey River. As usual, I was camped on a stool peering at the radar scope. Nothing showed. There was no coast line, no ship to be seen, nothing. The mate came into the wheel house and dolefully announced that visibility was zero.

"No problem, Mr. Mate. This little beauty can see for 20 miles. I'm expecting to pick up the pilot boat any minute now."

The sweep kept rotating around and around. Nothing showed. I knew everything was OK, though. Nothing could fool this gadget.

Suddenly the mate burst in, shouting: "Captain! You'd better go Full Astern! The shore line is just ahead!"

Full Astern we went, barely in time. That damned radar looked as if it was working, but it wasn't. I learned my lesson fast: there would never be a substitute for careful plotting and caution.

– 21 –

THE LIBERTY SHIP AT HER BEST

One time during the war I made a "pier head jump." That's seagoing lingo for a last-minute emergency personnel replacement on a ship about to sail.

I had just paid off a ship as chief mate and gone home. The day after I arrived home, the phone rang. It was my nemesis (sometimes known as my keeper), the marine superintendent. He turned on his usual persuasive charm. A ship was lying in Baltimore, fully loaded and ready to sail. The mate had either gotten sick or disappeared. I was ordered to catch the earliest train out of Boston and join the ship.

This guy was really something! He had worked this stunt on me before, and I have no doubt he was working it with other officers daily. That's probably why he was so good at it: constant practice.

Damn it! My two kids were growing up without me. I had become practically a visitor in my own home. But as you've probably already guessed, off I went to Baltimore and still another lousy Liberty ship.

Rattling along in a dirty day coach, I tried to take stock of myself. I was making good money. With overtime, I frequently made more than the skipper. So financially, I was in pretty good shape. My health was excellent, and I had been very, very lucky. A lot of my friends and shipmates were dead, either bombed or torpedoed. Many of my childhood friends who had either enlisted or been drafted in other armed forces had been killed, reported MIA, or maimed. The price I was paying was in my personal life. But, I rationalized, so were millions of other young men. And a lot of them, unlike me, were dead.

Setting all this philosophy and speculation aside, I stepped out into the Baltimore railroad station. I flung my ever-present suitcase, sea bag, and sextant into a cab and directed the cabbie to the Western Maryland piers down on the Baltimore waterfront.

The cab wasn't allowed inside the gates at the entrance to the terminal, so down the pier I walked, loaded with luggage. Up ahead I spotted my new home, another tired old Liberty. They all looked alike: rusty peas in a pod. Yet something about this one looked odd. Instead of her accommodation ladder leading down to the pier, a short brow led from the pier down to the ship. She looked as though she were resting on the bottom. My God, had she sprung a leak?

There was no sign of life about her decks. The whole ship looked deserted. There wasn't even a watch on the gangway.

Finally I saw a Navy guard meandering down the afterdeck. "Hey, where is everybody?" I hollered.

"We're due to ship the merchant crew tomorrow. What few are left are ashore, I guess."

"Where's the gangway watch?"

"That's me."

"Is your officer aboard?"

"Yes, sir. He's asleep."

What kind of damned ship is this! Fuming, I stumbled down the brow to the midship deck and found my way up to the mate's room. It was empty. *Somebody* had to be here. Dumping my stuff on deck, I went looking for the gunnery officer. Sure enough, he was sprawled out on his bunk, asleep.

"Wake up, Guns," I said. Slowly, he came to life.

"Who are you?"

"I'm the new mate. Where is everybody? Where's the Old Man? What kind of cargo is in this ship? Is she overloaded or resting on the bottom?"

"Well, Mister, since the old mate left, the crew, what few there are, come and go as they please. The Old Man is staying at the Lord Baltimore Hotel," he added with a leer. "He has company, if you know what I mean."

"Guns, lend me your waterproof flashlight, will you?" Navy armed guards were equipped with dandy flashlights that worked underwater.

"Over there in my desk."

Armed with his flashlight, I headed back to the gangway. All ships are marked amidships on each side with what is known as a Plimsoll mark. It was named for an Englishman who devised this universal mark to show the legal limit to which a ship could be loaded. Every ship in the world was so marked, and God help whoever loaded her deeper than her allowable mark. Overloading could make the hull and cargo insurance null and void. It could also cause her master and anyone else involved to be heavily fined and lose their tickets.

When the war came along and all ships were painted gray, each ship's Plimsoll mark was deliberately painted over. There was some nonsense about the mark aiding the enemy. But that didn't matter much because when the ship was built, the shipyard chiseled the Plimsoll right into the steel plating.

I went out on the dock and lay down on my stomach. I knew exactly where to find the Plimsoll, opposite the second porthole of the crew's mess room. I rolled up my sleeve and stuck the flashlight beneath the filthy water. I started looking just under the surface, feeling with my other hand for chisel marks. I got way over my elbow before I found them.

The Plimsoll wasn't just a single mark. It was cleverly contrived to have a more descriptive mark. Ours read WNA: Winter, North Atlantic. "W" meant winter, "S" for summer, "T" for tropical. Uppermost was a fresh water mark, for loading in fresh water. We were going into the North Atlantic, meaning that we should have been carrying far less cargo than we were since that was the lowest mark. Somebody was guilty as hell, but it wasn't going to be me that took the rap.

Up the pier I headed, this time for Coast Guard headquarters uptown. Since the war the Coast Guard had taken over the functions of the Steamboat Inspection Service, administered by the Department of Commerce. They ruled the roost as far as merchant shipping was concerned.

By the time I got there, I was steaming. I had had no sleep on the train, no breakfast, and by now it was way past lunch time. I grew even more steamed as I was shunted from one office to another. Each time I launched into my complaint, whoever was listening cut me off and sent me to Lieutenant So-and-So. Finally, one lieutenant heard me out. He looked like a high school kid: dead white skin, delicate, pale hands, all poured into a beautifully fitting tailor-made uniform. It seemed unreal for a kid to be wearing a stripe and a half.

"Now then, Mr. Mate," he said, sounding real, all right, and looking down from his great height of supreme authority. "Maybe you've overlooked the obvious fact that there is a great war raging out there. In wartime we always take calculated risks ... and some that aren't calculated."

My safety valve blew off with a roar. "Me, you little pipsqueak! Why, I've been booting these rotten ships across the oceans since 1931. When 1939 came along and you guys took over, things started getting hairy. Who convoyed us? You and your outfit? No, sir. The British and Canadians took care of us, some of us, at least. I'm one of the lucky ones. I'm still here.

"Where were you then? In grammar school, that's where. Your damned eternal inspections, your nitpicking insistence on 'Regulations.' It was us that took care of the cargo handling gear and the lifeboats. It was our engineers and black gang that kept the plant going. Not you, nosiree.

"What about your damned regulations now? You're willing to sweep it all under the rug and send a dangerously overloaded ship into the North Atlantic in the middle of winter. I'll be on that ship, Junior, with 70-odd more souls. And where will you be? Parked behind that desk on your skinny backside telling some other poor dope, 'There's a war on, don't you know.'"

Oh, I poured it on. All the frustrations I had been hoarding came rushing out. I really made an ass of myself, especially since I was talking to myself. This young squirt was probably as dedicated in his way as I thought I was in mine.

He terminated our "discussion" by saying I could go see his commander. *Now*, I thought, *finally I'll get somewhere.*

Shortly, I was ushered into the commander's presence. Unbelievably, he looked even younger than the lieutenant! He was slicker, though.

"Mister Mate, I'll send an inspection team down at once. We do not, repeat do not, send ships to sea in an unseaworthy condition, war or no war."

"Fine, Commander. When can I expect them?"

"First thing in the morning. Will 0800 hours suit you?"

"Fine, Commander. Thanks for your cooperation." I left, feeling somewhat mollified, and returned to the ship.

Just as I boarded the ship, it dawned on me that I had forgotten an important step in reading the Plimsoll mark. The marks are on both starboard and port sides. If the ship had just a little list, the reading on one side would be different from that on the other side. Proper procedure called for a stage to be rigged on the offshore side, that side to be read, and the two to be averaged.

As soon as I got aboard, I got the gunnery officer to loan me a couple of his kids and we rigged a painting stage over the offshore side. Armed with my trusty flashlight, over the side I went. I'll be damned if the ship wasn't on a perfectly even keel. Both sides read the same. Wow! Were we ever overloaded!

I decided to go up to my room and see if I could find the loading manifest. Hopefully, the previous mate had left it in his desk. Sure enough, it was there. I unfolded it and started to study it, hatch by hatch.

We were loaded with solid iron! We were carrying several thousand tons of steel railroad rails, hundreds of tons of rail spikes, and the splice plates which connect the rails together. Rail car wheels and axles, spare parts for locomotives and gondolas filled the rest of the holds. We were a floating railroad! Or almost floating. A fine cargo to go thrashing around with across the Western Ocean in midwinter.

Wearily, I folded the manifest and cargo plan. I might as well eat supper. I was starved. Entering the saloon, I met the saloon mess man. He looked half drunk, or hung over, or both.

"What's for supper, Mess?"

"Fried eggs and potatoes. Are you the new mate?"

"Damned right I am, and if you don't have a clean, white coat on by breakfast I'll fry you right down the gangway. Tell the steward that goes for him too, if he ever shows up.'

I was halfway through my eggs when a man walked through the door.

"Are you the mate?" he asked.

"Yep. Who are you?"

"I'm captain of the tow boat alongside. We're shifting you over to Cottman's heavy lift pier."

"Now just a minute," I objected. "We don't have steam up. I don't even have a crew to take the lines in."

"I know. Your agent has sent a shore gang to handle your lines, and I've got a second tow boat on the way."

"Why are you shifting us?"

"Damned if I know. Maybe they need this berth."

Shift we did. I felt foolish parading around the bridge while the tow boats pushed us over to a long, open pier over which two enormous lift cranes towered. In no time, we were tied up. I checked our moorings carefully. As deeply laden as we were, if a sudden blow broke us adrift we'd be hard to stop. There was nothing more I could so, so I hit the hay. I needed the rest.

The next morning things seemed more nearly normal. The steward's full department were back on board. The black gang were down below getting ready for sailing. Most of the deck gang had trickled down from the union hiring hall.

I set the bosun to work lowering the booms and battening down for sea. I wondered where the skipper was, then put him from my mind. I had a lot to do. There were stores to check. I had to meet with the purser, assign watches. I also had to find the second and third mates. Some well organized ship this was! Furthermore, we hadn't received our sailing orders yet. But for all I knew the Old Man could be on his way to the ship with them.

About mid-morning I stopped for coffee. In the saloon I met the chief engineer and first assistant. During a lull in the conversation I heard some sort of commotion out on the forward deck. Looking out one of the saloon portholes, I was astounded to see one of the shore cranes hoisting aboard a draft of 12 x 12 timbers. Now what!

Up forward I went. A gang of men were already laying out the timbers on deck on each side of the hatches. Four welders were welding big pad eyes to the deck. Up over the side came a sling load of great turnbuckles and lengths of chain.

"Who's the boss here?" I yelled. "What's going on?" My voice was drowned out by the rumble of a locomotive pulling a string of flatcars out onto the pier. Each car had either a locomotive or tender on it. *It can't be! Not on this ship!*

Just then an Army captain bustled onto the scene, shouting orders and waving a sheaf of papers.

"Captain, what the hell's going on?" I demanded.

"Out of my way," he snapped. "We're loading four locomotives on the forward deck and four tenders on the after deck."

"Oh, no, you're not," I snarled. "This damned ship is almost under water now."

By God, where was that Coast Guard inspection team! Down the gangway I flew, heading for the nearest phone. Furiously I dialed the Coast Guard.

"Give me Commander Johnson."

"Sorry, he is out in the field and won't be available for the rest of the week."

"Out in what field? I'm the one that's out in the field – left field! Let me talk to that Lieutenant, his assistant."

"Sorry, he is with the commander."

I was hopping with rage and frustration. I slammed the phone back on its hook and stormed out of the booth, smack into a blinding apparition dripping with gold braid. Four stripes on his shoulder boards and scrambled eggs all over the visor of his cap. Grabbing opportunity when it knocked, I quickly spilled my tale of woe.

"Captain, we've got to do something," I pleaded. "We'll be going to sea like a damned submarine!" Nothing I said seemed to faze him.

"Oh, we'll be all right, Mister. Besides, it's too late. We're sailing just as soon as the deck load is secured."

Right then, I threw in the towel. If I could have done so without losing face, I'd have packed my bags and quit. Maybe that's what the previous mate had done.

All four locomotives were loaded on the foredeck. They were secured by chains and the big turnbuckles, which in turn were shackled to the pad eyes welded to the deck. The same thing was done for the tenders on the afterdeck. We were so deep in the water you could just step overboard. We resembled a loaded tanker. The only difference was, tankers were supposed to sit low in the water when loaded.

We were ready to sail. All the lashers went ashore, a tow boat pulled alongside, and the bay pilot came on board. Just as I moved to give the order to take in the brow, the Army captain squealed up in a jeep, jumped out, and hurried aboard.

"Here, Mate," he said, thrusting a big, looseleaf notebook at me. It was as thick as a big-city telephone book. "These are the lubricating instructions for your deck cargo. Several pails and drums of oil and grease have been secured on the after deck. This schedule of daily greasing must be adhered to exactly. We wouldn't want these locos to arrive in anything but perfect condition, would we?"

"Oh, dear me, no, Captain. Where are the diving suits?"

"I don't understand."

"Once we get to sea, the entire forward deck will be taking green water aboard. The same goes for the after deck. It'll be a miracle if they don't all go overboard long before we get to where we're going!'

He looked crestfallen.

"Cheer up, Captain," I consoled him. "It's not your fault. If they do go over the side, just send the bill to Lieutenant Commander Johnson, care of the Coast Guard. So long. And give my very best to all the generals."

This Liberty ship had only a light load of locomotives. Fortunately, she wasn't badly overloaded the way we were; her decks are well clear of the water. Note the torpedo nets fitted to heavy-lift booms on her deck.

"All hands, fore and aft." The old familiar cry echoed through the ship. I went forward to take in the lines, the bosun at my heels, a chew of tobacco snuggled firmly in his cheek. While we waited by the lines, I gave him strict orders.

"Bosun, this ship is loaded way too deep and a lot of water is going to come over our bows. I want all the mooring lines stowed below. I want all the cargo booms stripped of their guy tackles. They, too, are to be stored below. Take off all the hatch ventilators and lash them between the winches. Don't swing out the boats. Leave them in their chocks and put round turn lashings on them. Put extra lashings on both accommodation ladders."

He looked at me silently. I continued.

"Cement shut both hawse pipes and make sure the turnbuckles on the devil claws are snugged up. Clear the boat deck of the bags of potatoes, onions, and any other bags or boxes. Have the steward's department stow 'em below. I'll want lifelines rigged on both forward and after decks. We've got about 20 hours down to the Virginia Capes, so keep all hands at it. And, Bosun ..."

He looked at me questioningly, working his jaw.

"After you've finished and sent the hands below, call me. You and the carpenter and I will start on the fo'c'sle head and work our way aft to the poop, making damned sure we're battened down and secure. This is going to be a wet – and I do mean wet – voyage. Can do?"

He shifted his chew and said, "Aye, Mister."

He'd do.

Next day we dropped anchor in Lynnhaven Roads, a fine natural anchorage just inside Cape Henry. Dozens of ships lay at anchor around us, waiting as we were to join an eastbound convoy. The deck gang stayed busy checking all the lashings. I had the other mates at it, too. I knew they thought I was being an old woman about this, but I kept them at it anyway. I had developed a very healthy respect for the Western Ocean in wintertime.

I warned the steward and chief engineer to make sure there was no loose gear anywhere that could go shooting around, smashing things up.

The next day we got a blinker message summoning the Old Man ashore for the convoy conference. Flags, our Navy signalman, hoisted the "Launch Wanted" signal and away went the Old Man, dripping gold braid as usual. I swear he slept in full uniform.

The captain returned late in the afternoon, loaded with the usual pile of instructions: convoy signals, zig zag diagrams, radio listening schedules, etc., etc. Both of us were old-timers, and this was all too familiar. I was pleased that he and I were hitting it off so well. We had never met before, but both of us had been with the line for several years, and had many mutual acquaintances in the company. He had been with them longer than I had, starting as a deck cadet and serving his time well. He was a good seaman.

Late that afternoon we hoisted anchor and steamed out between Cape Charles and Cape Henry, bound for southern France. We fell back quickly into the routine of convoy life: maintain station, strict blackout at sundown. As usual, I studied the other ships through binoculars, comparing their rig to ours.

We were headed north and east, up toward the Great Circle route. By the second day, the winter seas started to make up. As we gradually bore more toward the east, the northwest winds began hurling the seas against our port quarter. They broke green over our bows. As I had predicted, the seas flooded down the forward decks, waist high.

The first thing to carry away was the box containing lubricants for the locos. The whole shooting match just washed over the side. *Good riddance!* Nobody could live through this on the forward deck anyway. It was just as bad aft. I worried about the Navy gun crew quartered all the way aft, under the poop. They were a young, green, devil-may-care bunch, forever running back and forth, not using the lifelines. It was becoming a game with them to see if they could outrun a broaching wave. I kept after the gunnery officer to stop them. He tried, but never did entirely succeed.

We were about two days south and east of Newfoundland when the first real problem hit us. The weather had moderated temporarily. I was in the wheel house standing my usual 4 to 8 watch. It was about 4:30 in the morning and black as pitch: overcast, and no moon. I couldn't see two ship lengths in any direction.

My eyes were getting tired searching for the ship ahead. The windward wheel house door opened and in surged the dim form of Flags.

"What's up, Flags?"

"Mister Mate, would you step outside? I'm hearing a funny noise."

"Sure. Let's go."

I followed him out onto the port bridge wing and crawled after him into the 20 m.m. gun tub. The gale had died down considerably.

"Listen," he said."

By God, I've never heard such a noise! Loud, screeching, it sounded like a giant hand scraping fingernails across a blackboard. It fair tore my ears off, seeming to rise and fall as the ship rolled and pitched.

The pair of us hung over the splinter shield, trying to locate where it was coming from. It definitely was coming from somewhere on the forward deck. We crossed to the starboard side and listened again. Nothing. It was coming only from the port side.

"Great," I said grimly. "Probably one of those damned locomotives coming adrift. If we're lucky, it'll hurl itself over the side and we won't get half drowned or squashed trying to secure it."

That was the best guess we could make. Since we couldn't do anything about it if it were true, we went back to the business of the night.

Dawn comes late in the winter time. When it broke the next morning, I was busy getting the ship back into station through the rolling seas. Flag signals flashed over from the commodore: "Close up. Take proper station. True course to be maintained." It was the same every morning in every convoy.

I was so occupied, I didn't notice the Old Man out on the port wing. He came running into the wheel house, shouting, "Mister, don't you hear that noise?"

"Sure, Captain. I've been listening to it for the last two hours."

"Look down there at the port bulwarks, Mister."

Oh, my God! The bulwark was cracked wide open, and was opening and closing as the ship worked in the rolling sea. The ungodly noise kept on unabated.

The skipper scribbled a message for Flags to blink over to the commodore, telling him our trouble. I asked the Old Man to relieve me and raced for the crew's mess room.

"All hands, bosun. Unlash the lifeboats, uncover them, and swing them outboard. Make sure the plugs are in. Rig the boat ropes. Remove the heavy weather lashings from the rafts. Tell the steward to get any men off watch out of their bunks. All hands are to keep their life jackets with them."

Quickly, I roused out both mates and ordered them to check the contents of the boats, especially their water supply. "Have the men put extra warm clothing on, too," I said. "The deck gang will wear oilskins." *Great windbreakers, oilskins.*

I raced back to the bridge and reported all of this to the captain.

"Guess what, Mister," he said in answer. "The commodore wants to know if we're seaworthy! Seaworthy, he says! How the hell do I know? Do you?"

"No, sir. But at least the crack hasn't gotten any worse."

Flags ducked into the wheel house with another message from the commodore. It wasn't exactly what we wanted to hear. "Fall out of convoy and proceed independently at best possible speed to Halifax. Escort will meet you there."

The Old Man almost had a stroke. "Best possible speed?" he spluttered. "What the hell does that mean? Damn his Limey soul. Quartermaster, come left easy. Half Speed ahead." He turned to me. "Here we go, Mister."

We fell out of the convoy and watched the rest of the ships disappear over the horizon. A terrible, desolate feeling fell over all of us. We were so alone. We were also making only five knots. Talk about a sitting duck!

I pulled the lookout down from the crow's nest and stationed him on the bridge wing. The third mate took the wheel, allowing the helmsman to act as an additional lookout. Guns posted all his men at battle stations, putting them on lookout as well. If a sub spotted us, we were cooked.

Then a surprising thing happened. The crack stopped opening and closing.

"Reduction in speed," the Old Man reasoned. I agreed. We breathed easier then, but not much. I was scared to death, and I knew I wasn't the only one. We were a prime target and we all knew it.

Somehow we made it to Halifax. None of us went to bed on that trip, just napped in our clothes wherever we happened to be. For the first time in a thousand years, the weather remained perfect. Slight seas and just a light breeze prevailed, unheard of in the Western Ocean in mid-winter.

It wasn't until we raised land that a Canadian corvette came out to meet us. "Welcome," she blinked. "Follow me." And we did, right into Bedford Basin where we dropped the hook. Safe and sound at last. It sure was a great feeling.

The steward did himself proud that night. He spread out a turkey dinner with all the fixings, even mincemeat pie!

The crash of something colliding with us jarred me awake before daylight. It was the first time in a long while that I had taken my clothes off and really let go. Still in a stupor, I dragged my clothes on and stumbled out on deck. It was freezing cold and dark. My first thought was that some ship had dragged her anchor and drifted down on us. Visions of smashed lifeboats, propeller and rudder gone, holed below the water-line, swam through my head. I had become the consummate pessimist in those bleak days.

Hearing voices up forward, I slid down the ladder to the foredeck. There was some sort of large craft tied up on the port side. Men were running around on her deck throwing up heaving lines to our deck.

I bumped into the third mate. "What the hell's going on, Mister?"

"Mr. Mate, that's a floating heavy lift barge, here to remove the locos."

"Well, God bless me, Mister, that's the best news I've had since I arrived in Baltimore. In fact, it's the only good news. Good riddance. They never should have been loaded in the first place."

Things were looking up. I went back midships to the saloon. The mess boy was dozing in the captain's seat.

"Mess, where's the coffee?"

He opened one insolent eye and drawled, "Right in front of you. Help yourself."

One of these days, I thought, *I'll fix this bird's clock. That is, if he doesn't poison me first.* And he would, too, in a minute. I wasn't too well liked on this cruise ship. No matter. The big thing was, we were getting rid of those damned locomotives.

"What's for breakfast, Mess?"

"The usual."

I should know better.

The skipper appeared for breakfast. He was as overjoyed as I was when I gave him the news.

"Mister, without the deck cargo, if we don't have serious structural damage we shouldn't be here too long. What's for breakfast?"

"Don't ask."

Right after breakfast I went back to the forward deck. Canadian workers were releasing all the turnbuckles holding the locomotives down. Others were rigging the hoisting slings. In short order, the hoisting engine huffed to life and swung the first monster out over the side. The derrick barge was shifted forward, abreast of 1 hatch, and the second locomotive went over the side.

I felt a tap on my shoulder and turned around. It was the Old Man. He had three civilians with him. The first one he introduced was from the American Bureau of Shipping. The second was from the War Shipping Administration and the third from the Canadian Government Bureau.

"Mister, if you'll open #3 hatch, these gentlemen want to assess the extent of our damage."

I blew my whistle for the bosun and told him to open up the after end of #3. When it was open, we all piled down the ladder into the 'tween deck. The bosun sent down a couple of cluster lights. Our guests prowled everywhere, constantly writing in little notebooks. They were a very thorough trio. They scraped every weld clean. I stuck my nose between every frame right behind them, studying both the frames and the shell plating for signs of fracturing. After what seemed a long time, up the ladder they went.

Nosy me. "What's the verdict, gents?"

"We'll be in touch with your captain as soon as we draw our conclusions. Good day to you."

Off they went in their launch. There was nothing to do but wait it out. I put in the rest of the day prowling the ship, sticking my snoot into everyone's business but my own. To tell the truth, I was uneasy. I don't ordinarily subscribe to premonitions, but I had one this time. A big one. About what? I didn't know. There was just this strong feeling of something ominous. *Best to put it aside,* I told myself. Easier said than done.

At supper my appetite deserted me. The Old Man sat down opposite me and downed an enormous meal. Belching contentedly, he leaned forward and peered at me.

"Out with it, Mister. Something's bugging you. What is it?"

"Captain, I wish I knew."

"Cheer up. We're going to get a clean bill of health. Things looked pretty good to me, down there in #3."

"Yeah, they did to me, too. But I just can't shake this feeling."

"I've got just the cure for you. Come on up to my room. I've got

My heart wasn't in it, but I went along. We had two or three good snorts. I was poor company, though, and didn't stay long.

"Good night, Skipper," I said. "Thanks for the booze. And thanks for your concern."

The next morning I was up forward as usual. A gang of long-shoremen had topped the #3 booms and were shifting cargo in the 'tween decks away from the port side shell plating. About midmorning a gang of ship repairmen arrived in a big work boat. They proceeded to hoist aboard the biggest turnbuckles I ever saw, each the diameter of a five-gallon pail and three or four feet long. Welders were welding enormous pad eyes on the deck abreast #3 hatch. The same thing was going on down in the 'tween decks on the port side. When all the turnbuckles were in place, straddling the cracked area, they were simultaneously tightened. Little by little, the ship was dragged together. Heavy stiffeners were welded in place. It was a fine piece of work.

While this was going on, I noticed that the heavy lift barge with the two locomotives on it was still alongside. I went looking for the superintendent.

"Say, when are you going to remove the two locos from the starboard side and the four tenders from aft?"

"We're not removing anything," he said. "As soon as the welders finish and the work's approved by the A.B.S. man, we'll be hoisting the two locos back aboard."

"Well I'll be damned to hell and gone! Here we almost broke in two out there, and now we're right back where we started!" I moaned and ranted to everyone I could get to listen. I practically got down on my knees to the Old Man.

"Mister, we'll be OK," he assured me. "These people are experts. Trust them."

I have never been so frustrated in my life. One voice crying in the wilderness. That's all I was.

And so they did it. They hoisted the damned things aboard again, chained them down, and away we went in another convoy. I hated to admit it, but we crossed the Atlantic without incident, steamed through the Straits of Gibraltar to Marseilles where we discharged our floating railroad.

When we steamed back home, I promptly paid off. My luck had held in spite of my pessimism and dire predictions. I didn't know how well it was still holding. When the ship sailed on her next voyage to Murmansk with another mate, she was torpedoed and sank.

After the war, we all heard tales of Liberty ships breaking in two. Various theories were put forward. One seemed to prove that the steel used in their construction had either too much or too little manganese, causing the metal to crystallize in cold weather or cold water. Another held that the ships were driven too hard in heavy weather, keeping up with the convoy being more important than prudent seamanship. As far as I know, overloading was never advanced as a possible cause. Needless to say, I have my own theory about that.

– 22 –

SAILOR'S LUCK

I've often mentioned what good luck fell my way both before and all during the war. It held long afterward, too. Two particular pieces of luck stand out in my mind.

I was chief mate on a Liberty ship about midway in the war. We had just returned from a run across the North Atlantic and were tied up to the dock, safe and sound. The fear of enemy spies reporting ships, cargoes, and destinations was rife. Therefore a vessel's destination was very hush-hush, sometimes not announced until at sea. But we had become adept at guessing our destination by the type of cargo being loaded.

The day after we docked, a swarm of ship repairmen descended on us. Some of them started insulating the deck steam lines feeding the cargo winches. Others started ripping out the walls in the staterooms while more came behind them with insulation. They even removed the radiators in the rooms, insulating the pipes. The handwriting on the wall was plain to me: we were bound for Murmansk.

Murmansk, located in Russia around the northern tip of Norway up in the Arctic Circle, was a fearsome place to take a ship in those days. Not only were there German submarines, but Norway, which had been captured by the Krauts, was a perfect base for their Stutka dive bombers. On top of that, the temperature of the waters was in the 30s. A seaman didn't live more than a few minutes if his ship was sunk.

Old Stalin was hounding both Churchill and Roosevelt for war material, so convoy after convoy headed for Murmansk, nearly always with disastrous results. The bottom of the ocean up there was carpeted with ships, freighters, and their escorts. What crew was left on our ship took all this pretty philosophically. That we were going to Murmansk was a fact. We would get through OK, we thought.

The mate's room on a freighter is also his office, and a busy place it is. On those Libertys it was only as big as a large closet. My room looked as if a bomb had hit it. By now all the walls were torn out, pipes were strewn on deck, there was no heat, and it was wintertime. It's a custom on all ships under repair and not feeding to pay a daily "shore subsistence" to the crew. That supposedly provided enough money to pay for meals and lodging ashore. Since conditions aboard were intolerable for me, up I went to the port captain's office and requested shore subsistence. He scoffed at the idea and suggested I sleep in the ship's hospital, a dingy, stinking hole. I got on my high horse and shot my big mouth off.

"I'm chief officer and I'm damned if I'll stoop to bunking in the hospital!"

Things got pretty hot between us and before I knew it they reached the point of no return. Neither of us would back off. The next thing I knew, I'd quit. Back to the ship I went, fuming. I packed my suitcase and seabag, grabbed my sextant from the chart room, and was off for home. My big mouth!

Two weeks later the Boston agent for the steamship company phoned. All was forgiven, he said. There was a ship waiting for me. Back I went, of course. As soon as I got back, the first thing I did was to catch up on the latest company gossip. *God Almighty!* The ship I had walked off of had sailed with a new mate. She got about three days east of Newfoundland when the Germans caught up with her. At 4:30 in the afternoon a torpedo hit her abreast of #3 hatch, just forward of the bridge. The chief mate was out on the wing of the bridge, on his 4 to 8 watch. He was blown overboard and never seen again. For once, my big mouth had saved my life.

Another significant piece of luck happened on April 16, 1947. I had completely forgotten the significance of that date until 30 years later when I read in detail what happened then. I was idly scanning the magazine section of the Sunday paper. My eye was caught by a picture and article describing what happened that day.

Some weeks before the event, I was given command of a Liberty ship lying in Boston. A few days after I reported aboard, she got orders to sail for New York. The war was over and shipping was slacking off. Off we went, in ballast. Arriving in New York, we bunkered and sailed for Galveston, Texas, for orders. We had a fine trip south. Good weather all the way was a godsend, because there was not a stick of cargo in her and we were light.

We made a fast passage to Galveston. Fast, that is, for a weary old Liberty ship. With the ship secured to the dock, I went up to the agent's office and received orders to proceed up the Houston Ship Channel to Texas City. There we were to load a full cargo of grain for Emden, Germany.

The chief mate put all hands to work cleaning the holds for grain. We arrived at the grain elevator and commenced loading. Because this ship had carried grain on her previous voyage, all the shifting boards were in place and in good condition. Loading grain is fast work anyway with three or four spouts pouring grain into the holds.

That evening after supper, the agent came flying down to the pier. Hurrying to my room he told me there was a very good possibility of the Seamen's Union going on strike the next day. If my ship got caught in a safe harbor by a strike, she would be tied up for the duration. If we got to sea, the strike couldn't affect us.

He and I ran down the gangway and up to the office of the grain elevator superintendent. The agent persuaded him to put more spouts aboard and increase the volume of grain pouring into the holds. He agreed, and by midnight all holds were full and trimmed. The feeders were filled, too. The minute the spouts swung ashore, I called for all hands, fore and aft. The mate came piling up to the bridge, complaining bitterly.

"Captain, all the hatches are wide open and the booms are swinging. We can't sail until the ship is secured for sea."

He was right, of course. No well-managed ship ever leaves the dock until "in all respects ready for sea." However, I wasn't about to get caught in a long strike.

"Mister," I said, "there's a tow boat alongside and the pilot's on the bridge. Pull up the gangway and let go, fore and aft. Keep all hands and secure for sea. If you're not done by the time we reach the Galveston breakwater, you can finish out in the Gulf of Mexico. Let's go!"

That was midnight, the 15th of April, 1947.

The poor mate worked all hands until breakfast, then the sea watches took their turn. It wasn't until the following day that Sparks brought me a brief news bulletin telling of the tragic explosion that blew Texas City right off the map. The French ship loaded with ammonium nitrate fertilizer that blew first was berthed right near us. Had we been there, we'd have gone sky high. Nobody would have survived.

As I look back on my career at sea, I realize I had to have been the luckiest seaman ever to have sailed.

Yet my log book reflects none of this. It says simply:

> "Galveston for orders. Loaded full load of wheat, Texas City."
> "Departed Texas City, midnight April 15, 1947, bound for Emden, Germany on the Great Circle route."

There was a lot unsaid between these brief entries.

On April 16, 1947, the ammonium nitrate fertilizer-laden French freighter Grand-camp exploded at the Texas City, Texas, dock with a force more powerful than the bombs at Hiroshima and Nagasaki. In a chain reaction, two miles of waterfront oil refineries, tin smelters, and tanks of chlorine gas, sulphur, and nitrate also exploded or caught fire, sending up gigantic roils of smoke and flame. Huge ships were blasted out of the water, people in downtown Texas City were hurtled through the air, and windows were shattered 10 miles away in Galveston. In all, 462 people died, 3000 were injured, and 50 remained missing.
The author took his freighter full of grain out of this dock only hours before the explosion. Here, with the flames still raging, the Coast Guard cutter Iris at lower left is pouring water into the inferno at the dock.

Another time when my luck was holding fast didn't come to light until 40 years later. I was reading Captain Moore's outstanding book, *A Careless Word – A Needless Sinking.* In there I found out for the first time that over 40 American ships were either mined, bombed, or torpedoed in the Mediterranean from 1943-44. I was shuttling around the Med all that time, right in the middle of it. How many other ships and shipmates went down on my North Atlantic runs, I don't know. I guess I don't want to know.

Another stretch of luck carried me through the Normandy Invasion. To me, doing those runs was a piece of cake, even though we griped a lot and conditions were often bad. We all knew it could have been far worse for us than it was. Much later, I learned just how bad it was. Twelve American ships were torpedoed, bombed, or mined during that action:

SS *Louis Kassuth* – torpedoed, English Channel, 8/24/44.

SS *H.G. Blasdell* – torpedoed off St. Catherine's Point 8/29/44, 76 killed.

SS *James A. Farrell* – Torpedoed off St. Catherine's Point 6/29/44, 4 killed.

SS *John A. Trentlen* – torpedoed off St. Catherine's Point 6/29/44, 10 injured.

SS *Lee S. Overman* – mined off Le Havre 11/11/44.

SS *William L. Marey* – torpedoed by German E-boat off Juno Beach, at anchor, 8/7/44.

SS *Charles Morgan* – bombed off Utah Beach 6/10/44, 1 killed.

SS *Charles W. Elliott* – struck two mines off Juno Beach 6/28/44.

SS *Edward House* – torpedoed off St. Catherine's Point 6/29/44.

SS *Frances C. Harrington* – mined off Juno Beach 6/7/44.

SS *Sea Porpoise* – torpedoed off Utah Beach, 7/5/44.

SS *Theodore Parker* – mined off Humber River, 11/16/44. Repaired and returned to service. The *Parker*, years later, became my last command.

I knew nothing about these sinkings at the time. When I found out, I wondered how many British and Allied vessels went down also.

Today, we would probably find out such things in an instant by satellite communication. But then our sources of information were limited to scuttlebutt while in port. At sea, gossip passed throughout the convoys by Navy signalmen with blinker lights. It was crude and it was slow. In retrospect, because it was such awful news, perhaps that was just as well.

Some are weatherwise,
Some are otherwise.

Benjamin Franklin

– 23 –

TROUBLES IN COPENHAGEN

Sometimes my problems involved the entire crew. That's what turned one voyage to beautiful Copenhagen into one that I could have just as easily done without.

It was midwinter, bitterly cold and miserable the day we docked at the Langelinie Piers. Copenhagen's most famous statue, "The Little Mermaid," perched on a rock in the inner harbor just a short distance away.

Prior to docking, the mate, chief engineer, and I had made the usual search for contraband and the appropriate entries in the official log book. As usual, we had a full load.

Immediately after docking, longshoremen swarmed aboard and got busy rigging the booms and opening the hatches for discharging. Our agent, Axel Petersen, and I were having coffee in the main saloon. The chief mate, Mr. French, came slamming through the door.

"Captain, about 15 Customs men have just come aboard, all loaded down with shovels. They've chased all the longshoremen ashore and are down in #3 lower hold digging in the coal."

Mr. Petersen and I immediately headed for #3 hatch. The head Customs honcho was leaning over the hatch coaming, yelling at his men. Petersen nudged me to keep quiet as he engaged the man in conversation. Finally, turning to me, he translated.

"Captain, he claims to have received a tip that there is considerable contraband hidden on your ship."

"Baloney," I said. "We searched the ship before we ever docked. Naturally, we couldn't paw through 10,000 tons of coal, but we sure searched everything else."

Just then there was a commotion in the hatch. We peered down through the coal dust. By God, they were lifting out case after case of cigarettes. *Boy, oh boy!* Here was big trouble. It's practically universal that whenever undeclared contraband is discovered, the fine is double the value plus confiscation of the goods.

Further, if the guilty party is not apprehended the fine is levied against the ship. As the master is the legal representative of the ship, that meant me! My owners, being very proper, conservative Bostonians, would never pick up the tab. They'd dump it right back in my lap and out of my pocket it would come. *I'd better move fast!*

Rounding up the mate, I sat down and we worded a strong notice to be posted in the crew's mess room and the officers' saloon: "Guilty party or parties must come forward at once. Severe disciplinary action will be taken unless ... " etc., etc.

The mate was too optimistic. "I'll catch the bastards, Captain. Leave it to me. I've got ways."

"Now wait a damned minute, Mister. This is a strong union crew, and I don't want any of your rough stuff. You start any of that and the union will hang us when we get home. We've got to work with the head instead of the strong arm. Put on that notice that the guilty ones have 24 hours to own up. After that, don't be surprised at anything. That'll start 'em squealing on each other." Or so I thought.

The next morning Mr. Petersen came aboard with the bad news. I was required to appear at the Customs House before noon and pay a fine which amounted to $670 in American money. He was prepared to advance me the amount in Danish kroners, charging the same to the ship's account. I could reimburse the ship upon arrival home. Having no choice, uptown I went and paid His Majesty's Danish government the 670 clams.

On the way back to the ship, I kept getting madder and madder. I even started talking to myself. *Some crew I've got! The ungrateful bastards, I'll fix 'em. I'll catch the guilty snakes if it's the last thing I ever do!*

When I got back, the mate was waiting for me at the gangway. "Captain, we've got more trouble."

"Yeah? More cigarettes?"

"No, the longshoremen are threatening to go on strike."

"Come on up to my room and fill me in where we can talk without the damned crew evesdropping."

These Liberty ships had been designed to carry a naval gun crew of 27 men and one commissioned officer. Quarters for the enlisted men were built all the way aft, complete with showers and heads. After the war, when there was no further use for them, the pipes were drained to prevent freezing and the doors were padlocked.

Now the longshoremen had broken the locks and were using the latrines even though there was no water to flush them with. They had also taken over the living quarters, eating, drinking, and smoking during the frequent discharging delays while they waited for loaded lighters to be towed away and empty ones brought alongside. All hatches were discharging, but the lighters just couldn't keep up and I guess they figured they'd take advantage of a good situation.

Mr. Petersen and the mate and I headed aft to look the situation over. What a mess! What a stink!

"Mister, put new locks on these doors," I ordered. "If necessary, have the first assistant weld them shut. Mr. Petersen, tell these dirty apes they've got five minutes to get their asses out of these quarters."

The next thing I knew, Mr. Petersen and two loutish-looking Danes were hollering and yelling at each other to beat the band. Finally Mr. Petersen turned to me, explaining that these were the stevedore superintendent and the union representative. They insisted I make the gun crew quarters available to them or they'd strike the ship. Their argument was that the ship was berthed at an open pier with no warehouses and that it was an unusually cold winter. The men had to have shelter. I countered by pointing out that they never even asked, just broke in and took over, making a terrible mess to boot.

They walked off and there we lay, strike-bound. What next?

At supper, I spelled out my smuggler-catching strategy to the mate. By law, whenever a ship is in safe harbor, the master is required to open the slop chest once a week to allow the crew to buy tobacco and cigarettes.

"Well now, Mister, we're just going to break that law. No more smokes until somebody owns up. That'll fix the buggers. Put up a notice to that effect."

Next morning all three union stewards were banging on my door.

"Ah, gentlemen," I said, "what's bothering you?"

Oh, did they rant and rave! They'd blackball the ship when we got home, they swore. They'd blackball *me*. No union man would step foot on a ship where I was master! On and on they went.

When they finally ran out of breath, I told them that when we got home they could do their damnedest and be damned to them, but here in Copenhagen I was the boss. Just to rub it in, I observed that maybe they were raising such a stink because they were the guilty ones. And well they might be, too. Anyway, I said, this was only the beginning. Tomorrow I was taking another step.

Actually, I was in a pickle with my ship on strike. My owners would raise holy hell when they heard about it. And I was already out 670 bucks. To make matters worse, Mr. Petersen showed up the next morning with a copy of Copenhagen's leading newspaper. There we were on the front page. Mr. Petersen was reluctant to translate the copy, saying only that it was most uncomplimentary toward me.

I stormed up to my office and dashed off a rebuttal, insisting that Mr. Petersen take it to the offices of the newspaper. Sure enough, they printed it the next day.

But that still didn't catch my smugglers. I had to figure out something else to do. Another maritime law says that whenever a ship is in port over 24 hours, the crew shall be given a "draw" on their wages not to exceed half of what they'd earned to date.

I called for the first mate again. "Mister, put up another notice: no draw until the guilty ones come forward. That'll fix 'em good. Copenhagen is one of the best liberty ports in the world."

"Captain, you can't! We'll have a mutiny on our hands and this time the union will crucify us."

"Put it up, Mister. I've reached the point of no return."

For two days we were at a stalemate. The crew went wild. No smokes, no money. The longshoremen were parading out on the dock, flinging curses at me whenever I appeared on deck, puffing cigarettes just to torment the crew. The stalemate showed no signs of breaking. Mr. Petersen was holding daily meetings with the longshoremen's union reps. I was hiding out in my room, keeping the pressure on, refusing to talk to the crew's delegates.

It got so bad I worried that the steward would poison me with his slop that wasn't fit to eat anyway. So I took to going ashore every afternoon. I'd amble up to the Hotel d'Angleterre where they had a nice bar. I'd dump a few, then have a leisurely supper.

Two days after the "no draw" I told the mate to pull in the gangway. No more shore leave. Boy, my neck was out a mile this time!

Docked, idle – no more shore leave at the Langelinie pier
until somebody confesses.

The storm that had raged over the "no slop chest and no draw" was nothing compared to the wrath that now descended on me. I had to stop parading around puffing smoke at the crew. I was honestly afraid they'd try to dump me overboard.

The poor mate was wringing his hands, pleading for me to give in. I sympathized with him. He was in a terrible position. He had had a good rapport with the entire crew, and they really put out for him. Now he was the enemy as much as I was.

Unable to get any further on board, I went ashore for a while. That afternoon I was sitting at the bar in the hotel, idly thumbing through a *Time* magazine the bartender had loaned me. In through the door came a most attractive dame. She took a stool a little way down from me and ordered an aperitif. I, of course, was looking her over out of the corner of my eye. She was very stylishly dressed, obviously not an "on the make" barfly. She wore a fashionable little hat with a black veil covering her face.

While I watched, she extracted a cigarette from her purse. Sticking it through the veil, she touched a match to it. *Pfft!* In an instant the veil flashed into flame which went streaking up her face and into her hat and hair. Quick as a mongoose I swatted her with the magazine to put the fire out. At the same time, the bartender flung a pitcher of water at her, soaking me instead. The place was bedlam.

The poor woman was on the verge of hysterics. Between the bartender and me, we got a hooker of brandy into her and she quieted down somewhat. Then she got a glimpse of herself in the back bar mirror and started wailing again. All the hair on the front of her head had been burned off.

It took a couple of more brandies, but at last she quieted down and we got to talking. She spoke excellent English, though with a heavy Polish accent. She was a concert pianist, in Copenhagen to give a concert. Her agent had gotten his wires crossed and the affair was scheduled for three days hence. So here she was, checked into the hotel with nothing to do but wait until the hall was available.

Figuring that fortune was smiling on me, I asked her for dinner. She accepted and off we went to Copenhagen's finest restaurant, Wivex What a place! It rated the tops in northern Europe and the astronomical prices reflected it. But what the hell. Nothing ventured, nothing gained. We waded through about a month's pay. Then on we went to a plush nightclub.

While winding our way back to the d'Angleterre, like a fool I suggested a repeat performance for the following night. She accepted. Going up in the elevator, I congratulated myself on being such a Lothario. She unlocked her door, slipped through, then *Clang!* As I heard the bolt and chain latch into place, I came back to earth with a resounding thud.

Walking back to the ship, half frozen and broke, I resolved that some way, somehow, I had to get out of the next night. Before I went off to sleep I had my answer.

Our young third mate was a super lover boy. If you didn't believe it, you had only to ask him. His incessant boasting about his conquests were enough to make me sick. I had listened to so much of it at the dining table that I was thinking of banishing him to the engineers' table. To make it worse, he was more good looking than any man had a right to be: black, curly hair, a little black mustache, tall and lean. Oh, he had it all. Trouble was, he just wouldn't shut up about it. But now I was about to fix him for good.

At breakfast, very casually I told him just parts of the events of the previous evening, stressing the pianist's beauty and charm and how amenable to any suggestions she was. I could see his eyes start glistening. Then I let it drop that I was tuckered out and wished I didn't have to go out again tonight. He snapped up the bait like a starving shark.

"Captain, if you'd like, I'll fill in for you. I'm not doing anything tonight."

"That's very kind of you, Mister, because she's expecting to go out. Matter of fact, she said she would buy a new dress for the occasion. Now here's how we'll handle it. I'm supposed to meet her in the bar at the Hotel d'Angleterre at 5:30. At exactly 5:45, you come flying through the door and say there's been an emergency on the ship and the mate wants me right away. I'll introduce you, duck out, and you're on your own."

It worked like a charm. He showed up right on time and put on a great show about the "emergency" back on the ship.

Next morning at breakfast I sneaked a look at him. He had a face that would sour milk.

"Nice evening, Mister? Hope you went to Wivex. Marvelous place."

"Aah," he snarled, flinging down his napkin and storming out.

The mate asked, "What's the matter with Lover Boy?"

I told him the whole story and he laughed heartily.

"Captain, in such a discouraging, gloomy week, that's like a ray of sunshine."

That same day Mr. Petersen reached a compromise with the longshoremen's union. We'd let them use the Navy quarters but not the heads or showers. I also realized I wasn't going to catch the smugglers, so I opened the slop chest, gave a draw, and put the gangway down again.

I never did get a satisfactory end to this matter. On our next trip we were ordered to Aarhus and Kosoer in Denmark for discharging. Both are just small towns. When we docked at Aarhus, there was old faithful Mr. Petersen. He came into my office, beaming. With a flourish he plunked down a bottle of good Danish aquavit and said, "Two large glasses, my good Captain. I have good news."

We each had a snort. Then, grinning from ear to ear, he reached into his briefcase and slapped down a big handful of Danish kroners.

"How about that? I was able to pull a few strings at the Customs House and got your fine reduced by two-thirds. This is all yours."

"That sure is good news, Mr. Pete, but what am I going to do with Danish money? This port and the next one have little to offer."

We mulled over the matter while having a couple more belts of aquavit.

"I've got it!" I shouted, a new scheme suddenly forming. "Give the money to Mrs. Petersen. She's got good taste. Have her invest it all in Royal Copenhagen china. Next trip we'll surely hit Copenhagen. I'll hide the stuff real good and smuggle it ashore in the States."

He agreed and stuffed the dough in his briefcase. But from that day to this, I have never been back to Denmark. By now, that beautiful Royal Copenhagen china has reached the antique stage and is probably resting in the china closet of one of Mr. Petersen's daughters.

Praise the sea
But keep on land.
Proverb

– 24 –

JUST ANOTHER VOYAGE

Once again we were bound for a Scandinavian port with a full load of coal. It seemed as though northern Europe had an insatiable appetite for coal once the war was over. I had been running back and forth for the past couple of years from Norfolk or Baltimore to either Sweden or Denmark. Back home I'd go with a full load of iron ore from Narvik, Norway, in the winter and from Lulea, Sweden, in the summer.

Each trip, both westbound and eastbound, we transited Pentland Firth between the north coast of Scotland and the Orkneys. It was a lousy place to take a ship, but it saved a good day's run. Every trip so far I had struck the Firth just right, gaining clear weather and a slack tide. This time, however, it was not to be.

My log book entries for this trip are unusually sparse. And well they might be. It took me three damned days to get through. It was the fog that got me.

Aug. 18 – "0100 – Cape Wrath bearing 180 – Course 090 T, speed 10 knots."

"0500 – Thick fog – steaming 090 T, 270 T between Strathen and Dunnet – speed slow."

The weather had started to worsen when we came up to Cape Wrath, but we heard the lighthouse horn. Sparks had reported intermittent fog forecast for the area, but there was nothing intermittent about this. It was thick! We couldn't see the fo'c'sle head. *It'll clear up shortly,* I consoled myself. *Besides, there's no wind, the sea's calm. It's just a temporary delay.* So I thought.

The long, slow hours crept by. All day, all night, and all day again I prowled the bridge like a caged animal. *It's got to clear soon!* I was driving poor Sparks nuts asking for more and more weather reports. I should have known better. This godforsaken part of the world always had fog.

Only once in a while was there a clear day or two. I'd just had better luck than I deserved for the past two years. What to do?

We were coming up to the third day. Cold sandwiches and gallons of coffee were finally letting me down. My legs were trembling. My feet were so swollen I had taken to padding around in my stocking feet. I was just about at the end of my rope. The mate and I were poring over the British chart of the area. Poor bottom, too deep to anchor. *Damn!*

The mate nudged me and stuck the dividers into a spot to the northeast. By God, there was a tiny little spot with a sandy bottom. It was no more than a ship's length in diameter and not quite as deep as the water around it.

"Mister, we'll get a good RDF bearing of Sule Skerry. We'll have the second mate on the fathometer. When we're right over the spot, just creeping along, you'll back off the starboard anchor nice and easy and *Presto!* I'll get a couple of hours' sleep."

And it came to pass. There we were, all 10,000 tons of us, at anchor practically in the Atlantic Ocean.

"Mister," I said, "I'm going to collapse on the chart room settee. If the sea starts to make up, get me up if you have to use a club." Sounds crazy, but I had no choice. I was exhausted. My last thought before passing out was, "What will the crew think? Anchored in bad water and thick fog and he goes to sleep!"

Three hours later the mate grabbed me by the shoulders and sat me upright. "It's clearing, Captain. The carpenter's got the anchor coming up."

It's amazing what three hours of sleep will do. I hobbled out onto the bridge and away we sailed. I must say, that damned Pentland Firth showed me who was boss.

We shot through the rest of the Firth in fine style and squared away for the Skaw. Sparks brought me a message from our charters nominating Oxelosund, Sweden, as our port of discharge. Located south of Stockholm, it's indicated as a small port according to the Sailing Directions, fairly easy to enter.

Down the Kattegat we slogged, making our usual 10-1/2 knots. The sea was calm and the air balmy. When we got down near Copenhagen the peacefulness broke when we damn near collided with a ferry boat running from Malmo, Sweden, to Copenhagen. These ferries run day and night, acting just like the Staten Island ferries in New York Harbor – as though they own the sea. I guess most ships automatically steer clear of them, because they sure don't give way.

Soon enough, we picked up a pilot and threaded our way through countless islands to the port of Oxelosund. It's a tricky business navigating through these islands. These waters freeze solid almost every winter. Removing hundreds of buoys each fall, then setting them out again each

Discharging coal in Oxelosund into coal barges from the Theodore Parker. The coal is going to electric light plants all over Northern Europe.

spring, is just too big an undertaking. The Swedes solve the problem by setting out only a few buoys, filling in the rest of the channels with saplings. Right – saplings: small trees, anchored. Not too bad an arrangement in clear weather, but they must be hell at night. There are no lights on them, of course. And it gets pretty confusing because side channels are forever branching off and all saplings look alike.

On the way in, the pilot very kindly invited me to supper at his home. After we tied up, he waited while I changed into my shore-going suit. Down the gangway we went, and my education in that Socialist government began.

The pilot walked over to a very nice car, unlocked it, and motioned me in. As we drove out of the docks I complimented him on his fine car. He shrugged. I remarked that Oxelosund was such a small port, he must have plenty of leisure time. Again a shrug. I asked him if he had another job during the long winter when the port was frozen in.

He looked at me in surprise. "My job is a Federal one. It pays me a very adequate salary until retirement, whether there are any ships to pilot or not." Some job, handling a dozen or so ships a year.

He pointed out his home up ahead. It was magnificent. It was made of natural wood, hanging out over the water on a high, wooded point. The kitchen was right out of a magazine, all stainless steel with all the latest gadgets. And this was way back in the late 40s!

He introduced me to his wife. He also introduced me to his three daughters, all of whom had braces on their teeth.

"The dentists must keep you broke."

"Not at all," says he. "No Swede pays anything for dental or medical care."

"Who does?"

"The king, or government."

Socialism has serious drawbacks, but I envied him. Swedes sure seem to have things going for them. And they stayed out of two world wars to boot.

After a fine supper, served right out over the water, I reluctantly returned to my ship.

The next morning at breakfast, the chief engineer laid a beaut on me. "Captain, tomorrow's Sunday. Let's put the motor lifeboat in the water and have a picnic on one of the islands. We'll get the steward to put up a lunch. We'll have to invite the belly-robbing bastard, but at least he won't be able to poison us, seeing as how he'll have to eat it himself. How about it?"

"Chief, that's the first good idea you've had this trip. Who should we invite?"

"Well, there'll be you and me and the steward. How about the first assistant engineer?"

"And chief mate," I countered. Couldn't let the engineers out-number the deck crew. "And Sparks. That's enough."

"Great," says he. "We'll get underway at 9 o'clock, right after breakfast. That'll give the steward time to put up a fine lunch."

We leaned back, beaming at each other. A fine prospect.

Then an ugly thought intruded. "Now wait a damned minute, chief," I said. "Tomorrow is Sunday. We'll have to pay the bosun and some sailors overtime to rig up the falls to the winches. You know that old skinflint, Norton (the company comptroller) will have a fit and make me pay for it."

"Phooey, Captain. You're a poor schemer. Your education has been sadly neglected. Charge it up to securing boats during heavy weather."

He had such a smug look on his puss that I felt like dunking him in his oatmeal. Only engineers would eat the damn stuff anyway. But it was set. The steward went for the idea and promised a fine feast. The others were discreetly invited and accepted with alacrity. Everything was set for the next day.

Way before breakfast that following morning, the mate had yanked all the surplus junk out of the boat and piled it on deck. While the rest of us were eating breakfast, the steward was loading the boat with enough food for an army. He even had an enormous fresh salad made with Swedish vegetables bought the day before. He had Swedish meatballs, yet, and lots more.

The mate told the bosun that as soon as we lowered the boat he was to rig the falls to # 3 and #4 winches to be ready for hoisting on our return. We screwed the plug into the bottom of the lifeboat and rigged the bow painter forward. Everybody climbed aboard.

"Lower away, bosun!" yelled the mate. Down we went. The falls were unhooked. I spun the engine crank and she fired on the second try. We cast the painter off, engaged the clutch, and away we chugged. I headed for the entrance to the harbor and started following the saplings. Two or three times we headed up side channels, just for the joy of exploring them. It was a beautiful morning, cool and bright with clear sunshine. There I sat with one arm draped over the tiller, lord and master of all I surveyed.

"Say Captain," the chief engineer said, "there's a likely looking island right over the port bow. There's even a little white beach where we can eat."

"Right, chief, coming port easy." Right then and there I did one of the most foolish things of my life. I put the helm over and cut inside one of the saplings. My feeble mind reasoned that they were there for ships, not lifeboats. *Crunch!* The boat lurched and we were hard aground!

Those Liberty lifeboats were made of thin tin, maybe aluminum, tacked together with little rivets at the seams.

"She's leaking! We're sinking and I can't swim!" screeched the chief.

"Shut up. The water's only six inches deep."

He was stamping his feet on a split seam through which water was pouring. Before I could stop him, he ripped off his shirt and stuffed it in the hole. Dear God! We had enough talent in that boat to sail the *Queen Elizabeth* around the world. Both the mate and I held unlimited masters' tickets. Both the chief and first assistant held unlimited chiefs' tickets and Sparks held a first class commercial radio operator's certificate.

What a disgrace! This was my fault. All thoughts of a picnic were abandoned. We started back with the chief planted firmly on the leak, his big feet holding his shirt in place.

Now the cover-up began. We swore each other to secrecy before we got back to the ship. When the boat was hoisted aboard, we wouldn't say a word about the ruptured bottom. On the way home when we hit some bad weather I would make log book entries to show that during a gale #1 lifeboat pounded against her chocks and split a seam.

The trouble with lying is that inevitably one must tell more lies to justify the first one. And so it was here. All the way home we had good weather. In desperation, we resorted to making false weather notations, building up over three days to a full gale. If only I could do it over, I would just tell the truth. The only damage would have been to my damned pride. This was a sorry piece of business indeed. I paid a high price for a picnic that never took place and probably never should have.

But that fat engineer did look damned funny trying to stuff his shirt in the hole with his feet.

A few days later I received word from the ship's agent that upon completion of discharge we were to proceed to Stockholm for bunkers. From there we were bound for Lulea to pick up a full load of Swedish iron ore for Baltimore.

As soon as the last scoop of coal was hoisted, the hatches were battened down. My friend the pilot boarded and off we went, out through those damned saplings, for Stockholm.

It was only a short distance to the pilot station outside the Sharragard, the deep belt of islands that protects the entire coast of Sweden. The Stockholm pilot boarded us for the somewhat longer trip through the islands to Stockholm. The scenery was beyond words. Amid all those wooded islands and rocky shores were hundreds and hundreds of pleasure boats, all finished in natural wood. They looked nothing like boats in the States, which are mostly painted white.

We tied up at the oil docks. There I was told there would be a delay in bunkering. We had arrived in the midst of a major holiday and no pump men were available. Sweden seems to have more holidays than work days. Some country!

The pilot said he'd stay on board overnight, taking us out the following noon. The mate and I decided to take a look at the town. We went on a long walking tour of the cleanest city I've ever been in. The streets, the buildings, everything was spotless.

Feeling the need of a little refreshment, we popped into a nice-looking place and ordered two Scotch and sodas. The waiter explained that Sweden had a sort of Prohibition. If we wanted a drink, we had to order one with a meal.

"But we're not hungry," we protested. "We just had lunch."

The waiter smiled and winked. "Be right back, gents."

Back he came with the two drinks and two plates with lamb chops, mashed potatoes, and green peas.

"Waiter, we told you we're not hungry."

He picked up the plate, and with a flourish turned it upside down. The food stayed right on the plate! It was all made of wood, very cleverly painted.

"There," he said. "That covers the law. You are now having a drink with your food."

So much for the law.

The next morning we finished bunkering. The lines were let go and we headed out through the islands again. It was Sunday and there were even more sailing yachts than before. Hundreds of them were going every which way.

A recent *Rules of the Road* change now gives deep water vessels traveling in a a restricted channel the right of way over pleasure boats. Back then, though, a sailing vessel *always* had the right of way over a steam vessel.

Shortly, a large yawl appeared on our port bow, heading to cross in front of us. She was one of those beautiful natural wood boats. All her sails were set and she was making knots.

"Pilot, how are we going to avoid her? If we come left to pass astern of her, we'll be out of the channel. Is there enough water?"

"No. We've got to hold course. If we don't, we'll run aground."

Hold we did. It was obvious that the big sailboat was trying to pass ahead of us. It was also all too obvious that she wasn't going to make it. She swept under our port bow. What her foolhardy skipper hadn't realized was that our high sides would kill her wind. We were light and high in the water.

All in an instant, her sails went slack. Her momentum carried her just beyond our stem, but when she came in sight under the starboard bow we saw that she was capsized with her masts and sails lying in the water. We could see at least six people either in her cockpit or clinging to her rigging as we swept by.

"We can't stop, Captain. They'll be all right. Plenty of boats are coming to her rescue."

"My God, Pilot, you can't just leave them!"

"Yes, we can. This isn't the first time this has happened. Maybe someday they'll learn to stop playing chicken, as you Americans say."

I made a full report by radio to our Swedish agents and our owners, and made a written report for the pilot to give to the Swedish Coast Guard or whoever he thought should get it. Yet from that day to this I never heard another word about it, not even from my owners. I often think that if we had hit that yawl broadside with our bow, it would have been a tragedy. Undoubtedly, all aboard it would have been killed.

As soon as we got outside the last island, our pilot left us. I rang up Full Ahead and we squared away up the Gulf of Bothnia for Lulea. This body of water is practically landlocked. In this good summer weather it was just as flat as a lake.

Being light, our propeller was half out of the water and made a big, thrashing wake that stretched for miles astern. We were following the usual sapling buoys, relieved every five miles or so by a proper lighted one. The lights weren't needed, though. At this time of year in these latitudes it was daylight all night long. The sun never sets in the summertime.

I spent all my time sitting in my high chair out on the windward bridge wing. It was peaceful except for one thing. When light and going Full Ahead, these ships vibrate something fierce. The smokestack stays and the mast shrouds were flapping and humming like strings on a fiddle. I could feel it through my feet, in my bunk, everywhere. The plates in the dining saloon crept right into my lap if I didn't keep one hand on them. And yet it was a nice feeling because we were making knots instead of bucking weather.

Our bunkering in Stockholm had been carefully calculated right down to the last barrel. As soon as the war was over, chief engineers reverted to their old practice of hiding oil "up their sleeve." Our marine superintendent, Captain Litchfield, a very canny bird and more than a match for a room full of chiefs, had come down hard on the lot of them. He had sent each chief a letter, which they were required to acknowledge, telling them bluntly that the practice would stop at once or they'd be on the beach.

For every ton of oil they hid we sacrificed a ton of cargo, representing a sizable loss of income to the line. I even heard of one chief who, by poring over the ship's blueprints, discovered a blank space underneath the forward fire room bulkhead between the fire room and the double bottom underneath #3 hold. He drilled holes and ran pipes himself. He could hide 30 or 40 tons of oil in it. These chiefs were all like damned squirrels, hiding nuts.

Captain Litchfield was too smart for them, though. He patiently worked through the log abstracts from every ship in the fleet. Thus he established the average fuel consumption for each ship in good weather and bad, loaded, half loaded, or light. Then he calculated the fuel requirements for each voyage, allowing a 20% surplus as insurance that any prudent seaman would be content with. By the same process, he told each chief mate and master exactly how many tons of cargo they were expected to load. Our particular ship had a pretty steady fuel consumption of .7 barrel per nautical mile. So we knew to the ton how many tons of ore we would load in Lulea.

On my first trip to Lulea, I was puzzled by the absence of any reference to pilotage in the *Sailing Directions*. After steaming around for a couple of hours, I found out that pilots didn't board until after the ship entered the harbor.

This time I boldly steamed right in. There was our pilot sitting in his little boat, smoking his pipe and reading his newspaper. Leisurely stuffing the paper in his pocket, he fired up his engine and came alongside. Tying his boat to the ladder, up he came, all business.

"Morning, Captain. Hard left and Half Ahead if you please."

In no time at all we were alongside, all fast. The mate had opened all the hatches before coming alongside, so in a matter of minutes the loading chutes were swung aboard and ore was roaring down into the lower holds.

Lulea is the soul of informality. No going to the Customs House to enter the ship and all of that stuff. We had come from a Swedish port anyway, so what formalities there were occurred at shipside and were brief.

As soon as I could, I was off for town in the best transportation ever. The ship's chandler was a widow, and what a character! She met the ship on an ancient bicycle, getting the steward's order for fresh milk, bread, vegetables, and whatnot. I perched on the rear luggage carrier and off we went, me trying to keep my feet from dragging in the dust of the dirt road. I don't know if other skippers felt it beneath their dignity, but I loved it! There I was, cruising along listening to either broken English or broken Swedish. I felt like a kid again.

With loading proceeding at a fantastic pace, I only had time for one meal ashore. Afterward, I bought my son a "kick sled," a strange sled by our standards. Two long, flexible runners extended way out in back of its little seat. The operator stood on the runners, steering it by shifting his balance. I was told that all through the long, snowy winter such sleds are the principal means of transportation in Sweden.

So much for sightseeing. By now we were loaded deep with almost 10,000 tons of dense, heavy Swedish iron ore, destined for Bethlehem Steel Company's gigantic Sparrow Point steel mill. Located outside of Baltimore, this is the largest tidewater steel mill in the world.

The crew were already busy replacing hatch beams and covers, battening down for sea. We would have to creep out of the harbor at Dead Slow because there were only 12 inches of water under the keel. The chief mate had loaded every last pound the ship could lift. He didn't want Captain Litchfield breathing down *his* neck.

Back down the Gulf of Bothnia we wallowed. Homeward bound – a great feeling. We steamed out of the Gulf, up the Kattegat, across the Skagerrak, back through that damned Pentland Firth, this time in good weather. Finally, we stuck our rusty snout into the Atlantic, bound on the Great Circle track for the States again.

After an uneventful passage, we entered the Virginia Capes bound up for Baltimore. When I first picked up the flashing lights of Cape Henry and Cape Charles in my binoculars, it was raining cats and dogs. The night was pitch black, but in spite of the rain the lights were clearly visible. I put the ship on a Slow bell and kept sweeping the horizon for any sign of the pilot boat's blue light. Twice I had the third mate set off a blue flare signifying "I need a pilot."

At last I spotted a dim blue light. "Great! There she is, Mister. Half Ahead."

"Half Ahead, aye."

It was a cold rain pouring. All I had on was a pair of pants and a khaki shirt so I stayed nice and dry in the wheel house. Slowly we approached the pilot vessel. As we got closer, her blinker started signaling.

"Mister," I hollered at our very young, very new third mate. "Get out there on the light and see what he has to say."

"Captain, I'm not sure I can read blinker."

Damn! All of us who had just gone through a long war had, of necessity, become somewhat adept at flapping the lamp. In convoy, messages flashed throughout the convoy all day long. It was sort of a seagoing party line.

Out I dashed, switched on our big signal light, and acknowledged.

"What ship and where bound?"

"SS *Theodore Parker*, Baltimore," I answered.

"We do not have a Baltimore pilot at present. Follow me and anchor when we signal. We will have a pilot board you from the next outbound vessel."

Back into the wheel house I slogged, soaked to the hide. "Mister," I said to Jack through clenchéd teeth, "my compliments to the chief mate. Have him get the anchor lights ready, then stand by to anchor. And you, Mister, better go back to school. One of the requirements of a deck officer is that he be proficient in the use of the signaling lamp. Move it!" I admit I was rough on him. But hell, I was so cold and wet I could have killed him.

We were still creeping along in the downpour, following the dim blue light. The mate phoned from the fo'c'sle head and said the anchor lights were hoisted, all ready to be plugged in, with both anchors cleared.

That chief mate of mine was a very efficient man. He had drilled the bosun and carpenter in the anchoring procedure like we were on a battleship. They were to hoist both anchor lights, one on the forestay, the other aft. The bosun was to stand by the forward light, the carpenter the after one. The minute they heard the chain rattling out they were to plug in the lights to a deck receptacle. The third mate would snap off the running lights and we'd be at anchor.

Just about then, the pilot boat started blinking. I ran out and acknowledged. "Anchor where you are."

"Stop Engine, Mister. Let go forward."

Down splashed the starboard anchor. The third mate snapped off the running lights. *Damn!* No anchor lights came on.

"Get those anchor lights on, Mister."

"Can't, Captain. The plugs are shorted out by the heavy rain."

Just then, something made me look aft. *Dear God!* There was a ship heading right for us, her red and green side lights gleaming brightly, her range lights right in line, and us with no light at all!

I raced into the wheel house, snapped on our running lights, and blew the danger signal on the whistle. Back I raced to the port bridge wing to watch helplessly as the unknown ship went full astern, her bows slicing by us. *Whew!* She sheared to starboard, missing us by less than a ship's length. She was one of those big, self-unloading coal colliers, running in for Norfolk. She didn't have to stop for a pilot. Those coal boats did all their own piloting.

While all this was going on, the anchor lights suddenly blazed forth, and us with the running lights on while at anchor.

"Mister," I said to Jack. "Get some anchor bearings on the Capes. I'm going below to get some dry clothes on."

When I came back, Jack was plotting our position on the chart. Peeking over his shoulder, the enormity of what had just happened bore down upon me.

First, we had come to anchor without displaying any anchor lights. Second, I had blown the danger signal, which was only permitted in inland waters. Our anchor bearings now showed us outside a line drawn between Cape Charles and Cape Henry, the dividing line between inland and international waters. Third, I had snapped on the running lights while at anchor, an absolute violation of the rules. And last, the anchor lights had come on while we were still showing our underway lights.

In the space of minutes, I had violated at least four Rules of the Road. If that collier had hit us, the inspectors would have buried me for a thousand years. Wearily, I straightened up and pondered: *Am I in the wrong business? Maybe I should go ashore and raise chickens.*

As we lay at anchor, waiting for a pilot, I reflected on the damage I'd done on the voyage now ending: ripped the bottom out of the motor boat, swamped and capsized a sailboat full of people, and now damn near got sunk while anchored. What little egotism I ever had leaked out forevermore.

Shortly after dawn an outbound vessel dropped off her Baltimore pilot and boarded us for the trip up the bay. He started moaning about overwork, up all night, no sleep, a hell of a way to make a living. On and on he went.

"Oh, for God's sake, shut up," I said unfeelingly. "You think you're the only one who has troubles with these lousy old ships? Move over, Chum!"

"Let The Lower Lights Be Burning"

Old hymn

LIGHTSHIPS AND LIGHTHOUSES –
GOD BLESS 'EM

An entry in another of my log books reads:

> "8 p.m. Thick snow – impossible to see beyond the wheel house – on course – proceeding up the Bristol Channel for Breaksea Lightship."
> "8:35 p.m. Anchored in 11 fathoms awaiting favorable weather."

In between those lines there lies a tale of luck which I didn't deserve. It happened this way.

I was master of a fine new ship. It was a cargo ship again, but with every modern convenience and superbly equipped with every aid to navigation available. After discharging in a North European port, we were bound for Newport Mons for ballast. Newport is at the head of the Bristol Channel in Wales. It was wintertime, late January, and night came early.

Heading down the English Channel, I was reassured by the faint yellow gleam of the Eddystone Light on the starboard bow. "The Eddystone," it's called by seafarers. I've read somewhere that the Eddystone is the oldest constantly maintained light in the world. For centuries it has cast its gleam seaward – sometimes feeble, sometimes too late. Good ships and brave men have foundered and been lost because of that. Whenever I hear the sailor's hymn, "Let the Lower Lights be Burning," I think of the Eddystone.

Tonight, as the mate busied himself with the bearing of the light, I felt among friends. All down the Channel these lights had appeared. By day they eased into sight as small fingers, gradually changing to fat, stubby chimneys, each with its distinctive marking. At night, they appeared first as dim orange glimmers, then as sweeps across the black horizon, finally bursting as occulting or flashing sentinels, clear and unmistakable. "On course and all's well," they seemed to say, these signposts of the sea.

But though all was well out there, we were having problems on board. Engine trouble plagued us most of that night and the next day. What with the chief engineer having to stop several times, it was evening before we came up to Lundy's Island and squared away up the Bristol Channel.

By now the mate and I were comfortably toasting our shins against the pilot house radiators, discussing stowage of the ballast we were to load the next day. Because of the delays caused by the engines, we were already 24 hours behind schedule. Since we would lose another day bunkering in Swansea, I was anxious to hurry along. So when the mate said it was starting to snow, I grunted, "Keep her going," knowing that his next observation would be a suggestion to slow her down. Continuing was perhaps bad judgment, but her owners expected me to keep our schedule. And wasn't I known through the company as "Drive her, Johnny, drive her," after the famous old sea chanty? Overconfidence won over common sense and drive we did into a pitch black night with snow pelting against the windows, reducing visibility to zero.

The watches changed at 8 o'clock, with the third mate relieving the first mate. The first mate wrote up his log in the chart room, then returned to the wheel house.

For the past two hours we had been trying vainly to pick up the Breaksea Lightship on our radio direction finder. It should have been coming in loud and clear, yet we hadn't heard her signal once. I couldn't understand it. I wondered if there was something wrong with the receiver. Sparks looked it over and reported it in apparently good working order. Entering the chart room, I put earphones on and tried again. Not a peep. On other frequencies, I could hear other lighthouses and lightships far away, but from Breaksea there was dead silence.

Snapping off the RDF, I stepped back into the wheel house. Snow was still obscuring the windows. The third mate, as was proper, was out on the lee bridge wing trying to listen and look through the snow blowing in his ears and eyes. A premonition of danger made me uneasy. I opened a window and peered out. Snow stung my face. The howl of the wind in the rigging went up and down the scale as the ship rolled alternately from leeward to windward.

"Mister," I said, "this doesn't look too good. By our reckoning we should be coming up to Breaksea. Can't raise her on the DF. I think we'll just back off the starboard anchor nice and easy and steam to it for the night or until the weather clears. There's quite a tide here and the water's too deep for the pick to hold us in this wind. You go forward and back out the anchor. We'll use the engines on a slow bell to keep her from dragging. Better get warm clothes on first. Give me a shout when you're ready."

The mate was evidently a lot more worried than I was, for in a very few minutes he phoned from the fo'c'sle head that he and the carpenter

The last lightship in U.S. waters at Nantucket Shoals,
the "graveyard of ships."

had the anchor cleared for lowering. The third mate put the telegraph on Stop.

Having plenty of sea room, I didn't back her to take the way off, but let her coast along until, by the feel of her roll, I knew all headway had been lost. The mate then backed off the chain, link by link, since it was too deep to let her go on the run.

For the rest of the night we lay to, using an occasional touch of Slow Ahead to keep her from dragging. Time dragged through the long, cold night. All during the second mate's watch the snow piled down. Every now and again one of the lookouts imagined hearing a faint horn. One of them even reported hearing a deep whistle somewhere ahead. But there was nothing else.

When the mate came on again at 4 a.m. it was blowing harder than ever. Over steaming mugs of coffee, we discussed our situation. The anchor was dragging despite our efforts with the engine. We were veering and yawing badly. The time was fast approaching when we would have to do something, but what? We weren't sure of our position, and the Bristol Channel is not too wide. Strong winds and a wicked tide could have thrown us off course. For all we knew, the beach was close aboard.

While we talked and considered, darkness gradually changed to gray. Dawn was coming, and with it the snow was letting up. We decided to wait for full daylight before getting under way. Pretty soon it was light enough to see the foredeck, then the bows. The snow was slowing, coming only in flurries now, driven by the wind.

Suddenly, the sailor on the bow shouted. We could see him frantically waving his arm ahead. There, not half a ship's length dead ahead, lay the Breaksea Lightship.

"God A'mighty!" the mate breathed. "A few minutes more last night and we'd have cut her in two. We're lucky, Skipper!" Lucky we really were to be spared a disaster after having used such bad judgment in holding on in a blizzard, not knowing for sure where we were.

We hove the anchor home and got under way. We were finally sure of our position. We'd almost been *too* sure.

There were other times when floating signposts were not so welcome. Once we were clawing off a lee shore on the west coast of Norway in full winter. A hard westerly gale was blowing. We were in ballast, heading north.

For two days, try as we might to counteract it, the ship was being carried eastward. A wicked beam sea was running and the ship, being light, was rolling her bulwarks under. I reckoned that if we could weather the next cape we would lick the gale. We had the alternative of heaving to, of steaming to the west into the wind, but our destination was northward.

Shortly after midnight, the second mate picked up a faint glimmer ahead.

"Must be a fisherman," I muttered.

The wind was still blowing as hard as ever, but visibility was excellent. The stars were shining and the horizon was like dark velvet.

Soon the dim light on the starboard bow brightened, then disappeared. When the ship rose on the next crest, we saw the light flashing brightly and unmistakably. It was definitely a lighthouse. And it was almost dead ahead. Since we were being driven to leeward faster than we were making headway, it was all too obvious that we would not weather the land.

My disappointment was hard to swallow. It was one of the few times I mentally cursed my owners. It was they who had refused to spend the money for a pilot inside the Sharagard, the belt of islands completely enclosing the entire Norwegian coast.

Inside these islands there is a fine, deep water passage all the way from the southern tip of Norway to the North Cape. It's protected from all winds and a ship can steam along safely in all kinds of weather. It was especially favored by ships in ballast as we were, but our owners felt that the pilotage was an unnecessary expense.

They didn't realize, or hadn't attempted to, that a ship in ballast in the dead of winter off the coast of Norway was well nigh unmanageable in a gale. For one thing, the high sides of the ship were exposed to the winds. But worse, the propeller and rudder were thrown clear out of the water with each wave so that she wouldn't answer the helm.

When this happened, as it was happening to us now, the stern kicked up out of the water, the wind smashing against our weather side. The helmsman put the wheel hard up, but inexorably the bow fell off, paying to leeward. There we lay, four or five points to leeward of our course, until the propeller and rudder again buried themselves deep enough to bring her head back again. Sometimes this took half an hour. All the while we were being set toward the coast.

There was nothing to do but head out to sea and weather it out. We hauled the ship's head around to the west and commenced climbing up the face of the big, vicious seas. First the bows dipped down, then the stern tossed up clear of the water. The propeller raced madly until the engineer standing throttle watch cut the steam.

After an hour, it became all too apparent that we couldn't keep on. The engines would shake themselves to pieces, or the forward end would pound the rivets out of her. What to do? The glass was still falling, confirming the latest weather report: winds of gale force continuing for at least another 48 hours.

The chief engineer, the first assistant, the mate and myself held a powwow in the saloon. We finally decided to slow the engines considerably and see if the ship's motion and laboring eased any. If it didn't, we would ballast the after holds with sea water, something to be attempted only in dire emergency.

Returning to the bridge, the mate and I watched as the first assistant signaled on the engine room telegraph that he was slowing to half speed. The noise of the wind howling around the wheel house dropped from a high whistle to a low-throated muttering. The violent pitching diminished appreciably.

"Well, now," I remarked. "This is more like it. She's riding like a gull." Just then, a mighty gust of wind poured through the open port door of the wheel house.

"Watch your helm!" I bellowed at the quartermaster. "She's falling off to starboard." And fall off she did, faster and faster until she was almost broadside to. The wheel was hard aport, but she wouldn't answer. She just lay like a crippled whale. "Full Speed," I ordered. Slowly her head came back to the sea.

Now we were faced with a serious maneuver. The effect of a large amount of water in a ship at sea can be disastrous unless the water completely fills the compartment it's in. If the compartment is only partially filled, the water shifts from side to side as the ship rolls, creating havoc with the ship's stability even to the point of capsizing her.

Our after holds were bisected longitudinally by the shaft tunnel. We all agreed that they could be safely flooded to the height of the tunnel without too much danger. The shaft tunnel would act as a barrier to the motion of the water as the vessel's motion in the seaway sloshed it back and forth.

The chief arranged to let sea water into the holds through the bilge sections. In a short time, the water came pouring in. Fortunately, the holds had been thoroughly cleaned at the end of the last trip, so there was no debris to hamper pumping out later on.

The mate stationed a man with a flashlight in each 'tween deck to watch the water as it rose. When the water reached the top of the tunnel, they notified the engine room to shut off. This process took only a few hours, but we kept pitching up and down alarmingly all the while. The propeller was still threatening to tear itself off.

Gradually, as the weight of the water in the holds increased, the stern settled deeper in the water. The rudder began to take hold and the propeller eased its thrashing.

We hauled back onto our northerly course and the rolling started again. But this time it was different, easier to handle. In spite of the rolling, we were now holding our course.

And so, by a difficult maneuver executed in time, thanks to the gleam of a lighthouse seen from the crest of a wave, another voyage was completed, another log book survived to be filed away in the archives, and a little more experience crawled under our belts.

– 26 –

WOMEN ON A SHIP – BAD LUCK

As long as ships have been sailing the sea lanes, sailors have been saying women on a ship are bad luck. I've said it, too. Only once did I have the misfortune to be on a ship with them, and they *were* bad luck, in more ways than one.

The war was over and business on the sea lanes was back to normal. The convoys, the escort vessels, and the fears were all behind us. At long last we were back in the business of carrying the world's commerce. It was a good feeling. The nightmares were over and buried in the past.

I was master of one more tired old Liberty ship. She had been spruced up. All the guns and gun mounts were gone. The wartime battleship gray was painted over. The hull gleamed with peacetime black, the deck houses sparkled in white, and the masts and booms sported their fresh buff color. Our fancy Maritime Administration uniforms disappeared. Only the cap remained, its insignia now a replica of the company house flag. My cap still had the "scrambled eggs" on the visor. I guess I was just vain enough to want to keep one visible sign of master, a title I was very proud of and one I'd worked hard to attain.

We finished loading in an East Coast port and took our departure for Marseilles. It was full summer, and for once the North Atlantic was behaving. All the way to Gibraltar the weather remained fine. Day after day the log book entries hardly varied: "Sea slight; light breeze from the west." A real pleasure cruise, it was.

I lolled around the bridge day after day. Celestial navigation was a hobby of mine, so I was forever taking sights. Stars morning and night, and sun sights all day. I know it annoyed the mates that I spent so much time up there with them. But I'd had too many years of winter gales, convoys, and submarine scares, so I was taking full advantage of this pleasant interlude.

One day I even got a three-way fix: sun, moon, and Venus. Because Venus and the moon are unreliable, they're seldom used. But that day they were in just the right position. By pre-computing Venus's height and azimuth, I got a pretty good fix. An unnecessary exercise, but I enjoyed it.

Another thing contributing to the joy of this pleasant voyage was the food. It was marvelous! Shortly before the war ended, I switched companies from American Export to the Eastern Steamship Line, an old Boston company. For many years before the war, Eastern operated a coastwide passenger service renowned for its cuisine.

On this ship I had inherited a complete steward's department from one of the passenger ships. The crew was entirely black, second generation men from the Caribbean islands. What cooks they were! If I ordered fried eggs for breakfast, they were fried right on my plate. The chief steward, Hudson, was lord and master, but they loved him. They were a close knit group, always sailing together. In port they didn't get drunk. Instead, after supper they would sit out on #4 hatch and sing gospel hymns. Many a night I was lulled to sleep by their soft, deep voices singing in perfect harmony. Yeah, man. This was *some* cruise!

We were approaching the Straits of Gibraltar, so it was time to put the sextant away. Indeed, early next morning, just after sunrise, there was Gib, dead ahead. The chief mate was busy taking bearings on the pelorus. I slipped below to have another look at the chart: *Cape Trafalgar, Tarifa, Punta Carnero, Europa Point*. How familiar those names were. And what memories of the war they brought flooding back – scurrying through the Straits under cover of darkness; slipping into Gibraltar harbor for orders, usually to some stinking hole in North Africa early in the war, later to Italy or the Persian Gulf.

Today it was different. Here we were steaming along in the bright sunshine like a bloomin' cruise ship, boldly sticking our bows right down the middle of the Straits.

On those earlier voyages, back in the war years, I felt I needed to prove myself to my crew. After all, since I was master of the ship I had to act like one. Part of the mystique of being a skipper is the act of being all-knowing. I was no exception to indulging in this bit of playacting. In fact, I had become pretty adept at it.

One of my tricks was keeping a private course and distance book in which I meticulously noted routes from the time I was a young mate. None of the mates knew I had this book, so prior to making a course change or landfall I'd bone up with it. Then I'd stroll into the wheel house and observe that when such-and-such a lighthouse was bearing so-and-so, course should be changed to such-and-such. The mate on watch would scratch his head and mutter to the quartermaster, "Now how does he know that? He hasn't been in the chart room for two days."

Sometimes, just to impress them further, I'd order that no course lines be drawn on the chart. Then I'd peek in my little book, pop out and change course. They thought I had it all in my head, and were suitably impressed. Or so I hoped. Vanity at its worst. But it got me through.

Some of those notes that were so clear and important then, that I really depended on, have grown fuzzy over the years. For example, one quote from the book reads:

> "Europa Point and Punta Almina abeam, steer 099 T, 114 miles to Cape Tres Forcas abeam, distance off 15 miles, c/course to 060 T, 114 miles to Point Abuja abeam, distance off 4 miles, c/course to 060 T, 95 miles to Cape Tenez abeam bearing 112, 17 miles off."
> c/course to 954 T, 27 miles to Pt. "PH."
> c/course to 999 T, 196 miles to Pt. "PJ."
> c/course to 330 T, 32 miles to Pt. "PK."
> c/course to 234 T, 6 miles to Position 1.
> c/course to 007 T, 10 miles to Position 2.
> c/course to 072 T, 3-1/2 miles to Position 3.
> North to "Anchorage."
> Note: PT. "PH" – Lat. 39-20N, Lo 5-40E.
>   PT. "PJ" – Lat. 42-30N, Lo 5-40E.
>   PT. "PK" – Lat. 42-58 N, Lo 5-20E.

What all this means is that when Europa Point to port and Punta Almina to starboard were abeam, the vessel was through the Straits and had entered the Mediterranean eastbound. So far, so good. My next step was to steam easterly 228 miles until Point Abuja was abeam to starboard 4 miles off.

Now, Abuja is the Port of Oran in North Africa. What the hell was I doing 4 miles off the coast of North Africa on the southern side of the Med when I was bound for Marseilles in southern France on the northern coast of the Med? And what did "P.H., P.J., P.K." mean? And Position 1, 2, and 3?

I've wracked my brain, but it remains blank. The only thing that comes to mind is that for several years after the war ships had to follow specific routes, particularly in the English Channel and the North Sea, because there were still hundreds of mines that hadn't been swept up. Were the same procedures being practiced in the waters around the southern coast of France? That would account for these cryptic notes. Perhaps some of my colleagues from those days remember this better than I do. Me and my fancy navigation! I was glad I didn't have to depend on that for this voyage.

We reached Marseilles without incident, and picked up a pilot at the anchorage. A short time later we were alongside the dock, ready to discharge. I rang up "Finished with Engines" and hurried below to the saloon. It was Sunday. Ever since we got our new steward's department, Sunday night was steak night: porterhouse grilled to taste.

"Charred on the outside, red inside," I ordered, fairly drooling. I couldn't believe our good luck. We hadn't eaten like this for five years. That steak was so good I almost growled over it like a hungry dog. Though I can't remember why we steered the courses we did to get to this same port 40 years ago, I can remember the very taste of that steak.

Belching with contentment, I leaned back and beamed at the mates. "Some ship, hey? Make a note of it, Mister. These days are too good to last."

The saloon door opened and in came a diminutive Frenchman. He was all dressed up in a suit. He even had a velvet vest on, for God's sake! As he approached the table, we were enveloped in a cloud of French cologne.

"*Le chief mate, s'il vous plait,*" says he.

The chief mate shook hands with him, wrinkling his nose.

"*Je suis votre stevedore, messieurs.*"

Stevedore! He looked and smelled more like a queer! He and the mate jumped deep into a discussion about discharging our cargo, number of gangs needed, tons per hour, estimated time of finish, etc. He smelled too powerful for me, so I left.

As the days passed, I found out that things were much different in Marseilles than they were in New York or Baltimore. My first evening ashore I sauntered up the main drag, Rue Canbierre. There were dozens of fancy cafes. Slipping into one, I ordered a drink and looked around.

My God! There were several ladies of the evening, sipping Pernod, I guessed. What floored me was their appearance. They were very stylishly dressed, but their hair! One had kelly green hair, another purple, another a bright canary yellow. Still another had flaming orange. And that wasn't all. Each had a full sized poodle dog dyed the same color as her hair. There sat those damned mutts, each as big as a police dog, squatting on their backsides.

Ah, but the food! That's where the French put us to shame, even our steward. It has been said that the French can make an old crow taste like pheasant. As far as I know, I never ate old crow, but I have no doubt the statement is true.

A few days later I was summoned to the agent's office. He had received a cable from my owners setting forth our sailing orders. Upon completion of discharging, we were to proceed to Oran, Béni-Saf, and possibly Nemours to load for the States. It sounded great to me: southern waters and good weather all the way home.

Then the agent dropped the boom right on my noggin. Two female passengers would board tomorrow for passage to the States. He told me what little he knew about them. They were White Russians emigrating to the United States, an elderly mother and her middle-aged spinster daughter. *Oh, God!* And this was to have been the most pleasant voyage of my life.

Sure enough, the next noon they arrived at the gangway in a cab, loaded with suitcases and boxes. Homely? Wow! They looked like two old buzzards.

The steward had assigned the women to the cadets' stateroom up on the bridge deck on the port side. My quarters occupied the starboard side. The only other person on this deck was the radio officer. The next deck below was for the mates and engineers who shared a common shower and head. There was no head on the bridge deck except my private one.

I stayed busy all afternoon clearing the ship and settling accounts with the agent. Meanwhile, the mate was lowering the booms, battening down the hatches, and securing for sea. By the time I returned, watches had been set and the lines had been singled up. The third mate had tested the steering gear, telegraph, and whistle, and had read the draft. As soon as I came up the gangway, the bosun sang out, "All hands, fore and aft." Up came the gangway. I made my way to the bridge, shook hands with the pilot, and off we went, presumably through "P.K., P.J.," etc.

Somehow or other, I found my way over to Oran. As soon as we docked, the agent came aboard. He told me we were to bunker, then proceed up the coast to Béni-Saf, there to load for Savannah. It turned out that he had been the agent for American Export Lines, my old company, for many years. We had mutual friends and were soon exchanging anecdotes. When it came time for him to leave, he very kindly invited me to have dinner with him and his wife.

I was really looking forward to that. But first I had a matter on board to attend to. Ever since we left Marseilles, I hadn't laid eyes on my two passengers. I had spent all the trip so far on the bridge, eating from a tray. Now, however, my troubles began.

I was in the saloon having coffee with the chief engineer. He fiddled with his spoon and cleared his throat a couple of times, all the while peering at me kind of sly-like.

"Out with it, Chief. What's bugging you?" I settled back, prepared to suffer through a long, boring tirade against the seaman's union, the lousy engines in those old Libertys, about what a rotten hole Marseilles was, and who knew what else. But he surprised me.

"Well, Captain, it's about these passengers."

"What about them? They're too homely even for you, and you've never been too particular. Why, I remember one night you and I went ashore ... "

"No, dammit. No! I don't mean in *that* way. See, they've been using the engineers' washroom. The second went in there to take a leak.

They were in there and started screeching bloody murder. And this was 4:30 in the morning."

"Well, for God's sake, what do you want me to do about it? They sure as hell can't piss over the side. Tell you what, Chief. You're either in the engine room or sitting on your ass here in the saloon. Let 'em use your head."

"I will not! And you'd better do something. This has been a happy ship, but it won't stay that way for long."

"OK, OK. I'll do something about it tomorrow. I've got to go up and take a shower and change my clothes. I'm having dinner ashore with the agent and his wife."

Knowing the layout of the ship helps explain the rest of this story. The captain's quarters on a Liberty ship run fore and aft. First comes his office, then his stateroom and bath. Thus, getting into the stateroom requires going through the office first. There's a second door opening from the stateroom into the alleyway, but it stays locked. I never even had a key for it on this ship. Also, on all ships during the war every door except the watertight ones had kickout panels at the bottom. Kickout panels were even set into the partitions between staterooms. If a torpedo hit warped the door frame, the occupant could escape anyway through the panel.

When I got up to the bridge deck, damned if my office door wasn't closed and locked. I never closed or locked that door except when I was going ashore. The key was inside on my desk. Something fishy was going on here.

Just then, I heard my shower running. *Oh, that dirty skunk of an engineer!* I banged on the door and was met with a flood of Russian.

"Open this damned door!" I roared. No answer. In desperation, I belted out the kickout panel with my foot. I got down on my hands and knees and crawled through the hole. Before I could get up, my unabridged edition of Bowditch, complete with tables, bounced off the side of my head. I rolled over, covering my head. There stood that old witch of a mother with a book in each hand – big ones: *Farwell's Rules of the Road* and my old Dutton's. Damn her, she was winding up to let me have another one, all the while screeching in Russian.

"Me, I am captain," I croaked in my best waterfront pidgen English. "What the hell are you doing here?"

She got it. "Oh, very nice engineer say OK."

"He did, hey? Well these are my quarters. Get out!"

"No. My daughter, she in the water, there," she said, pointing to the door leading to my stateroom.

"Well, get her out. I've got to change my clothes and go ashore."

She fired off a stream of Russian at the door, then turned to me. "Two minutes, Captain."

Twenty minutes later the daughter came out, looking as though she'd drowned a month ago. They glided off down the alleyway like two spooks.

I looked into my shower. What a mess! Wet towels were strewn all over the deck. There wasn't a dry one left. Damn their souls, they'd not get in here again!

At a New Year's Eve party in Copenhagen with the ship's agent.
(That's me standing at the far right.)
Women off the ship were O.K.

I changed into my one shore-going suit and hurried up the gangway where the agent and his wife were waiting in a tiny, beat-up French car. I folded myself into the storage compartment that passed for a back seat. With considerable coughing and spitting, the car came to life and we clanked out of the docks.

We went to a fine-looking restaurant where the cooking was half and half – half French and half Arabic. I should have stayed aboard. Steward Hudson's cooking made this stuff pale by comparison.

I was still feeling hungry when we parted company. I thanked them very sincerely. It was very kind of them to think of me, even though I knew the cost of the evening would be cleverly hidden when he rendered the ship's account tomorrow.

I took a taxi back to the ship. As I went up the gangway I decided to slip into the saloon. I was still hungry and there might just be some night lunch left. Also, the chief engineer might be in there and I had a score to settle with him. Sure enough there he was, just finishing up the last of the cold cuts, damn his scheming soul.

Those two women were a plague, all right, but they weren't my only problem. The next morning I was having breakfast with the chief mate. Something had been nagging at me all the way across the Atlantic. "Say, Mister," I said, "have you noticed anything funny about the saloon messman?"

"Can't say as I have, Captain. Why?"

"Well, watch this." I finished my first cup of coffee and flagged down the messman.

"Yes, sir, Captain. What'll it be this morning?"

"The usual, Mess."

"And what would that be, sir?"

"What I have every morning – bacon and eggs."

As soon as he headed for the galley, I said, "See, Mister? Every morning of my life I have the same: bacon and eggs. I never vary. Now watch what happens."

In sailed the messman and plunked down a stack of flapjacks.

"There we are, Captain. A dash of syrup?"

"See," I hissed. "He never fails. There's something screwy about this bird. He's as neat as a pin. Can't be booze; his eyes are clear as ice. But his head is way off somehow."

In the business of getting underway I put the messman, the damned passengers, and my revenge on the chief engineer in the back of my mind. We were bound for Béni-Saf to load some kind of ore. Béni-Saf is just up the coast from Oran, and it didn't take us long to get there. A little pilot cutter was lying well off the entrance. We hove to for him to board.

The Mediterranean is a beautiful place in the summertime: sparkling blue, almost too blue to be true. There was just a trace of slight sea today. The ship hardly rolled at all. This still could be the best trip of my life. Doubts were creeping in even as I was thinking that. But it could be. It still could be.

We docked at a sort of bulk cargo pier. There was a big gantry crane mounted on wide railroad tracks running the length of the pier. Because our gangway would be in the way of the crane, the mate rigged the pilot ladder to get ashore. It was only a rope ladder with wooden steps, hanging down the ship's high side, but it would suffice for the few days we'd be in port. We were scheduled to load only a part cargo, so two days should see us homeward bound. Béni-Saf is just an out-of-the-way two-bit port. There were absolutely no attractions ashore, so I decided to stay on board, reading and snoozing. Besides, it was so hot you could fry an egg on the compass.

As soon as we were tied up, I headed for my quarters. The two passengers were there waiting for me. What now? Broken English spilled out of the old one. The gist of it was that they just had to use my bathroom. Any arguments I had were pretty feeble. They did have a point. They couldn't be expected to share the engineers' head, could they? Against my better judgment, I relented. I set time limits: 8 to 10 in the morning and 6 to 8 in the evening. I'd be on the bridge anyway during those hours. That settled the matter – or so I thought.

The next afternoon, I was sprawled on my settee writing a letter to my boy. The sound of the second mate bellowing out on the foredeck interrupted my thoughts. The roaring of the big crane prevented any understanding of what he was yelling about, so I just ignored it. Not for long, though. He burst into my office all out of breath.

"Captain, there's been an accident!"

"Yeah? What happened, Mister?"

"The saloon messman just fell off the pilot ladder. He got all the way to the top and was climbing over the bulwarks when over he went, right down to the dock. They just took him away."

"Took him? Where? Is he dead?"

"No, he isn't dead. At least I don't think so."

I pulled on a shirt and climbed down the ladder looking for the stevedore boss. I found him holed up in a little tin shack, fast asleep. I got him awake, told him what happened, and asked where the hospital was. He offered to drive me, and I gladly accepted.

Soon we pulled up in front of a small, dirty one-story building. It looked more like a garage than a hospital. I made inquiry of a dull-eyed native clerk.

"He's in there," he said, pointing a limp finger.

Sure enough, there he was, sitting on a stool.

"How do you feel, Mess?"

"Kind of weak, Captain. Busted my shoulder."

"It's a miracle you're not dead! You been drinking some of this North African rotgut?"

"No, I don't drink. Just lost my balance."

The doctor came around the corner and spoke up. "You can take him back to the ship now."

"Doc, I can't do that. We're sailing tomorrow. I haven't got anyone to take care of him. He'll have to stay here and catch another ship when he's cured."

The doctor patiently explained that this was only a small clinic, with no facilities to care for him. He'd have to go with us.

I knew when I was licked, so the stevedore boss and I crammed him into the little car and rattled our way back to the ship. How were we going to get him aboard? He couldn't climb that ladder. We solved the problem by dumping him into the ore bucket hanging on the end of the crane. Up he sailed, for all the world like "Rub-a-Dub-Dub, One Messman in a Tub."

I was anxious to get back to sea, away from dirty little ports, the heat and bugs, the noise and confusion. I couldn't wait to drop the pilot and pick up a clean sea breeze.

The bosun and a couple of the hands broke out the big black washdown hose. The engine room gave them 125 pounds of water pressure and they blasted away all the dirt and debris with clean sea water. The old ship got clean and quiet again. She was rolling easily now. All would be well. A comfortable old shoe she was; tranquility would enfold us.

It almost worked out that way, too, except for those two women. We slipped through the Straits of Gibraltar and out into the Atlantic, headed for Savannah, one of my favorite ports. I looked forward to a pleasant end to the voyage. I settled down to the comfortable rhythm of life at sea.

Before dawn, I joined the mate on the bridge. We were old friends and there was little formality between us. We enjoyed gabbing about ship business and drinking coffee. When the first signs of dawn appeared behind us, I went below to get my sextant for dawn star sights. On most ships, the mates and skipper kept their sextants in the chart room. But mine was that British beauty I'd bought in Scotland during the war. Jealously, I kept it in my office. I didn't want any young squirt of a third mate fiddling with it.

On the way, I stopped off in the chart room. The previous evening I'd calculated our dead reckoning position at dawn and figured out the altitude and azimuth of three stars. I picked up those notes, felt in my pockets to make sure I had my stopwatch, and turned the knob on my office for my sextant. By God, it was locked again!

I hammered on the door. No answer. "Open this damned door, you crazy Russians. I've got to get in there!"

I could hear water running and my radio blaring out Spanish music from Morocco. Sparks poked his head out and said, "They won't come out, Captain. I was just coming out of the radio shack when I saw them going in. I tried to stop them, but they just slammed the door in my face and locked it."

Back I tromped up to the bridge, cursing like a wild man. The mate tried to console me by loaning his sextant. But there's an unwritten law of the sea than an officer never borrows, loans, or otherwise parts with either his sextant or his razor. That law is always respected. It holds that you must have a razor to look presentable enough to get a berth. If you're fortunate enough to get the berth, you must have your sextant in order to do your job.

I was furious. But even this wasn't the last of my troubles. The following day the second mate came up and asked me to come have a look at the messman.

"Why, Mister?"

"You'll see soon enough, Captain."

I followed him down to the main deck. The messman's room was right next to the saloon on the starboard side. We ducked in. I stared aghast. The mess was sitting on the edge of his bunk. His face was emaciated and the color of putty. Sweat streamed down his face. His hands and legs were trembling something awful. He smelled as bad as he looked.

"Mess, for God's sake! What's the matter with you?"

He just moaned and pointed his finger at his suitcase. The second mate opened it up. "Look what's in here, Captain. I found these this morning. This guy's a hophead."

I looked. There was a hypodermic syringe, needles, a bottle of alcohol, and a vial of morphine pills.

"I'll just throw this stuff overboard, huh?"

The messman was wailing and pleading. He got so loud you could hear him all over the main deck.

"Mister, give him the goddam stuff. We can't have this screeching all the way to Savannah."

"He can't stick the needle in himself because of that big plaster cast."

"Well then, you stick it into him. I'll not have him going bananas on us. It's bad enough that he can't work and we have to carry our own grub from the galley and make our own coffee. Why, I've even got the third mate cleaning the pantry!"

So much for the "most pleasant voyage of my life." Spoiled, ruined, by those two women and the dopehead messman. I *knew* there was something screwy about the messman, but I never suspected dope.

The two women caused more trouble on their own. Two or three days later the old one came up on the bridge during the second mate's watch and accused him of trying to rape her daughter. I had to take the wheel myself while the quartermaster dragged her off the bridge. I knew what had started that problem. The daughter had complained of a sprained back, so I had asked the second to have a look at her. Now the second never was too particular, at least by reputation, but even he wouldn't go so far as to try anything with that miserable daughter.

In all the aggravation, the beautiful summer days slipped by almost unnoticed. I had to move my sextant to the chart room. To make matters worse, I was reduced to using the mate's head and shower. I timed my meals to avoid those two witch passengers. I found myself furtively peeking into the saloon. If they were in there, I'd sneak away. My high hopes had been so thoroughly dashed that even today, so many years later, it's distasteful to write about it.

Despite everything, at last we sighted the Savannah Lightship and the pilot boat. We picked up our pilot, an old acquaintance, and steamed up the river to our berth.

After the formalities of Customs and Immigration had been completed, we got rid of the two witches and the saloon messman. The passengers went to a destination unknown, the messman we sent to the U.S. Public Health Hospital. Good riddance to them all!

An eye for an eye,
and a tooth for a tooth.

Matthew v, 38

– 27 –

ONE BAD APPLE

To tell the whole truth, women weren't the only bad apples I had to face. There was one bird, a ship's carpenter, who was as bad on board as those Russian dames.

It was shortly after the war and I was master of another Liberty ship. This one had first been converted to an assault troop carrier, then switched back to a cargo carrier.

Her elaborate hospital and medical facilities from her troop carrier days were still intact. Because these facilities were of little importance to us, they usually remained locked. Once in a while our second mate, the unhappy holder of the title "ship's medical officer," got the key from me for aspirin, iodine, or perhaps band aids. But except for such minor use it remained an almost forgotten part of the vessel.

In due time we went on loading berth, loading our reconverted ship for the Mediterranean. On sailing day, by the time I got back from the New York Customs House the mate had the ship battened down for sea and the lines singled up. I joined the pilot on the bridge. With a command of "Let go forward, let go aft," the pilot backed her out of the berth and swung her around. Off we went, out through the Narrows, outward bound for Ambrose Light and the pilot's station.

As soon as the pilot went down the Jacob's ladder at Ambrose, the first mate (let's call him Josh Steiner) came up on the bridge announcing that the three union delegates among our crew wanted to meet with me. As usual, each department – deck, engine, and steward – had selected a spokesman. Their request to see me at the outset of the voyage was unusual. Ordinarily they would go to the chief mate, chief engineer, or steward with their departmental beefs.

"I'll see them in my office as soon as we get squared away on our next leg and clear of incoming traffic, Mister. You be there, too."

I rang up Full Ahead on the telegraph and hauled around on a course for Nantucket Lightship. A quick look around the horizon assured me that all was clear.

"She's all yours, Mister," I said to the second mate. "I'll be in my room if you need me." Slipping down the ladder, I headed for my office. Steiner and the three delegates were waiting. Opening the door, I ushered them in. "Sit down, men. What's on your minds?"

The ship's carpenter stepped forward, commencing a loud, belligerent tirade. He was such a miserable looking critter: thin to the point of emaciation, undersized, with a pinched, narrow face resembling a ferret's. The gist of his yelling was that he had been elected chief delegate and was speaking for all departments. He intended to run a proper union ship.

"You're mistaken," I said, interrupting. "I will run this ship. We're on the high seas. You and everyone else on board are under Articles and subject to my orders until such time as we return to a U.S. port and the crew has been paid and signed off. Let's not have any misunderstanding about that, Chips. Any and all complaints will be duly noted. If I can mediate such beefs, I will. If not, they'll be settled on our return."

He ranted and raved that he'd have me blackballed or worse. That was it. I had had enough.

"Chips, there's the door. Get out!"

He stormed out still screeching threats.

"Well, Mister," I said to Steiner. "Looks like we've got a beaut in this bird. Can you keep him busy?"

"That's a tough one, Captain. Usually the carpenter works along with the bosun, but not this bird. He pulls the union agreement on me every day. Won't do a thing if it's not involved with wood."

"Here's a thought, Mister. It worked for me a few years ago when I was mate. Have the bosun hoist a big draft of dunnage out of #1 'tween deck. Make sure he dumps it on the windward side of the main deck where it will get the most spray. Also make sure that each board is hardwood. Then tell Chips you have a big project planned and that you'll need at least 500 pieces of dunnage, each one foot long. Tell him to sharpen his saw and go to work, 8 to 5 every day. That should chill him down. Then, each night when you come off watch, slip forward and throw his day's work overboard as rejects."

Boy, oh boy, did we have a tiger by the tail! Chips sawed away all the first day. When he went forward the next day, all evidence of his work had disappeared. He was no dummy. He figured out what the mate was up to.

I was on the bridge with the third mate. I could hear him yelling at Steiner down below somewhere. Then he burst onto the bridge, roaring at me.

I adopted a lofty air. "Quiet down! I'll have no yelling on this bridge. If you have a union beef, I'll be most happy to attempt a settlement. Meanwhile, go back to work." I thought he'd bust a gut, but I was firm. "That's all, Chips. Get off this bridge or I'll have you dragged off."

Off he stormed. I watched him making his way forward. By God, he started heaving the dunnage over the side! I sent for Steiner and pointed to what Chips was up to.

"Mister, get up there and tell that carpenter his pay will be docked for every stick of ship's property he throws overboard."

I watched intently from the pilot house as Steiner made his way up the spray-drenched deck. I could see Chips waving his arms like crazy. Turning around, I caught the man at the wheel trying to wipe a big grin off his puss. I grinned back.

"Captain," he said, "I'll deny I ever said it, but that guy's a real nut. I'm a good Union man, but all he wants is trouble. The whole crew is fed up with him."

"Thanks, Sailor. I didn't hear a word you said." But of course I did hear, and took heart from it.

As the days went by, Chips's campaign continued. Steiner had to discontinue the wood sawing project. The weather was worsening. Since we were deeply laden, green water was coming on deck and Chips was

Chips was in danger of being washed overboard during
heavy weather in the North Atlantic.
That's a Russian transport ship passing right astern.

in some danger of being washed overboard. Come to think of it, leaving him on deck wasn't a bad idea at that. Maybe I should have.

A few mornings later the chief engineer, mate, and chief steward came to see me again. They were at their wits' end with the beefs streaming from the carpenter. Like me, all three of them had been sailing since long before the war. We were well aware of the abuses, privations, and starvation wages of those bleak times. None of us ever wanted those conditions to prevail again. All the unions – NMU, SIU, MEBA, and MM&P – had worked to bring about changes for the better. In fact, we had participated in that ourselves. But – and it was a big "but" – here we had on our hands a zealot who was blinded to all of that. What to do?

The chief engineer finally suggested that I have a private meeting with Chips to try and reason with him, to point out that we had sailed in fo'c'sles much worse than he had ever imagined.

"Chief, why me? As master, I represent everything he hates. I haven't got a chance in hell of getting through to him. Why don't we be patient and hope the crew will clean their own house?"

No dice, the chief said. The others agreed with him. I said I'd try.

The next day was Sunday, a no-work day for Chips. I was on the bridge before daylight as usual for star sights and coffee with the mate. Peeking up from the compass, I asked the man at the wheel to tell Chips I wanted to see him at 10 o'clock.

Promptly at 10, I heard a hammering on my door. I opened it and there stood Chips.

"Come in. I'd like a word with you."

"Captain, if you want to talk to me I want two hours overtime."

"You do, hey? Last Sunday you woke me up with yet another of your phony beefs. Did you get overtime for that? Not likely. But I'll tell you what I'll do. I'll give you your two hours this morning, but in return I'll expect you to listen to *my* beefs without interruption. Deal?"

He nodded and slouched through the door.

I pointed to the settee and said, "Take off your cap. You're in my home."

He flung his cap at my feet. This was going to be *some* session. He was so full of hate and defiance I knew it was a lost cause. But I had to try.

His hands were shaking as he lit a cigarette. He was looking even worse than usual. Now I had been sailing these ships for a lot of years and had become pretty good at reading signs, especially in sailors.

"Chips, do you drink a lot?"

"None of your fucking business."

"Fair enough, but you look awful. You should take better care of yourself. You're starting to look like a dead man."

Diplomacy at its worst, huh? Yet with that bad beginning, I waded in. I reviewed the whole union movement, starting with the Wobblies, the

the IWW, Communists to the core. I told of their recruiting efforts, how they'd get up on a stool in the fo'c'sle and make fiery speeches, passing out literature which always had a cartoon of the ship owner in a tall hat, swallowtail coat, striped pants, and a big, fat cigar.

I told of some of the worst lines. I told of the Morgan Line cherries, actually stewed prunes, which were fed to the crew day after day. I told of some paying only $29 a month for able seamen, good ones.

Then I told of one of the worst cases, the Luckenbach Line, a big intracoastal outfit. Its ships had a forest of booms that had to be topped and lowered at each port. They instituted two watches, six on and six off. They always carried several workaways, out-of-work seamen wanting to get back to the other coast, willing to sign on for a penny a month. I told him of the rumors, which I believed, that things were so bad the Luckenbach mates were even firing the workaways.

The Munson Line was even worse. How any self-respecting sailor could sign on one of their hell ships was beyond me. But some would do anything to get off the beach. I told of how those men were bunking in flophouses and living on soup down at Sailor's Haven, for which they usually had to listen first to a religious sermon.

I described in detail the rotten food we'd had to eat ourselves; of six A.B.s, two ordinaries, and one or two deck boys living together in cold, dank fo'c'sles.

I wound up by pointing out that through bitter strikes and too much violence, things got better. We finally earned one watch to a room, overtime, better pay, and a host of other benefits.

"But, Chips, don't push your luck too far. There's a happy medium. The war is over. It's the foreign flag vessels that are out to bury us now."

The little misguided rat did hear me out. But when I finally finished he defiantly threw a lighted cigarette on my nice carpeting, stubbed it out with his foot, and left, slamming the door as hard as he could swing it. Two hours of overtime went with him, right down the drain.

At supper that night I told the chief and the mate what I'd done. "I tried but failed," I admitted. "In fact, I have an idea he'll be worse than ever now."

That night the weather started worsening. The seas mounted and the wind started to moan in the shrouds and around the wheel house. The ship was laboring pretty badly, so I reduced speed to 55 revolutions. By daylight we had a full gale on our hands. The ship was pitching badly and taking some heavy seas aboard. I reduced speed again, not wanting our cargo to get smashed up.

After a full night of battling the weather, I slipped below for a quick breakfast to get me going again. A bleary-eyed second mate was poking at his eggs. He stood the midnight to 4 a.m. bridge watch, but always dragged himself out of his bunk for a morning sun line.

"Mister, you'll not get a peek at the sun this morning," I told him, "but being as how you're up, why don't you accompany the mate when he comes off watch and make sure everything's lashed down? You might check our fancy hospital, too. It's chock-a-block full of all kinds of bottles of God knows what, and they could make some mess if they got adrift."

"Will do, Captain."

I finished my breakfast and crawled wearily back up to the bridge. The glass was still low. All signs were pointing to a stretch of continuing bad weather. *The weather has always changed before, so it will again.* That was all I could think of.

An hour or so later both mates came streaming into the wheel house. Even with oilskins and sea boots they were soaked through.

"Captain, everything is tied down and holding. But there's something you've got to see for yourself."

"What's that, Mister?"

"The ship's hospital has been broken into. Whoever did it has left some mess – broken bottles all over the deck, pills and instruments flung around. The deck is awash in iodine, gentian violet, and God knows what else."

The mate and I went down to have a look. The reports weren't exaggerated. We crunched our way through the broken glass. All the cabinet doors were swinging and banging as the ship rolled and pitched.

Just then the bosun stuck his head in the door, his eyes bugging out as he looked at the mess.

"Excuse me, Mister Mate," he said to Steiner. "I just came to tell you the carpenter's drunk and won't turn to."

A blinding light hit me. "Grain alcohol, Mister. That's got to be it." I turned toward the door. "Bosun, where's Chips now?"

"In his bunk, Captain. He sure is ossified."

"Let's have a look at him, Mister."

Josh and I followed the bosun down to the main deck where he and the carpenter shared a room. He was drunk, all right, lying in his bunk, muttering and laughing to himself.

"Search the room, Mister. I can smell medicinal alcohol."

A thorough search turned up nothing. The bosun pointed to an open porthole. "He must have deep-sixed the jug."

Steiner started rummaging around under the bunk. Triumphantly, he pulled out a pair of work shoes. They were soaked with that mixture of gentian violet and iodine.

"Bosun," I said, "let me know when he sobers up. I'll be on the bridge."

"Aye, Captain."

The next day the weather cleared, the seas flattened, and we were back on Full Ahead, making knots toward Gibraltar.

The bosun sent Chips up to see me. Chips swore up and down that he didn't break into the hospital. When confronted with the shoes, he told a pisser. He said he heard a noise up on the next deck, went to investigate, found the hospital door open, and stepped inside. No, he didn't have a flashlight with him, so he didn't see either the damage or the stuff all over the deck. Where did he get the booze? He said he had it hidden in his suitcase.

It was my word against his. All I had was circumstantial evidence. He had slipped cleverly out of the noose.

As the days went by I kept on brooding about the matter. *Every dog has his day*, I consoled myself. *My day will come.* Steiner, too, was becoming half cuckoo over this. Chips had shifted his attack to him. Every day the poor harassed mate kept pouring out a litany of the complaints coming from that skinny little bastard. Then Chips started on the chief steward. That was hitting below the belt, because stewards belonged to the same union as the crew. But he didn't care.

How one man could disrupt an entire ship's company so thoroughly and make our lives so miserable, I'll never know. But that carpenter managed to do it. I kept trying to smooth feathers with only partial success. The first assistant engineer, a big, brawny brute, finally grabbed Chips one day and damned near broke him in two. Fortunately, there were no witnesses.

I had mixed feelings when I talked with the assistant. "Don't make that mistake again," I said. "Even though you're bigger, if there's a next time, he'll get you and it'll mean your ticket. Be patient. He's got almost enough rope now to hang himself. There are some sensible citizens in the crew, and I'm betting they'll take care of him. You keep your big paws off him, hear?"

"OK, Captain, but it ain't going to be easy. Maybe I'll get him ashore some night."

"Now stop that kind of talk. Time heals all wounds."

"Balls, Captain."

Can't say as I blame him for saying that.

Not long afterward, we transited the Straits of Gibraltar and tied up at Marseilles, our first port of discharge. The agent told me our entire cargo was to be discharged there, meaning we would stay docked for six or seven days. That was fine with me. Then we could go right back home and hopefully unload the albatross around our necks: Chips.

Marseilles held no attraction for me except for the food. The chief engineer, first mate, and I ate supper ashore almost every night. On the way back to the ship we always stopped on a street corner where the inevitable pushcart vendor held forth, his cart piled high with succulent, fresh-from-the-sea oysters. We'd eat them as fast as he could shuck them. Then he'd count the shells, divide by two, and that was the bill. It was great!

The rest of the crew were having the time of their lives. Marseilles was one of the best liberty ports in the Med, full of high class, expensive French whores. They didn't just take you to bed and say "So long." They pretended to have "un affaire." There was dinner and drinks, then they'd let themselves be seduced. They put on an excellent act and the sailors ate it up. But it *was* expensive. I was giving a draw almost daily.

During our stay we never heard the first complaint out of Chips. He was always first in line for a draw. He also took several days off, which the mate wanted to log. But I prevailed, saying, "It's just more rope for him."

A couple of days before sailing I received orders to head over to North Africa for a full load of cork. The cork would fill all five hatches plus the forward and after decks. But being very light, even then we'd only have about 1000 tons. The chief agreed to press up all the deep tanks and empty double bottoms with sea water for ballast as soon as we got clear of the harbor and into clean water.

The crew said tearful good byes to their newfound lovers, promising to write, pledging their undying love and other such nonsense which neither they nor the whores believed.

We were one or two days out of a stinking North African port, loaded to the hatch beams with bales of cork. It was about 7 o'clock of a fine, sunny morning. As usual, I was on the bridge with Steiner. The bosun came up to get his orders for the day from the mate. They agreed that little could be done about the decks, since they were covered with cork. So they decided to concentrate on the crew's quarters, soogying them down and repainting them.

The bosun sidled over to me and said in a low voice, "Captain, the carpenter would like to see you privately."

"No way, Bosun. If he wants to see me, my mate will be present. Tell him to be in my office at 10." I turned to Steiner. "OK with you, Mister?" He nodded and the bosun left with his message.

Right on the dot Chips showed. The minute he came in he took off his cap. That was odd; usually I had to order him to take it off.

"What's the beef this time, Chips?"

"I ain't got no beef. This is personal and don't concern the mate."

"Well, Sailor, the mate's staying. Now what's on your mind."

"It's personal, Captain."

"Out with it. What's your problem?"

"Well, I think I've got the Old Joe."

"Ho, ho! Syphillis, huh? Drop your pants and let me see your dink."

"Not in front of him, Captain. Please." By God, he was starting to cry.

"Mister," I said, "I guess you can leave and attend to your duties." After Steiner left, I turned to Chips. He was absolutely terrified. "Down with the pants. Let's see now."

He dropped his pants and pulled out his dink. Sure enough, there was a big hard chancre.

"Chips, you've got the Old Joe. That's for sure."

"Oh, my God, Captain! Will I go crazy? Or get that loco thing?" Obviously, he had heard all the wild tales told in fo'c'sles the world over.

"Now, Chips, not to worry. I think I can cure you. Nowadays we have a miracle drug called penicillin. I think it will do the job. Come on down to the hospital."

We trekked down to the hospital and I rummaged through the cabinets. I searched as long as I could. Then, "Ah, I found it. Lucky for you." I never realized I had a sadistic streak, but there it was. I'm ashamed to admit it today, but I was actually enjoying myself. And I hadn't even begun yet.

"Now, Chips. We have to inject massive doses of this stuff into your backside every day all the way home. Down with the pants and shorts and put your hands on the bulkhead. Better put your head against it, too. Now bend over."

My God, he was so skinny! His backside looked like two shingles on a slab. I selected the longest, biggest needle I could find and fitted it to a syringe. Then I rammed that big needle all the way in, felt it grind against his pelvic bone. He jerked forward, banging his head against the steel bulkhead. Sounded like Big Ben in London.

Of course, he didn't need all the massive doses I gave him, but I figured they wouldn't do him any harm, either. We didn't have disposable syringes back them, so I rammed that same big needle into him every single day, all the way home. When one side of his ass got all black and blue, I switched over to the other side. I must have pumped a quart of the stuff into him. He was some mess. Told me he had to sleep on his stomach. Even his head was sore from clanging it against the bulkhead.

I expected bad trouble from him when we got back, but there was never a peep. He paid off and disappeared. I never heard from him again, thank God.

I suppose I should feel more guilt than I do, but I rationalized it as an even swap. Yet come to think of it, I only made *him* miserable. He made the whole ship's company miserable. Maybe it wasn't such an even swap after all.

He who loses his wealth loses little, he who loses his health loses much, he who loses his reputation loses everything.

Anonymous

– 28 –

THE GREATEST VOYAGE OF MY CAREER (AND IT NEVER HAPPENED)

For every bad time at sea, there were plenty of good ones. Some of them came pretty well disguised to begin with, like the time I was master of a ship that was bound, fully-laden, for New Orleans. We were steaming down the Florida coast, inside the Gulf Stream. It was summer and the weather was perfect.

Sailing south inside the Stream was very challenging to me. I had to maintain a rigid course inside the northern thrust of the Stream and outside of the reefs stretching from Point Judith in the north all the way to Key West.

I was like a kid with his Christmas morning toys – constant bearings, continuous soundings on the fathometer, meticulous course changes, all needing highly accurate steering by the quartermasters.

Navigation and piloting had almost become obsessions with me ever since I first assumed command. If a skipper is blessed with a good chief mate, he is blessed indeed. I had a succession of them, so I had plenty of time to play with my toys.

Life was good on this trip. Here we were steaming by sunny Florida, playground of the wealthy. Soon we would be rounding the Keys and heading up for Southwest Pass, the entrance to the Mississippi River. It was getting hotter by now, but I was loving every minute of it.

Even supper was a treat on this ship. On all ships the main meal of the day, served at noon, is called dinner. Supper was usually a stale salad and cold cuts with lots of ketchup to take the curse off. If we were lucky, maybe a piece of pie went with it. Not on this vessel. The steward did himself proud every night: charcoal broiled steaks or succulent lamb chops, even prime ribs or an outside cut. Good fortune was smiling down on us and I, for one, was very grateful.

It was just coming dark as we sighted the pilot vessel. Then: "Hard right. Stop Engines." The pilot scrambled up the rope ladder, carrying his little bag. As he came into the wheel house he handed me a day-old newspaper. I always appreciated this small courtesy. Then it was: "Full

Ahead. Come left, easy," and we began our overnight journey up the river to New Orleans.

It was a warm, bright moonlit night. The pilot and I slouched comfortably against the forward windows, gossiping. I remarked that there was very little outbound traffic coming down the river. What he said took me by surprise.

"Seamen's union's on strike. My orders are to anchor you off the port."

That didn't sound too good. We were an SIU ship, which of course meant that we were going to be bound by whatever the union did. *Well, I mused, time will tell.*

The next morning we swung out of the channel and dropped the hook. As soon as we finished with Quarantine and Immigration, I boarded a water taxi. At the boat landing I transferred to a land taxi and headed through the morning heat for our agent's office. There I got more disturbing news. There was no sign of the strike being settled. The crew was to be paid off, the boilers were to be blown down, and the ship was to lay where she was until the strike was over.

I arranged for the shipping commissioner to come aboard that afternoon to pay off the crew. Our Boston owners telexed that just the chief engineer and I were to remain on payroll. We were to be the ship's keepers. I didn't relish the thought of just him and me living aboard a dead ship out on that hot, steamy, muddy river. How would we eat? What if she dragged anchor? That river was running at eight or nine knots and we would have no steam to heave the anchor up. Problems, problems. Little did I know that an even greater surprise lay just around the corner.

I went to the bank, filled my briefcase with cash to pay off the crew, and headed back for the boat landing. The mate met me at the head of the gangway and I gave him the bad news.

"Now, Mister," I told him, "we'll delay the payoff while the chief gets steam up. Then we'll go Slow Ahead and drop our second anchor. Rig up a flag signal for 'I need a tow boat,' but don't hoist it. After all of you are gone, I might need that signal in a hurry."

I paid off the crew and signed them off Articles without incident. By 4:30 they were going down the gangway into water taxis with their suitcases and sea bags. The mate, steward, and I had a rather emotional scene in the saloon. Those two had been my good and faithful shipmates. God alone knew when we'd meet again.

Six o'clock found the chief and me leaning on the boat deck railing feeling sorry for ourselves.

"Captain, the hell with it," the chief said. "Let's catch a launch and go ashore and dump a few. We'll both go batty on this pile of dead iron."

"I'm with you, Chief. Just wait 'til I change my shirt."

It was way after midnight. We were sitting in an air conditioned bar, still feeling sorry for ourselves.

"Captain, we'll never get a launch this late at night. Besides, we'd roast out on that ship. Let's check into a hotel and be comfortable."

"Chief, you're a bloody genius. Let's go."

The next morning, after a huge breakfast, the chief announced that he was going to the agent's office to telex Boston that he was quitting. He felt useless here and wanted another berth.

I went back to the ship and spent the day wandering around the deserted passageways. It was an eerie feeling. All the familiar sounds and smells had stopped.

I sat at my desk and pondered. A few more days like this and I'd either go stir crazy or starve to death. What was I going to do about eating? I rummaged through the galley: nothing. Nothing in the pantry, either. The steward had done a thorough job of cleaning up. I hung around the bridge for a couple of hours, smoking cigarettes to help quell my hunger. Turning in, I decided that I, too, would have a talk with Boston.

The next morning I went ashore, hungry as a wolf. A plate of bacon and eggs perked me up. I set a course for the agent's office and docked at 9 sharp. Before I could say what I wanted, his manager ordered me to call the Boston office at once.

In a minute or two the familiar voice of my old friend and mentor, Marine Superintendent Captain Litchfield, came booming through the receiver.

"Hold onto your hat," he said. "As soon as the strike is over and your cargo is fully discharged, your ship will be sold to States Marine Line. Please stay with the ship until she's turned over. I'll write you details later covering joint inventory, obtaining receipts for the navigational equipment, ship's documents, all of that. Will you go along with this?"

"Of course, Captain," I said. "But one question. How does the future look for me?"

"Well, now, I'll be perfectly frank with you. The postwar slump in ocean shipping is the direct cause of your vessel's sale. But you've served this company well. Shortening sail as we must, it could be that the best I can do is step you back to chief mate again until a master's berth comes available. Don't give me an answer now. Think it over. And thanks for staying on down there. Talk to you later, my friend."

I sat there, stunned. Here I had just lost my fine crew, all good friends. Now I was losing my ship and my job. Sure, I could step down, sail as mate again. But I was so proud of being master. That had been my lifelong ambition. I gloried in my job, the culmination of many hard years of work. *Swallow your pride. Be practical. The economic slump is real.* It was a bitter pill that stuck in my throat and wouldn't go down. Nor could I cough it up.

I decided that as dismal as a dead ship was, I'd buy a couple of sandwiches, a thermos of coffee, and spend the night on board. Maybe I could come to terms with myself. Actually, I didn't have much choice. I had been with the same company for a long time. Whatever reputation I had was strictly "in house."

As I got back to the launch landing, loaded with enough grub to do me for the night, there was a picket line of white-capped seamen parading back and forth with SIU placards.

"Hello, men," I said. They formed a solid line and wouldn't let me through. "Hey, I'm no strikebreaker," I said. "I'm the master of that dead ship out yonder. Just going out to spend the night. You don't think I'm going to get up steam and sail her away all by myself, do you?"

I might as well have saved my breath. I demanded help from the headquarters of my own union, the MM&P, but they refused me, too. In a rage, I pulled out my union card, tore it into pieces, and stormed out.

Now what? My dough was running low, but it was too late to go to the agent's office. All I could do was check into a hotel again and put it on my expense account.

A week or more went by. Rumors were strong that ship owners and the SIU were close to a settlement. I sure hoped so. The days were beginning to pall. During the days I hung around the agent's office making a pest of myself. I spent evenings either in the hotel bar drinking more than was my habit, or reading in bed (the *Sailing Directions*, of course). With no solution in sight, I was getting morose and itchy.

One morning the agent told me the marine superintendent of States Marine wanted to see me at 2 p.m. After shaking hands and exchanging pleasantries over the New Orleans coffee to which I had become addicted, the superintendent hit me with a blockbuster: "Your ship has been fixed to load a full cargo of cotton in Peru, consigned to Egypt via the Panama Canal and Cape Horn. I'm offering you command."

I was stunned, quite unable to answer.

"Think it over," he said. "You don't have to give me an answer right now. However, this company believes a skipper is one of the main keys to the success of a voyage, so we try to treat them as well as possible. You will receive a substantial increase above the Liberty ship scale. Also, we're well aware that most masters despise paperwork and that pursers have been done away with. So we pay our masters an extra $200 a month to compensate for having to do the paperwork. We also pay them a rather good voyage bonus for efficient ship handling.

"Also, your living quarters will be enlarged, extending out to encompass the starboard alleyway and forward to take over the chart room and about a third of the wheel house.

"Think it over, Captain. We'd like you to come aboard."

We shook hands and I groped for the door, walking out in a daze. Never had anything like this happened to me. My ego was inflated to bursting. My mind was a turmoil of conflicting thoughts.

I walked over to a small, shaded park and sat down on a bench to sort it all out. First I reviewed the tangible benefits – absolutely great. Then I tried to examine myself. I had always been a strong company man with very deep loyalties. Captain Litchfield had pushed and supported me ever since I came to the line. Would it be disloyal to leave him? Stepping down to mate would affect only my pride. With overtime, the average mate made as much as or more than the Old Man.

When I finished, there was only one thing that overshadowed all the pros and cons: Cape Horn!

All my life there had lurked the hidden dream of booting a ship around Cape Stiff. It and Pentland Firth are generally accepted as two of the worst places in the world to take a ship. Voyages around the cold, remote, desolate Cape were commonplace in the days of the big wind ships. But since the advent of steam and the opening of the Panama Canal, that route was all but forgotten. Way in the back of my mind that dream, that challenge of rounding the Cape lingered. Here it was, ready for me to grasp.

Right then and there I made up my mind. I headed right back for States Marine and the superintendent's office.

"Didn't take you long to make up your mind, Captain. What influenced you most: the money or the quarters?

"Neither, Captain. It was Cape Horn."

He grinned. "I knew I had you figured right. Come on. I'm buying lunch."

Those dark thoughts of disloyalty, of walking away from Captain Litchfield's steadfast support, crept in to torment me. I put off calling Boston. After all, I'd be on their payroll until the turnover.

Misgivings buried, I started walking on air. With States Marine's permission I raided the Hydrographic Office, buying every chart available for the Cape Horn area and the Straits of Magellan. I bought an armload for the West Coast of South America, both coastal charts and detailed ones for entering any major port en route. I bought two copies of the *Sailing Directions* for our entire voyage, intending to memorize them before sailing day arrived.

Now I was itching to get back on board and into the chart room to start plotting courses. But since the strike was still on, I had to be content with spreading charts all over the floor of my room. I weighed down the corners of the charts with books. God knows what the maid thought. Every night I studied the *Sailing Directions*. The more I read, the more I

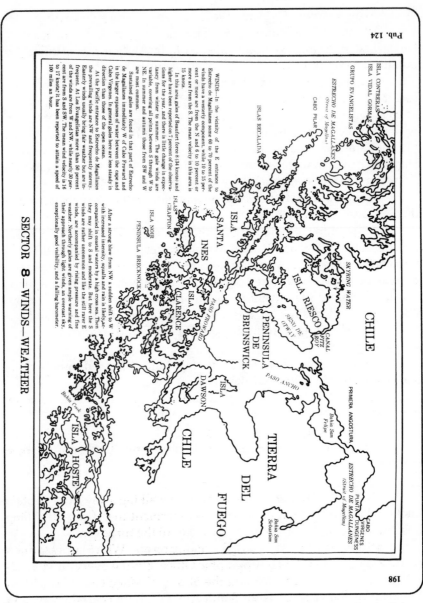

A first look at the Straits of Magellan – from the Sailing Directions for the East Coast of South America.

realized that those old-time clipper ships weren't exaggerating about Cape Stiff: it was no place to fool around.

Down there the southern oceans sweep completely around the globe unimpeded by any land mass. The prevailing winds are almost

199

SECTOR 8

ESTRECHO DE MAGALLANES

PLAN.—This sector describes the Estrecho de Magallanes (Strait of Magellan) from its E entrance between Punta Dungeness and Cabo Espiritu Santo, westward to its W entrance between Cabo Victoria and Cabo Pilar, 28 miles SSE. The distance between the E and W entrances of the strait, through the various channels, is 310 miles.

Bays and anchorages are described, in the order in which they are approached, from E to W.

GENERAL REMARKS

When passing through the strait an entire change in the features of the country, and probably in the weather, will be experienced in its various parts.

From its E entrance to Cabo Porpesse, 100 miles WSW, the land is comparatively low and covered with grass, but no trees are visible.

All over this E portion of the strait the most remarkable difference takes place in the appearance of the land according to the conditions of the light in which it is seen.

In the vicinity of Cabo Porpesse the land becomes wooded and its elevation gradually increases. The forest becomes more dense and the mountains more lofty as Cabo Froward is approached. These characteristics continue as far as the E part of Paso Largo. From here, though the mountains still border the strait, the trees become smaller, until towards the W entrance of the strait the shores are bare and rocky, only the ravines showing a stunted, though dense, vegetation.

East of Cabo Froward the land is comparatively level compared to that W of the cape, where there are steep mountains, bare on the upper parts, but covered with thick moss or dense forest on the lower slopes.

The passage through Estrecho de Magallanes is safe, but vigilance and caution are necessary. The difficulties and dangers in navigating the strait in either direction are the same that are experienced in narrow channels and close harbors of the same latitude elsewhere. But if the weather is thick, as is likely to be the case for more or less protracted periods, the passage is rendered more difficult because of in-

complete surveys, the lack of aids to navigation, the distance between anchorages, the lack of good anchorages, the strong currents, and in some cases the narrow limit for maneuvering of vessels.

The difference in the duration of daylight in summer and winter forms an important consideration. In December there is daylight from 0230 until 2030, while in June daylight will be limited from 0800 to 1600. Night is preferred to daylight, by some, for navigating Primera Angostura and Segunda Angostura, as the lights are more easily discernible than the beacons and other marks on land.

Paso Tortuoso is navigated by day and night by all regular trading vessels. Without local knowledge there is some risk in passing through this part of the strait owing to the strong tidal streams and the probability at any time of thick weather, either in the form of snow or rain. Anchorage should be found before nightfall, but large W-bound vessels with good radar can safely remain underway in Paso Ancho during night, to await daylight for the passage of Paso Tortuoso.

WINDS—WEATHER

Violent and unpredictable squalls are frequent all over the strait. Sustained gales are seldom encountered except in the widest entrances and passages.

In many of the countless narrow passages the wind follows the run of the passage, and has therefore, only two possible directions. It may be reversed abruptly when there has been a large shift of wind direction over the open sea.

The most dangerous winds are the violent and unpredictable squalls. The occurrence of one or more of these in succession from the same direction is no indication that the next will not be from some widely different direction. Moreover, of two possible anchorages a few miles apart, the more open may well be less subject to these squalls. These squalls depend largely, if not entirely, on the existence of strong winds or gales at sea or at a height of several thousand meters over land. As these winds strike the rugged mountains of the archipelagos they set up eddies of varying size and intensity. In a

Pub. 124

Beginning the detailed description of the Straits of Magellan in the Sailing Directions (Enroute).

always westerly, putting them advantageously abaft our beam. With an early fall departure from New Orleans, it would be summer there by the time we finished loading in Peru and were heading south for the Cape, since the seasons are reversed in each hemisphere.

I turned to the matter of cotton since that would be our cargo. Did it stow heavy or light? What was its stowage factor? The ship had 475,000 cubic feet available for cargo. The stowage factor and the total space determined the total long tons we could carry. This in turn enabled me to calculate the vessel's loaded draft. Would the ship be deep enough in the water to keep the propeller and rudder submerged when those terrible following seas swept under our counter down there off the Horn? Such seas they were! The highest waves in the world went roaring by Cape Horn.

My notebook was filling fast with hundreds of facts and questions. I checked and rechecked them again and again. Despite the fancy new quarters I was getting, I would still have a tired old underpowered Liberty ship with all its limits.

Wow! This voyage was requiring *some* logistical planning. States Marine would undoubtedly decide where we would put in for bunkers. All steamship lines had worldwide arrangements with the oil companies, so I knew they'd advise me in due course. Still, for a while I played around with the fuel oil requirements. These Libertys had three deep tanks: two in #1 lower hold and one in #4 lower hold. If I filled them with bunker oil, should I burn them on the way south and fill them with sea water (which is heavier than oil)? With a homogeneous cargo such as we were going to load, we should have as much weight as low in the ship as possible for stability.

I knew that the shore staff of States Marine would be grappling with these same problems. Still, I took my responsibilities as master very seriously. Let anything at all happen, and it was the Old Man's ass. There was no saying: "I was napping after having been on the bridge for three days and nights when it happened." No way! The Old Man is *always* on watch. That's the way ships are run.

Finally, I heard on the early morning news that the seamen's strike had been settled. I gulped down a quick breakfast and made a beeline for the office. The manager and I phoned the unions and ordered six temporary A.B.s, three water tenders, and two assistant engineers. They were to report aboard at 1 p.m. and get steam up. A tow boat was ordered for 3 o'clock. States Marine was sending out its chief engineer and mate. Things were starting to move.

I bought a shopping bag full of sandwiches and five pounds of coffee and headed for the boat landing. Fixed firmly under my arm was a big roll of charts, my ticket to Cape Horn. With no pickets in the way, I ran up the accommodation ladder straight to the chart room with my precious charts.

Soon the water taxi disgorged our temporary crew. While the black gang was firing off the boilers and the deck crew was laying out the mooring lines and spring wires, my new officers and I gathered in the saloon. We had enough steam up to run the pantry coffee urn, so the mate charged it up. Then we sat down and broke the ice over my big bag of sandwiches.

I was well impressed with the chief engineer and chief mate. They were longtime career men with States Marine, obviously capable, dependable officers. My luck was holding. These two could make life so much easier for me if they knew their job. Equally important, we were all compatible, a condition I was determined to nurture.

"Tell you what," I said, "soon as we get tied up, I'm springing for supper. We'll all meet at The Court of Two Sisters." They accepted dinner at the famous New Orleans restaurant enthusiastically.

Things were going great, but I knew I'd have to be careful to keep them that way. There is a saying that familiarity breeds contempt. It's probably true. However, there is a fine line in the merchant service that I never crossed. I have gone ashore and raised hell with many close friends: chief engineers, chief mates, radio operators, stewards. Yet back on board we were *always* formal. All officers were called "Mister" except for the chief engineer, who was called "Chief." I was always "Captain," never "Cap." That fine line stayed black and bold, the way it should be. I knew that dinner on shore with this crew would be relaxed, fun. Back on board, it would be business as usual.

The next day was filled with the sound of winches clattering as our cargo was hoisted out of all five hatches. A port captain and port engineer arrived from States Marine to begin the joint survey and inventory. We compiled long lists over the next two days: tools, stores, navigational equipment, narcotics, ship's documents. The long lists were taken ashore for endless copying. This ship, being government built, involved the War Shipping Administration, the Maritime Administration, and both steamship companies. Everybody needed copies.

Turnover day was drawing near. A full crew had been shipped, so the galley was manned and the ship was feeding again. Unfortunately, the food wasn't like it was before. This time the cooks were Hispanic and the grub reflected it: greasy, highly spiced, with chick peas daily.

But that was not my immediate problem. I had a lot of studying to do and time was getting short. I spent hours in the chart room with Bill Strunk, my new second mate, in interminable discussions about courses and distances, especially through the Straits of Magellan.

This waterway isn't a straight, wide passage from east to west (or, in our case, from west to east). Instead, it's a bastard to traverse, or so I was concluding after poring over all available information.

Before getting there we would have to steam from the Panama Canal down through 63 degrees of latitude, from 9 degrees north to 53 south – upwards of 3700 miles. To that we'd add the distance from New Orleans to the Canal. Then the thousands of miles from Cape Horn to the Cape of Good Hope at the southern tip of Africa. Then north in the Indian Ocean to the Red Sea, and through the Suez Canal to Egypt.

A real concern intruded: weather. It is common knowledge that the weather at Cape Horn is always bad. But what about the currents through the Straits of Magellan? Did fog ever prevail there? If so, were there any safe anchorages in the Straits? Did ships engage a pilot? Or were any available? Were they any good? What about the current charts for the Agulhus and Mozambique currents in the Indian Ocean?

What about deck stores? We should have plenty of spare tarpaulins and hatch covers. They should be stowed where we could get at them quickly – some forward, some aft. We'd need several topping mauls, several bags of hatch wedges. *Oh, the hell with it. We have an excellent chief mate. I'm dumping this problem in his lap. He'll handle it, and well.*

I had other things to do. I needed to speak to the mate about medical stores. The slop chest was also my baby. I'd load her up with plenty of cold weather gear: longjohns, oilskins, cigarettes for a year. On and on the list went. I needed to get ashore and lay in a full supply of pilot charts for every month for the entire route. To me they were the best source of weather information and I put great faith in them.

To make the planning easier, Bill and I divided the voyage into sections: New Orleans to the Panama Canal, the Canal to Peru, Peru to the Straits of Magellan, the Straits themselves, the Straits to the Cape of Good Hope, the Indian Ocean to the Red Sea, and the Red Sea through the Suez Canal to Egypt.

Even with turning many of the problems over to the chief mate, the planning threatened to overwhelm me.

"Mister," I finally said to Bill, "lock up this damn chart room. My compliments to the mate and the chief. If they're free, I'd be delighted if they'd be my guests for supper at Antoine's this evening. You, too, if you're not otherwise occupied." High-falutin' talk on an old Liberty ship, but I loved it. I never failed to observe all the niceties and the protocols that have held ships together since time immemorial. Besides, I had always had a weakness for French food and this town was deservedly famous for it.

When our drinks had arrived, I began. "Gentlemen, I have a confession to make. The planning for this voyage has got me buried. We're going practically around the world, coming home via the Mediterranean, and right now I don't know whether I'm coming or going."

Clearing his throat, the mate reached in his pocket, and pulled out a thick sheaf of neatly typed papers.

"Captain, I've been doing some planning myself. Here's my list of deck stores."

His put mine to shame! He had anticipated every contingency, every emergency, and then some. I was absolutely astounded.

The chief reached into his pocket and hauled out an even bigger stack of notes. "Captain, I've had several meetings with our port engineer. Here are all our fuel oil estimates, barrels per mile, distances between bunkering ports, the amount to be loaded, and the ports where we're bunkering. We're pretty sure of our figures."

Again I was flabbergasted. While I was trying to collect myself, Bill cleared his throat.

"Captain, I haven't got a list, but after you turned in at night, I plotted every course and distance from here to the Suez. I used recommended routing, all well clear of off-lying islands, reefs, and so forth. I think you'll find them quite accurate."

Well, now, I'll tell you I was touched.

"Waiter, another round," I called. Then, "Gents, I'm ashamed of myself. My 'hands on' style of management has caught up with me. I've neglected to take advantage of the most important management tool: good, capable people. I owe you my deepest apologies. I'm very grateful and proud to be your shipmate."

The capability and competence of my three top associates took a big load off my back. In all my years at sea, I had never once sailed the Pacific. They hadn't either, so we were all greenhorns. I consoled myself with knowing that good seamanship and prudence were the same on any ocean.

We'd need all our combined skills for this passage. As the *Sailing Directions* said:

> "The passage through the Straits of Magellan is safe, but vigilance and caution are necessary. If the weather is thick, as is likely to be the case for more or less protracted periods, the passage is rendered more difficult because of incomplete surveys, the lack of aids to navigation, the distance between anchorages, the strong currents, and in some cases the narrow limit for maneuvering of vessels.
>
> "The most dangerous winds are the violent and unpredictable squalls ... sometimes exceeding 100 knots."

The Straits are 310 miles long. This means at least one overnight, maybe more, to traverse them. The weather and tidal currents for that trip were concerning me most. There would be squalls springing up in minutes with winds reaching 100 m.p.h., then changing direction with no warning at all. There would be sea fog, sleet, and blinding snow squalls. There would also be tidal currents reaching up to 8 knots in the narrows and ranging up to 39 feet. *Wow!* A fine place to be trapped during one of those squalls!

A lot of my elation was fast leaking out. What concerned me even above the weather and currents was the ship herself, this beat-up old Liberty with only 2500 horsepower. Her high slab sides would be exposed to those gales. There was sea room of only 2000 yards shore to shore in the narrows.

I started figuring I must be nuts to *want* to go through what was ahead of us. If we did make it through the Straits, there was the Cape of Good Hope rearing its ugly snout 'way across the South Atlantic, waiting to pounce on us poor souls. *What was I getting into?*

A day or two later, a sleek, well-maintained British ship docked astern of us. She was an E&B ship, Ellerman Bucknell, one of England's oldest and most prestigious lines. I ambled over and introduced myself to the gangway watch, saying I had come to call on the master.

Moments later His Nibs bustled out of the passageway. "I say, jolly good of you to pop in. Come join me for a spot of gin before lunch."

We repaired to his opulent suite. His Indian "boy" hovered over us, mixing pink gins, a marvelous concoction.

"Cheers, old boy, " the British master said. "Do have another. I'm going to."

I told him of our impending voyage and of my trepidations.

"My dear chap, if I were you I'd be far more concerned about the Cape of Good Hope than the Straits of Magellan. Do you have a copy of the Admiralty book, *Africa Pilot*? No? Well, here. Take mine. I've been around that bloody Cape a few times meself and it ain't no picnic, as you Yanks say. Go ahead, take it. It will damned well scare the bloody piss out of you!"

I took it, of course. And after a fine Indian lunch with curries galore, hot enough to make my eyes water, I took my departure.

Later, curling up on my settee, I opened the *Africa Pilot* to the Cape of Good Hope section. I read and read, right through supper.

Oh, how right he was! This Cape was some dismal place, all right. I read of the Agulhus Current, pouring down between the East African coast and the big island of Madagascar at a rate of 3 to 5 knots. When this flow meets the terrible southwesterly gales sweeping around the Cape all the way from Antarctica, a veritable maelstrom is whipped up. Confused 60-foot seas go tumbling in every direction. Many are the ships that are overwhelmed and lost. *We're taking an old Liberty ship into those waters.* A sobering thought, to say the least.

Despite how bad all these problems sound, I was loving every minute of this. Lying in my bunk at night, I felt very privileged to have the chance at this voyage. *Cape Horn, here we come!*

The turnover of the vessel to States Marine was scheduled for two days hence. The next morning I headed for the agent's office, armed with yet another list of charts that we needed. There the manager and I sat drinking coffee and speculating on the weather: hot or hotter. New Orleans was fierce in the summertime. His secretary came in and handed him a note.

"This is for you," the manager said. "Captain Litchfield wants you to call as soon as possible."

Captain Litchfield! I hadn't even thought of him for a week. Must be more about the turnover.

The manager picked up his phone and told his operator to get Boston. Handing the phone to me, he said, "That man's energy would wear down an iron man."

The captain's voice came booming out, as usual. "That you, Captain? Understand turnover is for tomorrow, right? Now listen closely; I haven't got much time. I've stepped on some toes up here and hurt some feelings, but here's what I've got for you: command of the SS *Samuel Johnston*. She's laying in Philadelphia. Tomorrow night, get your ass on a train for Philly and take over. All the best to you in your new command. Write me! Bye."

Oh, my God! I dropped the receiver on the desk and went stumbling out the door. That conscience of mine roared up and engulfed me. For hours I walked the streets, my mind in turmoil, weighing the pros and cons.

Captain Litchfield had once again stuck his neck out on my behalf. He had always been behind me. His good counsel and rare praise had sustained me many, many times. So why leave him and go with another company? The answer was all too obvious: vanity. I wanted to show off, if only to myself, to hug myself and say, "I did it! By God, I sailed her around the Horn!" Ruefully, I had to admit that vanity was a poor swap for loyalty.

Wearily, I stopped my blind pacing and headed for the one place I had to go: States Marine and the office of the marine superintendent. I told him of my decision and why. For a while, he played with a pencil. Then he stood up, came around the desk holding his hand out, and said, "Your Captain Litchfield is one good marine superintendent!" *So are you,* I thought. *So are you.*

Blindly, I found the door.

The next night I was on a train for Philly. A lost dream? Maybe. I only heard of the ship once again. Did she make out OK on the trip to Cape Horn? I didn't hear that part, but I like to think so. At least she had enough charts! Far more important, she had three damned good seamen to guide her through: the chief engineer, the chief mate, and the second mate.

I did find something more about her recently, but I'm not particularly glad I did. I read in the newspaper that she had been towed out of the reserve fleet and sunk off Charleston, South Carolina, to create a refuge for fish. An ignoble end for a gallant vessel that had gone around Cape Stiff.

– 29 –

FINISHED WITH ENGINES

Inevitably, the time came when I had to make the most difficult decision of my life – to leave the sea and come ashore.

Ever since I had started reading I had only one goal: to go to sea, to be a seaman. All through my childhood that goal remained bright and steadfast, never wavering.

In high school we had counselors whose job it was to steer students into a profession suitable for their talents and aptitudes. My counselor was baffled.

"Why are you taking a college tech curriculum if you have no intention of going on to a technical college?"

"It's my folks' idea, not mine." A lame answer, perhaps, but there it was.

My counselor ranted, raved, and cajoled, but to no avail. Finally, he said, "You're wasting my time."

So away to sea I went.

Now, so many years later, with thousands and thousands of sea miles left behind in my wake, I was coming ashore. In truth, I felt I had no choice.

My wife became a casualty of the war. My son, then about ten or 11 years old, was sort of cast adrift. His aunt, to whom I had entrusted him, took over his charge most willingly. She and her husband never had any children, but she was more than equal to the task and devoted most of her time in my son's behalf. She enrolled him in a good private school in New Hampshire. Summers he spent at a boys' camp. He took holiday and vacation stints with Aunt Beaulah and Uncle Walter, who were very kind to him and loved him dearly.

But to me, it wasn't enough. I was experiencing severe feelings of guilt. I had left my family at the beginning of the war to the mercies of wonderful, well-intentioned relatives on both sides of the family. While I was floating around in convoys, they were making do somehow. Or so

I thought. Late in the war my wife suffered a personal tragedy that took not only her life but the life of our beloved little daughter, Marcia, then three. I never knew about it until months later, when I returned to those shores from yet another voyage.

Now, some years later, I had to face the facts. My boy had suffered traumatically from the death of his mother and little sister. He was at an impressionable age; I had to do something.

As the ship laid in New York waiting for her assignment at Pier 25, North River, I laid there too, taking stock. My boy deserved a home and family life, something I couldn't give him while floating around the seven seas as master of a tramp freighter. Yet the more I pondered, the more confused I became.

Finally, I decided to take things one step at a time. I'd come ashore, get a job, and take it from there.

The next morning I telephoned my mentor and staunch supporter, Captain Litchfield. As always he was most understanding, wishing me well. He sent a letter of recommendation for me to the John W. McGrath Corporation, the country's largest stevedoring firm. Armed with this, I made an appointment to see John McGrath, the president. He hired me on the spot!

My first assignment was as assistant superintendent on Pier 88, North River. This was the home of the French Line, the North German Lloyd, the Hamburg American Line, and the Polish Line.

With considerable trepidation I reported to the superintendent, Bill Buist. The pier was bedlam, day and night. Passenger ships were arriving and departing daily, with at least two cargo ships discharging and loading as well.

I rented a room in a family's home 'way up the West side, but could only use it one or two nights a week. Because I had no family or home, I volunteered for as much night and weekend work as I could stand. Occasionally the French Line let me use a stateroom on one of their ships where I could nap for a couple of hours.

As time went by and I became more familiar with the work, I was sent all over the port. I began spending a few months on the East River, then did stints over in Jersey, Staten Island, Brooklyn.

One day I was told to take over Pier 92, just north of Pier 88. This was bad duty. Known as New York's "hot pier," it was rife with crime. My head foreman was murdered one morning. Later my harbormaster was found in an alley, a bullet in his back. It was not a pleasant place to work in those days.

Yet one pleasant thing did happen. I met the girl who was to become my wife. I had begged three days off to go home and spend Christmas with my boy. In the seat next to mine on the airplane was a head nurse of a New York hospital, also heading home to Boston for the holiday. We started talking and got around to exchanging phone numbers before the plane landed.

Back on the job, I lost no time phoning her. Soon we started to date. Some dates these were! I'd be sent over to Jersey City to work a ship all night. She would ride the tubes with me, then turn around and ride back to the hospital. The next morning I'd be back on Pier 92. Somehow it all fell into place anyway, and six months later we were married. We had a week's honeymoon on Cape Cod, then the two of us moved with my son into an attic apartment in Bronxville. My hours were just as bad as ever, but now they seemed worthwhile.

Three months later my big break came. The Port of Baltimore was the company's largest as to tonnage. The manager there, Captain Black, had suffered a bad nervous breakdown and was retiring. I got his job. My family and I spent six very happy years there, making friends we still hear from today.

They were busy years. The stevedoring business almost never stops, day or night. The only exceptions were Christmas, Easter, and Labor Day. But I thrived on it. I was on my beloved ships daily. I associated with their captains, mates, and engineers. Like with the stevedore in Denmark, we spoke the same language.

It was almost like being at sea. Almost – but not quite the same. There has never been a day since I came ashore that I haven't yearned for command again. It has been in my blood too long. I'm now over 70, but it's still there. If the chance came I'd pack my old sea bag, pick up my sextant, and be off. Sounds like romantic drivel, but the call of the sea is still loud and clear in my ears.

Frequently, I sit on the beach gazing unseeing at the Atlantic, nostalgia washing over me. I hear the sounds and smell the smells of life at sea. Freshly brewed coffee in the wheelhouse wafts by me. The sweet, sickish stink from the fuel tank vent pipes slides beneath my nose. The myriad smells from open hatches in port mingle in the air, bringing memories of faraway places. The faint tinkle of the wheel house bell chiming the hours rings in my ears. So does the answering big ship's bell from when I stood lookout as a young A.B. I hear "Lights are burning bright, sir," from the fo'c'sle head. And my heart races with the harsh clamor of the General Alarm bells echoing through the ship.

Again that song rings in memory: "Ah, yes, my friend, those were the days. We thought they'd never end ... "

Yet for me, end they did. As they say, I swallowed the anchor. But it will remain stuck in my throat forever.

Captain Frank F. Farrar
Melbourne Beach, Florida
1988

A micrometer drum sextant used in the merchant marine.

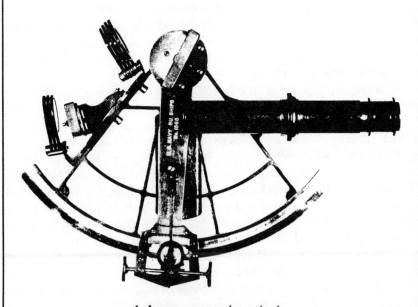

A clamp screw vernier sextant.

*Two of the many types of sextants that have been developed over the years.
The one at the top is just like the one I used in these stories. I bought the clamp
screw vernier model before I got the dough to buy the other one.*

GLOSSARY

ATS – Army Transport Service. British women's army corps.

Abaft – Toward the stern of the ship.

Able seaman (A.B.) – Experienced seaman who holds a certificate of proficiency. (Same as ablebodied seaman.)

Aft – Toward the stern of the ship.

Alleyway – Corridor.

Athwartships – From side to side across the ship.

Azimuth – True bearing.

Ballast – Rocks, sand, gravel, sea water, etc., loaded instead of cargo to give the ship stability.

Barge – Scow. Has a flat deck, no covering.

Batten down – Cover the hatches for sea.

"Belly robber" – Derogatory title for chief steward on hungry ship.

Bilges – Bottoms of holds, running fore and aft. They collect water.

Binnacle – Cover over compass. Contains a light for steering at night.

Bitt – Cast iron post for holding mooring lines; found both on deck and on the dock.

Bitter end – End of a rope or line.

Black gang – Unlicensed members of engine room crew.

Block – Pulley.

Boom – Cargo derrick.

Bosun – Abbreviation for boatswain. Foreman of deck crew.

Bosun's chair – Rig for hauling a seaman up a mast; looks like a child's swing.

Bottoms – Another word for ships. Most commonly used by shippers and Charterers.

Bow painter – Rope attached to the bow of the lifeboat.

Bowditch – Famous navigation book. "The Seagoing Bible."

Bridge – Navigating area; runs "athwartships" high on the ship.

Bridge wing – Open part of the bridge extending port and starboard from the wheel house.

Brig – Small, two-masted square-rigged sailing vessel.

Bristol fashion – Clean, neat, well-ordered.

British Ministry of War Transport – Same as our War Shipping Administration.

Bulkhead – Steel, watertight partition between compartments.

Bulwarks – Sides of ship extending above deck. Usually about 3 feet.

Bunkers – Fuel oil. ("To bunker" is to take on fuel oil.)

Cargo runners – Wire ropes for hoisting cargo.

Cargo slings – Slings which wrap around cargo for hoisting.

Celestial navigation – Finding ship's position by means of sun, moon, planets, and stars.

Chandler – Store that supplies ships.

Charter Party – Legal contract leasing the ship.

Chief steward – Seaman in charge of the galley and its crew.

"Chips" – Name for ship's carpenter.

Chronometer – Very accurate clock set to Greenwich time (Greenwich, England — zero degrees longitude).

Clipper ship – Fast, square-rigged sailing vessel (circa 1860-1890).

Coaming – Raised edge of cargo hatch.

Cockleshells – Frail, small boats.

Collier – Ship which carries only coal.

Con – Direct (a ship). Naval expression, primarily.

Corvette – Small destroyer-type escort.

Crew's mess – Crew's dining room.

Crosstrees – Platform at the junction of the mast and topmast. *Also*, point at which the mast meets the topmast.

Crow's nest – Steel, barrel-shaped container fastened high on the foremast to furnish protection from the weather for the lookout.

DF – Same as RDF; Radio Direction Finder.

DWT – Dead Weight Tonnage: the maximum capacity of the ship with full cargo, stores, and crew.

Davits – Steel framework from which a lifeboat is suspended.

Davy Jones's locker – Mythical place at the bottom of the sea where the souls of drowned sailors rest.

Deck gang – Able seamen, ordinary seamen, and bosun.

Deck houses – Compartments raised above the main deck.

Devil's claw – Iron hooks holding anchor while at sea.

Draft – Depth of ship in water.

Draw – Advance on wages.

Dry dock – Facility for ship repair. Water is pumped out after the ship sails in, leaving the ship's bottom available for repairs.

ETA – Estimated time of arrival.

Faking – Coiling rope flat in ever-widening circles. *Also* called "flaking" or "Belgian faking."

Falls – Rope reaved through pulleys.

Fan tail – Extreme stern of ship.

Fathom – Six feet.

Fathometer – Instrument to measure water depth by sound signals.

Fidley – Series of steel ladders extending up from fire room to deck.

Fireman – Seaman who works in the boiler room (fire room).

"Flags" – Generic name for a signalman.

Flying Fort – Four-engine bomber used in WW II.

Fo'c'sle – Abbreviation for forecastle. Crew's sleeping quarters.

Foredeck – Forward deck of a ship.

Foremast – Mast nearest bow.

Frapping line – Wrap-around rope to pull staging under the stern or bow. (Staging is planking to sit or stand on while working against the hull of the ship.)

Furl – Fold.

Galley – Kitchen.

Gangway – Ladder from the ship to the dock.

Gantline – Rope, usually about 1-inch, rove through a single block.

Gib – Gibraltar.

Gimbal – Device that allows a compass or other object to stay level when the ship rolls.

Glass – Barometer.

Great Circle Route – Shortest distance between two points on a sphere.

Greenwich Civil Time (GCT) – Same as Greenwich time. Time at Greenwich, England, used as the basis for the world's standard time.

"Guns" – Generic name for the gunnery officer.

Guy – Tackle to hold booms in place.

Gyrocompass – Shows true north (magnetic compass shows magnetic north).

Halyards – Ropes used to hoist signal flags.

Hatch – Opening in the deck through which cargo is loaded.

Hatch beams – Stiffeners over the hatches.

Hatch tarps – Canvas covers over cargo hatches.

Hatch wedges – Tapered pieces of wood driven against hatch tarps with a topping maul. They hold tarps in place.

Hawse pipe stoppers – Iron covers over holes that anchor chain passes through.

Hawser – Mooring line.

Heave the anchor – Hoist the anchor.

Hold – Cargo space.

Hook – The anchor.

Hove – Past tense of heave.

Hove to – Making just enough speed to keep the ship to the wind in a storm.

Jacob's ladder – Rope ladder with wooden steps.

Knot – Rate of speed. Equals one sea mile of 6,080 feet.

Lee side – The side of the ship away from the wind. (To "make a lee" is to turn the ship to provide a protected, or lee, side. Usually done for an approaching boat.)

Lap-straked – Overlapping boards on a small boat.

Lasher – Longshoreman specializing in securing cargo.

Launch – Small, open motorboat. *Also*, to put a boat in the water.

Liberty ship – A cargo ship built during the World War II era, weighing 10,500 DWT tons. In all, 2700 were built.

Lifelines – Ropes stretched along the decks in rough weather to provide a safety grip.

Lighter – Covered barge.

Limey – Britisher.

Local Apparent Time (LAT) – Time at the ship at any given location.

Longshoremen – Laborers who load cargo.

Lyle gun – Small cannon which shoots a line to another ship.

MM&P – Masters, Mates & Pilots (union).

Mainmast – Mast next aft of foremast.

Manifest – Official list of all cargo loaded in a ship.

Marlin – Tarred string, sometimes called "small stuff."

Master – The captain's legal title.

Mate – Deck officer. (There are first mates, second mates, and third mates, each with different responsibilities.)

Mercator chart (Mercator projection) – Type of chart with parallel meridians and increasing parallels of latitude.

Meridian – Line of longitude.

Mess – Dining room. *Also* applies to the seaman who serves meals.

Mess boy (man) – Dining room waiter (see "mess" above).

"Midships" – Command to quartermaster to place the rudder on the center line of the ship.

Milreis – Brazilian coin (see "Reis").

"Mister" – Form of address for mates.

Mizzenmast – Aftermost mast on three-masted ship.

Nigger head – Revolving spool on winch, used to pull wire and rope. Not now in good usage.

Notice to Mariners – Corrections to charts.

Oiler – Seaman who works in the engine room, oiling main engine and auxiliaries.

Oilskins – Foul weather gear (usually overalls, jacket, and hat) made of an oiled waterproof cloth.

"On the beach" – Out of work.

Ordinary seaman – Green hand (just learning).

Pad eye – Steel eye, or set of eyes, through which lines are run.

Palm – Leather partial glove which covers the palm, serving much as a thimble, protecting the hand from the pressure of large sailor's needles.

Pay off – Give the crew their wages after a voyage. *Also*, receiving those wages.

Pelorus – Dummy compass on the bridge wing, used to take bearings.

Pick – The anchor.

Pilot – Person licensed to guide a ship into and out of a port or other designated areas.

Plimsoll mark – Design on side of ship showing the deepest draft to which she can be loaded.

Pontoon – Steel hatch cover.

Poop deck – Raised deck over the stern.

Port – Left.

Quartermaster – The seaman who steers the ship.

Quay – Dock (British term).

RDF – Radio Direction Finder.

Ratlines – Foot ropes used to climb shrouds.

Reciprocating engine – Steam engine with pistons (usually 3).

Reef – To reduce sail area by rolling or folding part of the sail and securing it. *Also*, that part of the sail that is reduced by this method. *Also*, rocks, coral, etc. at or just beneath the water's surface.

Reeve – Thread rope through blocks (pulleys).

Reis – Brazilian money (see "Milreis").

Righting ability – Ability of a ship to return to upright after rolling.

Roaring Forties – Latitude 40N. Going southward to Cape Horn, the point at which a ship changes to winter storm sails.

SIU – Seamen's International Union.

STO officer – Sea Transport Officer (British).

Saloon – Officers' dining room.

Schooner – Fore-and-aft-rigged ship, usually having two masts, whose taller mainmast is nearly amidships. (Can have up to seven masts.)

Sea Transport Office – Port of British Ministry of War Transport.

Sextant – Hand-held device for measuring the angular height of a heavenly body above the horizon.

Shackles – 15-fathom lengths of anchor chain.

Shaft tunnel – Propeller shaft covering.

Shell plating – Skin or hull of the ship.

Ship's register – Official document containing information about the ship, such as tonnage, ownership, etc. Similar to a deed.

Shoot the sun (moon, stars) – Take sights on these objects with a sextant.

Shrouds – Heavy rope or cables supporting the mast.

Single up the lines – Release all mooring lines but two (one forward, one aft).

"Skipper" – Affectionate title for the captain.

Sledge – Sledgehammer.

Slop chest – Ship's store.

Snatch block – Block (pulley) that snaps open.

Soogy – Wash paint work with a strong solution.

Sounding – Measurement of water depth.

"Sparks" – Generic name for the radio officer.

Splinter shield – Guard around a naval gun for protection.

Starboard – Right.

Stay – Same as *shrouds*. Heavy wire or rope supporting mast. Also called "forestay."

Stem winder – Ship with engines and accommodations aft.

Steering sweep – Long oar, used to steer a rowboat.

Stevedore – Boss longshoreman.

Steward – Cook.

Stokes stretcher – Wire stretcher, used to transport the injured.

Stores – Supplies.

Swallow the anchor – Quit the sea and come ashore.

Taffrail – Rail around the stern.

Tail – Provide pressure by pulling on a line.

Tanker – Ship carrying oil.

"The Old Man" – The captain. Used only behind his back.

Ticket – License. (Master's ticket, mate's ticket, etc.)

Time ticks – Radio signals sent out over government radio. Can be heard all over the world. Consists of 59 'ticks' per minute; 60th tick is silent.

Topping lift – Wire tackle holding up a boom.

Topping maul – Sledge hammer with point on one end.

Tramp – Ship with no fixed itinerary.

Trolley line – Line rigged between two ships at sea on which objects are passed by means of a pulley from one ship to the other.

Turnbuckle – Tightening device using screw threads or threads and a swivel.

'Tween decks – Upper compartment of the cargo hold.

Vernier – Fine adjustment screw on a sextant.

Victory ship – Improved model of the Liberty ship.

WACs – U.S. Women's Army Corp.

War Shipping Administration – Federal agency which built and allocated ships during WWII.

Watch – Duty period for seamen, variable by the ship, but usually consisting of four hours on, eight off. *Also*, the seamen on duty during a watch.

Watch partners – Two, sometimes three, seamen who stand a watch together.

Water tender – Seaman who works in the fire room.

Way – Motion or speed of a ship through the water.

Weather side – The side of a ship toward the wind.

Well deck – That part of the main deck that is forward of the poop deck and aft of the fo'c'sle head.

West Coast Shipping Board – Organization which built ships on the West Coast during WW I.

Winch – Stern engine used to hoist cargo.
Windlass – Winch used to hoist anchor.
Yard – Place where ships are built or repaired.
Zone Time – Time based on Greenwich Mean Time (GMT), in which time advances or lags behind GMT for each 15 degrees of longitude east or west of Greenwich.

Fo'c'sle head   Poop deck

Forward well deck   After well deck

Midship housing

Typical deck locations for a freighter, shown on the SS Seattle Spirit.
This ship was torpedoed in the North Atlantic by a German submarine June 18, 1942,
en route from Murmansk, Russia, to New York via Reykjavik, Iceland.

ABOUT THE AUTHOR

Captain Frank F. Farrar

Frank Francis Farrar started out life on dry land, in Waltham, Massachusetts. He stayed right there for the early part of his life, graduating from Waltham High School at the age of 16. The moment he graduated he put his childhood – and dry land – behind him and set sail on the SS *Seattle Spirit* as a deck boy for the grand sum of $25 a month in wages.

Gaining the post of able seaman, he sailed continuously until World War II broke out. He sat successfully for his chief mate's license in time to take that rank with him through the war. Just at the end of the war, he got his first command, the SS *Augustus P. Loring*, a Liberty ship.

Some years later, having come ashore for personal reasons, Captain Farrar went to work for the John W. McGarth Corporation, the country's largest stevedoring and terminals operator. He retired as vice-president for operations.

Early in his retirement, Captain Farrar owned and operated a 400-acre dairy farm, milking 80 cows with the assistance of a single hired hand. (*"Nursemaid to a bunch of cows!"*) He gave that up for real retirement in Melbourne Beach, Florida.

He works daily writing about the sea and ships which have been such an integral part of almost his entire life. He has published stories in *Sea History* and *Sea Classics* magazines. He has also recently completed a novel about a ship caught in the tense current events in the Persian Gulf.

Captain Farrar is a marine member of the Boston Marine Society, the oldest such society in the world. That does not, however, mean that he is the oldest mariner in the world. He is only 73. He is, admittedly, a cat nut, having always been the one who saw to it that the ship's cats were fed. In fact, he and his wife, Dot, share living quarters with a cat. To be ecumenical, they share those quarters with a Yorkshire Terrier as well.